AF530824

An Early Self

Stanford Studies in Jewish History and Culture

EDITED BY *Aron Rodrigue and Steven J. Zipperstein*

An Early Self

Jewish Belonging in Romance Literature, 1499–1627

Susanne Zepp

TRANSLATED BY
Insa Kummer

STANFORD UNIVERSITY PRESS
STANFORD, CALIFORNIA

Stanford University Press
Stanford, California

Susanne Zepp, Original title: *Herkunft und Textkultur: Über jüdische Erfahrungswelten in romanischen Literaturen 1499–1627*, Göttingen, 2010

The translation of this work was funded by Geisteswissenschaften International—Translation Funding for Work in the Humanities and Social Sciences from Germany, a joint initiative of the Fritz Thyssen Foundation, the German Federal Foreign Office, the collecting society VG WORT, and the Börsenverein des Deutschen Buchhandels (German Publishers and Booksellers Association).

Printed in the United States of America on acid-free, archival-quality paper

Library of Congress Cataloging-in-Publication Data

Zepp, Susanne, author.
[Herkunft und Textkultur. English]
An early self : Jewish belonging in Romance literature, 1499-1627 / Susanne Zepp ; translated by Insa Kummer.
pages cm—(Stanford studies in Jewish history and culture)
"Original title: Herkunft und Textkultur : über jüdische Erfahrungswelten in romanischen Literaturen 1499-1627."
Includes bibliographical references and index.
ISBN 978-0-8047-8745-1 (cloth : alk. paper)
1. Romance literature—Early modern, 1500–1700—History and criticism. 2. Romance literature—Jewish authors—History and criticism. 3. Jewish literature—16th century—History and criticism. 4. Jewish literature—17th century—History and criticism. 5. Judaism and literature. I. Title. II. Series: Stanford studies in Jewish history and culture.
PN812.Z4713 2014
840.09—dc23

ISBN 978-0-8047-9314-8 (electronic)

Typeset by Classic Typography in 10.5/14 Galliard

Contents

Acknowledgments

This is an updated English translation of my book that initially appeared in German under the title *Herkunft und Textkultur: Über jüdische Erfahrungswelten in romanischen Literaturen 1499–1627* (Göttingen: Vandenhoeck & Ruprecht, 2010). In 2011, the book was awarded the Geisteswissenschaften International prize, which provides funding for German-English translations of publications in the humanities and thus aims to contribute to the dissemination of humanities research from Germany. I wish to thank the Börsenverin des Deutschen Buchhandels, Fritz Thyssen Stiftung, VG WORT, and the Federal Foreign Office for awarding my book this opportunity.

This book grew out of my work at the Simon Dubnow Institute for Jewish History and Culture at Leipzig University. My greatest thanks are due to Dan Diner, director of the Simon Dubnow Institute and professor of modern history at the Hebrew University of Jerusalem, who generously reviewed the manuscript and helped me understand the tectonics of early modern Jewish history. Both in method and scope, this book is the result of all that I've learned from him. Thanks to his achievements, the Simon Dubnow Institute is a true community of scholars engaged in the collective task of creating a distinctive approach to Jewish studies. This book would not have taken shape without him and my colleagues and friends at the Dubnow Institute. I'm also very grateful to Joachim Küpper, professor of Romance and comparative literature at Freie Universität Berlin, who helped me sharpen my methodological approach. Since I first had the privilege to work with Joachim as my doctoral advisor while writing on Jorge Luis Borges, he has consistently pushed me to develop my ideas further. Joachim read and reviewed more than one draft of this book and gave me important insights about my theoretical and historical presuppositions, for which I am very thankful.

I would like to thank my committee, Claudius Armbruster, Dan Diner, Hans Ulrich Gumbrecht, Andreas Kablitz, Katharina Niemeyer, and Barbara Potthast. In particular, I wish to thank Katharina Niemeyer for supporting the research from the very beginning. I greatly appreciate the help Andreas Kablitz offered with regard to the book's methodological orientation, especially regarding the chapters on Michel de Montaigne and Leone Ebreo. I'm very thankful to Sepp Gumbrecht for his stimulating comments on this book in particular and for our discussions regarding the future of the study of Romance literatures and languages in general; I always learn a great deal. Barbara Potthast, chair of the Iberian and Latin American Division of the Universität zu Köln's History Department, offered me valuable insights, as did Claudius Armbruster, director of the Portuguese-Brazilian Institute at the Universität zu Köln; I thank them both very much.

I have found an exemplary translator in Insa Kummer. I'm deeply thankful that she shared her expertise in language, grammar, style, and culture with me. She is an author's dream translator in every respect, and I'm very grateful for her thorough, incisive, and intellectually stimulating work and support. This book has also benefited greatly from Christine Gever's thorough and detail-focused copyediting. She has helped me to coordinate and think through the various aspects of this book, for which I'm very thankful.

My research assistant Lucrezia Delphine Guiot meticulously perused the English translations of the Spanish, French, Italian, and Portuguese originals of the literary texts and helped me to find an English Midrash Esther Rabbah in Berlin. I greatly appreciate her much-needed help. I would also like to thank my colleague and friend Victoria Prilutzky for allowing me to use her photo of Toledo for the cover.

As this book spans various disciplines, many colleagues and friends read and reviewed the manuscript from their different perspectives, in particular, Natasha Gordinsky (University of Haifa), Omar Kamil (Friedrich-Alexander-Universität Erlangen), Elisabeth Gallas (Franz Rosenzweig Minerva Research Center for German-Jewish Literature and Cultural History at The Hebrew University of Jerusalem), Arndt Engelhardt, Petra Klara Gamke-Breitschopf and Nicolas Berg from the Simon Dubnow Institute, and Dieter Burdorf (Universität Leipzig). A long conversation at the Wissenschaftskolleg zu Berlin with David Nirenberg (University of Chicago) helped me to understand the complicated research tradition on Spanish-Jewish history and culture, for which I am very thankful.

At Freie Universität Berlin, I'm enjoying a vibrant and encouraging research environment, for which I owe gratitude to our dean, Doris Kolesch, and to Freie Universität's Center for International Cooperation. I have been lucky to enjoy the friendship and continuing dialogue with Emilia Merino Claros (Universität Wuppertal), Andrea Weidenfeld (Köln), Natascha Pomino (Universität Zürich), Carola Hilfrich (The Hebrew University of Jerusalem), and Paola Traverso (Freie Universität Berlin) for many years. I'm very grateful for that privilege.

I want to express my deep appreciation to my successive editors in the Stanford Studies in Jewish History and Culture series at Stanford University Press, Aron Rodrigue and Steven Zipperstein, and David Biale and Sarah Abrevaya Stein. And my most sincere thanks also go to the staff at the press: working with Kate Wahl (publishing director and editor-in-chief) and production editor Gigi Mark has been a joy.

Finally, as always, to my family and to my partner Arne, I give my most profound thanks.

Introduction

At the heart of this book is the literary interpretation of five texts that originated in early modern Europe between 1499 and 1627. In this process, I examine Romance literatures from a perspective that closely links the change in genres and the characteristics specific to literary texts of the time with early sixteenth and seventeenth-century history. This study considers essential texts of the epoch, the interpretation of which has hitherto focused mainly on the Jewish, "New Christian," or Marranic[1] affiliation of their authors, whether alleged or actual: *La Celestina*; the *Dialoghi d'amore* by Leone Ebreo; the first picaresque novel, *Lazarillo de Tormes*; Michel de Montaigne's *Essais*; and João Pinto Delgado's poeticizing treatments of biblical texts.

It is the intention of this study to redirect attention away from the author's origins and toward an analysis of the texts themselves. Of particular interest in this context is the varying articulation of the early modern individual, portrayed in each of the analyzed texts in a specific way, yet always in interaction with Holy Scripture and the sphere of the sacred, in an act of artistic production. A particular role is attributed to the historical-theological backdrop of the Inquisition, the conversions, and the French Wars of Religion. The consciousness of autonomous productivity represented differently in each text is understood as a precondition for intellectual consciousness emerging into the modern age. The interpretations suggested here will not supply further arguments for the author's belonging; instead I will show that from a literary studies perspective, the development of early modern subjective consciousness can—at least in significant part—also be explained as a universalization of Jewish experiences.

For the purpose of examining the diversity of early modern Romance literatures, their Jewish components are useful both as striking examples and as a point of departure for comparison and contrast. Many aspects of cultural diversity in Europe are mirrored in the history of European Jewry, since hardly any other minority had to solve the question of "identity" as urgently and in as differentiated a manner as the Jews.[2] As a history of the transformation of belonging, European-Jewish history is able to provide analytical categories that facilitate the examination of other affiliations and their relations to each other.

In situating the epistemic interest of this study, these introductory remarks include a historical contextualization as well as a detailed literature review. Romance studies have engaged with the Jewish contribution to Romance languages and literatures in phases of varying intensity. While this has mainly meant the study of texts written in the Judeo-Romance languages, the coexistence of Arabic, Jewish, and Christian cultures was certainly acknowledged as a historical background for Romance literatures overall. Spanish literature represented the most common point of reference for such considerations. In the first half of the twentieth century, Américo Castro (1885–1972) vehemently emphasized the importance of the respective constellations in cultural history. In his books *España en su historia* (1948) and *De la edad conflictiva* (1961), Castro had pointed out the influence of the Iberian Peninsula's Jewish and Arabic history on the development of Spanish culture in comparison to the contributions of Visigothic culture. He analyzed Spain's post-sixteenth-century decline as follows:

> El motive era muy simple: la casi totalidad del pensamiento científico y filosófico y de la técnica más afinada había sido tarea de hispano-judíos, de la casta hispano-hebrea, integrada antes por judíos de religíon, y desde 1492 por cristianos nuevos. . . . El retrocesco cultural de los españoles desde mediados del siglo XVI no se debe a ninguna Contrareforma, ni a la fobia anticientífica de Felipe II, sino simplemente al terror a ser tomado por judío. En el capítulo II de la edición renovada de *La realidad histórica de España* (1962) hago ver,

> sin sombra de duda, que la famosa limpieza de sangre del siglo XVI, el prurito de cristianidad vieja y de genealogía sin mácula judía, son mera transposición hispano-cristiana de lo que secularmente venía aconteciendo entre hispano-judíos.[3]

This passage from Castro's study shows that he sought a greater acknowledgment of the diversity of fifteenth- and sixteenth-century religious and cultural configurations; that said, his argument is shaped overall by the discourses of his time. For instance, it is not free of essentialist expressions describing allegedly "typical characteristics" of Christians, Jews, and Muslims, and of *conversos* and Marranos, thus hindering Castro's understanding of matters beyond these essentialisms in his otherwise often-stimulating analyses.

Castro's student Stephen Gilman mainly focused on the converted Jews' contributions to Spanish culture in his literary scholarship. In his view, not only were the *conversos* of central importance for Spanish government administration and religious reforms, but, most important, "the converts had given the world" the novel, the main literary genre of the modern age. Mateo Alemán, Alonso Nuñez de Reinoso, Jorge de Montemayor, the anonymous author of *Lazarillo de Tormes*, Fernando de Rojas, Diego de San Pedro, and Alonso Martínez de Toledo had created this narrative genre.[4]

There was, however, considerable opposition to these perspectives that should be taken into account. In 1957, Spanish medievalist Claudio Sánchez-Albornoz,[5] exiled in Argentina, published his study *España, un enigma histórico*, which was conceived—among other things—as a reply to Américo Castro's theses. Sánchez-Albornoz summarized his rigorous rejection of Américo Castro's conception of history as follows:

> The Jewish has contributed to the creation of the Spanish not on the paths of light, but on dark paths . . . , and it can produce nothing which distinguishes it against us, for it has left us so much deformation and misfortune and has damaged our potential for development as well as our historical credibility.[6]

Claudio Sánchez-Albornoz's abrasive polemic against Américo Castro represents a dispute among historians that has affected literary studies as well. Following the end of the Franco regime and the subsequent democratization of the 1970s and 1980s, and since the five-hundred-year-anniversary celebrations of the epochal year 1492 at the latest, the study of Hispanic literature has increasingly turned toward analyses of Sephardic and Andalusian-Arabic culture and literature. Juan Goytisolo played a very significant role in the increased acknowledgment of matters concerning Spanish-Arabic relations. To this day, his literary, essayist, and journalistic works are aimed at opposing the denial of Arabic influences by Francoist Spain with an appropriate appreciation of its Muslim history and thus, as an author and essayist, contributing to a corrective appraisal of the Spanish past.[7] Taking a decidedly pro-Arabic position, however, Goytisolo considers the Jewish contribution to the development of the Iberian Peninsula's culture to be much less important than this study does.

Essential to a scholarly discussion concerning the significance of the Inquisition and Marranism for historical and philosophical study are Israël Salvator Révah's works on Portuguese literature and its connections with Judaism and Marranism. In their preface to an anthology dedicated to Révah (2001), Henry Méchoulan and Gérard Nahon acknowledge the importance of Révah's scholarly works on Uriel da Costa, Manuel Fernandes de Villareal, Miguel de Barrios, and Baruch Spinoza, on the Judeo-Spanish (Ladino) language, and on the procedures of the Inquisition, and they have attempted to make these works accessible to future generations of scholars.[8] Révah's studies on Portuguese crypto-Judaism and Marranism in Amsterdam had already been compiled and thus made accessible to a new readership by Carsten Lorenz Wilke and Henry Méchoulan in 1995.[9] The works of Révah's contemporaries Haim Beinart, Julio Caro Baroja, and António Domínguez deserve mention at this point as well.

Any survey of interdisciplinary studies must also make mention of the fact that these questions were in fact articulated at a relatively early point. In 1859, the Leipzig publishing house of Hermann Mendelssohn published a monograph titled *Sephardim—Romanische Poesien der Juden in Spanien: Ein Beitrag zur Literatur und Geschichte der spanisch-portugiesischen Juden* (Sephardim—Romance poetry by the Jews of Spain: A study on the literature and history of the Spanish-

Portuguese Jews), which directed attention toward the importance of Spanish-Jewish culture for Spanish and European literature. Its author, Meyer Kayserling, thus opened up a new perspective for the still-new German-language study of Hispanic literature in several regards. Kayserling's study combined historical and literary analyses, a combination that was programmatic for him: "History is as inseparable from literature as literature is from history: a principle that historians of Jewish history and literature in particular would do well to take heed of."[10]

The nineteenth century also saw the birth of *filología hispánica* in Spain. Beginning in the middle of the century, numerous scholarly works on literature were published; and scarcely ten years before Meyer Kayserling's book, Spanish Jewry's contribution to Spanish literature was acknowledged for the first time—albeit very briefly—in the *Historia crítica de la literatura española* published beginning in 1860 by Madrid's professor of Spanish literature, José Amador de los Ríos (1818–1878). He also authored a history of the Iberian Peninsula's Jews, *Historia política, social y religiosa de los judíos de España y Portugal* (1875/76). Similarly, in his studies on the Sephardic *romancero* tradition[11] and his cultural studies monographs *Origenes del español* (1926) and *La España del Cid* (1929), Ramón Menéndez Pidal (1869–1968) paid a great deal of attention to the particularities of the interactions among Christian, Jewish, and Muslim cultures in medieval Spain.

In post–World War II Germany, several overviews of the study of Hispanic literatures have been published since the mid-1990s that have provided the stimulus for further critical engagement with the productivity of Jewish culture in Spanish literature before and after 1492. Among these, the studies by André Stoll,[12] Manfred Tietz,[13] Dietrich Briesemeister,[14] Albert Gier,[15] Eugen Heinen,[16] Norbert Rehrmann and Andreas Koechert,[17] and Leo Pollmann[18] deserve to be mentioned. All of them have covered the pertinent thematic context from different angles and presented an overview. In Spanish-language Hispanic studies, the relevant works on this topic are those by Iacob M. Hassán and Ricardo Izquierdo Benito,[19] Felipe Pedraza Jiménez and Milagros Rodríguez Cáceres,[20] and Ángel Sáenz-Badillos and Judit Targarona Borras.[21]

The year 1492 not only stands for the discovery of a new continent, it also marks the end of the last Muslim empire on Spanish soil: the beginning of the year 1492 saw the fall of the Emirate of Granada following the capitulation of Boabdil, last king of the Nasrid dynasty.[22] Although the Catholic kings had guaranteed the Muslims and Jews of Granada protection in the Treaty of Granada, all Jews who did not convert to Christianity within four months had to leave Spain according to the edict issued by the *reyes católicos* on March 31, 1492. Thus ended the tradition of Jewish life in Spain that went as far back as late antiquity, for Jews had already settled in Roman Hispania, mostly in the southern part of the peninsula. In Tarragona, Tortosa, and Mérida, burial slabs document Jewish settlements between 100 and 50 BCE. Following the Jewish revolts under Hadrian and Titus, the destruction of the Second Temple of Jerusalem in 70 CE, the Bar Kokhba revolt, the capture of Jerusalem, and the diaspora after 135 CE, many Jews fled to Sepharad and other regions in the Mediterranean.[23] The first written evidence of Jewish life on the Iberian Peninsula appears in the canons issued by the Synod of Elvira (ca. 306 CE, near contemporary Seville).[24]

Following Roderic's defeat by Tariq Ibn Ziyad in 711, the era of Al-Andalus began. The coexistence of Jews, Muslims, and Christians was greatly hindered by the rule of the Almoravids (1046–1147) and the Almohads (1147–1269), as a consequence of which many Jews moved north to the Christian states of Castile and Aragon, at whose courts they enjoyed protection as a religious minority. From the eleventh to the fourteenth century, Spanish-Jewish culture and philosophy flourished. Beginning in the fourteenth century, conversions of Jews to Christianity increased as a result of growing anti-Judaism in Spain.[25]

The Ottoman Empire granted freedom of religion to the Sephardim in the aftermath of the 1492 Spanish Edict of Expulsion, as a result of which about 200,000 Jews migrated to eastern Mediterranean lands. Thessaloniki and the entirety of the Balkans became a center of Judeo-Spanish communities, who maintained their cultural identity and language.[26]

The historiography of Spanish Jewry first culminated in the 1848 publication of a work by Elias Hiam Lindo.[27] This was followed by a study by José Amador de los Rios;[28] and then, in the beginning of the twentieth century, by a work by Yitzhak F. Baer on the Jews in Christian Spain, the first part of which was titled *Aragón and Navarre*, published in Berlin between 1929 and 1936;[29] and a book by Eliyahu Ashtor;[30] as well as several more-recent studies on the history of the Sephardim.[31]

The subject of the Spanish Inquisition has been well researched from a historical perspective and well covered by several general works from recent decades in particular. The reference texts include Henry Kamen's repeatedly revised study,[32] the various editions of Cecil Roth's seminal book,[33] Benzion Netanyahu's works,[34] and John Edwards's history of the Inquisition.[35] Ángel Alcalá complemented these general works with his studies on the persecution of intellectuals by the Spanish Inquisition,[36] while studies by Charles Amiel[37] and Francisco Bethencourt[38] have provided vital information on the Inquisition in Portugal. A German-language study on the Inquisition was authored by Fritz Heymann.[39]

The essays authored by Jaime Contreras and Gustav Henningsen[40] as well as those by Jean Pierre Dedieu[41] represent the basic reference texts for the methodical analysis of the archival material on the Inquisition used for this study. The volume *Christians, Muslims, and Jews in Medieval and Early Modern Spain*, edited by Mark D. Meyerson and Edward D. English, compiles essential essays on the subject.[42]

Luce López Barralt's study of the influence of Islamic culture on Spanish literature[43] is of relevance for literary studies, since it sheds light on a continuing desideratum in Hispanic studies for an Arabic studies perspective. There is no shortage of works on Judeo-Spanish texts but of analyses examining the productivity of Jewish culture for Spanish literary history overall.

In 1967, an article by Eugenio Asensio on the "peculiarity" (*peculiaridad*) of *converso* literature was published in the *Anuario de Estudios Medievales*.[44] Ángel Alcalá Galve examined the image of Jews and *conversos* in the period between 1474 and 1516.[45] The publication of the anthology *Judíos, sefarditas, conversos: La expulsion de 1492 y sus consecuencias*, edited by Alcalá Galve, led to increased interest in the questions raised there. Twenty years ago, Eliyahu Ashtor had already provided a highly useful introduction to the Spanish-language documents found in the Cairo Genizah and held at the University of Cambridge.[46] Richard David Barnett,[47] Josep María Solá-Solé,[48] and Ron Barkai[49] attempted to give an overview of the cultural coexistence of Arabic, Jewish, and Christian lives. Studies published in the 1990s by Ross Brann,[50] Miguel Ángel Bunes Ibarra,[51] Enrique Cantera Montenegro,[52] and Bernard Dov Cooperman[53] reinforced the substantial acknowledgment in literary studies of the triangle of Spanish, Muslim, and Jewish cultural influences.

Evidence for lost Jewish and *converso* literature in medieval Castile and Aragon was presented by Alan D. Deyermond in 1996.[54] An important impulse for increased interest in the amalgamation of Romance and Jewish culture and literature on the Iberian Peninsula was provided by the exhibition *Ten Centuries of Hispano-Jewish Culture* organized by the Genizah Research Unit and shown at the Cambridge University Library on the occasion of the five-hundredth anniversary of the expulsion of Spanish Jews.[55]

Miriam Bodian,[56] Thomas F. Glick,[57] and Yosef Kaplan[58] have presented vital studies on the development of a "European" *converso* identity. A survey of literature originating from Spain during the period of *convivencia* titled *The Literature of Al-Andalus* was published in 2000. It attempts to merge three philological perspectives—the three editors are scholars of Romance, Hebrew, and Arabic studies, respectively.[59] The main focus of this important book is on Islamic culture, however. The foundations for a proper history of *converso* literature were laid by Gregory B. Kaplan in 2002.[60]

In addition to these general works, many individual studies[61] have been published in the past twenty years, the broad spectrum of which renders individual mention or discussion impossible. They are mentioned wherever they touch on the relevant context. Apart from studies on individual authors writing in the Hebrew, Judeo-Spanish, or Castilian language that are focused mainly on literary history, a number of studies on the image of the Sephardim in various literatures and cultures that concentrate on historical memory have also been published.[62] An entire spectrum of historical studies on the history of Spanish Jewry after the expulsion of 1492 have been published in

recent decades—following the groundwork laid by Cecil Roth, Salo W. Baron, and Israël S. Révah in the first half of the twentieth century. Esther Benbassa and Aaron Rodrigue,[63] Yosef Kaplan,[64] Jonathan Israel,[65] and Paloma Díaz-Mas[66] offer both in-depth overviews and vital contributions to the understanding of Jewish history at the transition from the early modern age to modernity. With their anthologies, Charles Meyers and Norman Simms,[67] Joshua Stampfer,[68] Howard Sachar,[69] Ross Brann and Adam Sutcliffe,[70] as well as Yedida K. Stillman and Norman A. Stillman,[71] have compiled essential works on the subject of Sephardic history. Finally, there are numerous studies on the countries which became destinations for the Jews expelled from Spain, such as the Ottoman Empire[72] and the Netherlands.[73]
As we have seen, vital studies on the present subject of inquiry have been published in the fields of history, cultural studies, and the history of philosophy. What they all have in common, however, is that they cite literary texts mainly in an illustrative capacity as sources. This study offers an integrative philological analysis not merely concerning itself with the coexistence of cultures but also considering, in particular, the dimension and function of the literary use of language in this context. Its underlying concept derives from the research agenda of the Simon Dubnow Institute for Jewish History and Culture, which is aimed at integrating Jewish history into general history in order to avoid isolating views from either non-Jewish or Jewish perspectives. With this in mind, the deficiency of some studies in particular becomes evident. Both Castro's studies and those based on his work do contain stimulating observations. However, their analytical sections invariably feature literary interpretations identifying the more or less precisely defined Jewish character of these texts either by citing the author's affiliation or a rather vaguely phrased "underlying atmosphere" of the texts. The methodological problems such an approach to literary texts entails provide the point of departure for the analyses presented here. What I am suggesting is a literary studies approach grounded in an interdisciplinary, philological close reading of the texts contextualized within cultural history.

Based on the sixteenth-century cultural constellations on the Iberian Peninsula, I will decipher emblems of affiliation contained in literary texts without reproducing the essentialisms which characterized Castro's works on early modern Romance literatures.

Historian and literary scholar David Nirenberg has stated that both cultural and social studies are all too willing to label all manner of phenomena as "Jewish" without sufficiently considering the conditions and consequences of such attributions. He declares the search for evidence of an author's affiliation in his or her texts as a continuation of the discourse of the Inquisition, in a certain sense. Nirenberg contrasts this "genealogical reading" with a philological approach adequately and methodologically reflecting the literariness of the texts and thus also the literariness of *converso* affiliations.[74]

In the field of philosophy, a thematically relevant study by Yirmiyahu Yovel was published in 2009, which claims that *conversos* and Marranos had contributed significantly to the emergence of European modernity.[75] In his philosophical-cultural history, Yovel describes the role of the Marranos in the emergence of early modern subjectivity as pivotal, and he suggests the term "split identity" for these contexts. According to him, it had grown from the particular situation of the (forcibly) converted Jews into the general condition of all modern human beings. While Yovel's approach of philosophical argumentation differs significantly from my own perspective, his theses have been an important inspiration.

Ernst Robert Curtius was convinced that the lines of tradition in the Romance literatures could only be understood by relinquishing the perspectives of national philology and epochal distinctions in favor of a comprehensive view of European literary history.[76] According to him, the collective memories he categorized in the form of topoi could not be attributed to national cultures of knowledge but formed a European literature as an "intellectual unit reaching from Homer to Goethe." Yet the European aspect of Europe's history reveals itself by means of a degree of diversity that cannot be reduced to Greco-Roman antiquity or the Christian tradition of the "Occident." The history of European literature is also characterized by the traditions of the encounter between Christian, Jewish, and Muslim cultures in medieval Spain. Medieval and early modern European culture constituted itself by its very diversity in areas inseparably and deeply linked with ethnic but also religious traditions; for many Europeans this mostly means Christian occidental tradition. As a result of the emancipation brought about by the Enlightenment, Jewish perspectives were integrated into this legacy; Islam has been included only since the end of the twentieth century. It is easily forgotten that the impact of both Judaism and Islam was present in European culture many centuries earlier: in the case of Jewish culture since the existence of Christianity and in the case of Muslim culture since the existence of Islam. Europe is founded on a cultural diversity that has only been recognized in recent times.

In this study I am trying, on the basis of five early modern literary texts, to understand the contribution of Jewish culture to the formation of modernity beyond generalizations and essentialist attributions. As a transnational community, Jews performed adaptations aimed at preserving as much of their own identity as possible, and doing so while appropriating as much foreign identity as required. Consequently, Jewish experience in the early modern era entailed a certain degree of maneuverability with regard to identities and belonging. This experience had the epistemic potential to radicalize the question of modernity itself. This specific cultural-historical configuration provides me with an analytical prism for the literary sources of this study and is also the reason why I challenge a rigid concept of hybridity. Language and literature are the primary emblems of cultural affiliation. While the term "literary hybridity" central to the basic assumption of this study evokes the continuous process of transformation and amalgamation of cultures, it is not without its problems regarding the period under consideration. In a way, it is only "correct" to speak of "hybridity" if there is homogeneity as well. Premodern societies were inherently hybrid, however, and the process of national and cultural homogenization is a characteristic of the path to modernity.

It seems that the key to the solution of this problem may be found in the sphere of the sacred, or more precisely, in liturgical-ritual and theological texts influencing literature and language. In the context of this study, the question that must be asked with regard to early modern literary texts is not about the affiliation of their authors but about the sacred emblems contained therein. Thus a dimension of cultural history and perhaps even of cultural anthropology is added to the literary studies perspective of analysis.

The sacred emblems themselves are divided into several layers: primary emblems such as biblical subjects or references to rabbinical texts, for example, require a different kind of decoding than those phenomena that cannot be clearly attributed because they oscillate between different cultural manifestations. It is here that hybridity finds its true expression, and in these cases it is secondary emblems of affiliation that must be decoded in the analysis of the text.

I begin my analyses with a discussion of each text's respective literary form. The narrating, lyrical, and essayist "I" is a phenomenon emerging in the sixteenth century. Chapter 3 interprets the emergence of this narrative form as a process in the universalization of Jewish prisms of experience in the early modern age. The procedures of the Inquisition, the conversions and theological investigations into ancestry, origin, and affiliation, are taken to be the framework, or rather the preconditions, for the constituting of subjective consciousness. Those literary texts of the period in which traces of Jewish experiences are contained are interpreted as sources for the emergence of early modern subjectivity, and while there is no question that early modern subjectivity has other cultural roots as well, these cannot be considered in this study owing to the necessary limitations of its subject matter.[77]

Dan Diner has pointed out just how much the premodern Jewish self-image changed from a religion permeating all areas of life to new forms of Jewish belonging: this change affected the symbols of affiliation, at varying levels in cases of elements of sacredness, and it prompted the Jews to formulate universal values; hence they went beyond a narrow representation of their own interests.[78] In his essay *Geschichte der Juden: Paradigma einer europäischen Historie* (History of the Jews: The paradigm of a European history), Diner shows how individual Jewish communities made efforts to interlace the sacred laws regulating most of their lives with those of the integrating society. It was important to reconcile one's own law with the stipulations of a "foreign" rule in a "foreign" place. This was accompanied by a change in the Jewish interpretation of history: the ties to the sacred and the sacred text receded into the background, while a profane and context-driven conception of history increasingly began to cover sacred textuality. Both the sacred and the profane realms of interpretation existed parallel to each other and interlaced with each other.[79]

I intend to render the consequences of my analytical findings productive for the development of Romance literatures in general. Based on a methodical engagement with the paradigmatic character of Jewish cultures of experience and knowledge, I will devise an approach that differs qualitatively from the rather additive attempts at unifying the various national literary histories as European.

Sixteenth- and early seventeenth-century texts reflect a peculiarity of Spanish history: the official homogenization beginning with the reign of Isabella I of Castile and Ferdinand II of Aragon seems like a modern phenomenon in the early modern era—just as the modern nation-states striving for ethnic homogeneity were to do four hundred years later, the early absolutist state attempted a definition of affiliations "by all means necessary" and through the institution of the Inquisition. In 1492, the Jewish communities, challenged by the circumstances of their time, had to choose between exile and conversion. With the transformative process of conversion, the emblems of affiliation changed as well. Thus the European perspective inherent in Jewish history may permit observations beyond the Iberian context.

I am testing my hypothesis outlined above using five different linguistic and period contexts from Romance-speaking Europe: the first text is the *Tragicomedia de Calixto y Melibea*, which has become known under the title *La Celestina*. Based on an acrostic in the dedication poem, this text is ascribed to Fernando de Rojas; however, there is no absolute certainty regarding the work's author. This closet drama is almost invariably described as a "threshold" or as a "work of crisis" (Manfred Tietz) at the transition from the Middle Ages to the Renaissance. The story of the tragic end to the love affair between Calisto and Melibea unites very different concepts of love, which are interpreted in various ways. The final act of this text, in particular, Pleberio's lamentation for his daughter Melibea, who commits suicide, has consistently been read as a symbol of the tension between the Middle Ages and the emerging modern age revealing itself in the text. Hartmut Stenzel has written the following on Pleberio's lamentation for the dead:

> The renunciation of the world staged at the end of this work, its [*La Celestina*'s] image of fortune's fancies and the world as a vale of tears[,] do indeed bear the marks of the late Middle Ages, yet they can be read as skeptical criticism as well. In this regard, it is telling that Fernando de Rojas hailed from a family of converted Jews, from the milieu of the so-called *conversos* . . . [; it is possible] that their skepticism and the constraints of persecution and the adaptive measures they were subjected to have shaped the path of Spanish literature into the Renaissance in a specific way. At any rate, the contradictions in *La Celestina* . . . can be read as evidence for a deliberation on the mechanisms of repression and exclusion which characterized Spain's transition to the Modern Age.[80]

This assessment serves to illustrate a peculiar aspect of many studies examining Jewish traces in Spanish literature. The analysis is not actually wrong, of course, for any articulation of skepticism and pessimism can naturally also be an articulation of "Jewish skepticism" and "*converso*" pessimism. However, it is hard to prove such a presumed "*converso*" ambience as described in the quote above by means of a philological analysis of the text—which is precisely what a literary studies perspective informed by cultural history would require. Based on the analysis of individual textual passages concluding with Pleberio's lamentation for his daughter, the first chapter elucidates the amalgamation of Jewish and Christian textual traditions in *La Celestina* instead of claiming them based on the insecure footing of the author's supposed origin.

The second chapter is dedicated to an analysis of Leone Ebreo's *Dialoghi d'amore* (1505/1535). Their author was Lisbon-born Judah Abrabanel, who came from a prominent Sephardi family and became known as the "Hebrew Lion." He ranked among the most important philosophers and writers of his time. At the center of his main work written in Italian are contemplations on the essence of love. In three dialogues, the two noble characters Filone and Sofia discuss love as a cosmic concept. In the existing scholarship on this key treatise of the Italian Renaissance, two dominant lines of interpretation have evolved that differ in their assessment of the Jewish perspective. Leaving this question aside, I will instead attempt to illustrate the simultaneous adoption of components from Christian, Arabic, and Jewish sources as a distinctive feature of this work.

The third chapter focuses on the picaresque novel. Although the author of *Lazarillo de Tormes*, the first work of this genre, remains anonymous, the specifics of this text have repeatedly been interpreted with the author's assumed Jewish or *converso* belonging in mind. In this case, I will offer a new interpretation of its literary form based on an archival discovery. My aim is to show that a historical experience far transcending the specific context of a Spanish *converso*'s life has been molded in this text. In fact, it seems that the hybrid textuality of sixteenth-century Spain is characterized by a plurality of literary memory.

The fourth chapter covers the main work of one of the most innovative early modern intellectuals. Deliberations on Michel de Montaigne's ancestry, origin, and belonging documented in writing began as early as 1622, about thirty years after his death. In a letter, royal councilor and member of the Bordeaux magistracy Pierre de l'Ancre considered contemporary knowledge of Montaigne's family background a matter of course: "Bien qu'on die que le siuer de Montagne estoit son parent du costé de sa mere qui estoit Espagnolle de la maison de Lopes."[81] As both Carola Hilfrich and Elizabeth Mendes da Costa have pointed out, in the late fifteenth, sixteenth, and early seventeenth centuries, the adjective *Espagnolle* meant "Jewish without saying it."[82] At the time Bordeaux was one of the central places of refuge for the Iberian Peninsula's converted Jews trying to escape the investigations of their "purity of blood" rigorously carried out by the Inquisition there. But did Montaigne know of his grandparents' conversion and flight? Is his not speaking of his mother in the *Essais* a deliberate strategy?

The case of Montaigne once again clearly illustrates the problems concerning part of the scholarship on sixteenth-century Romance literatures. Taking previous attempts to explain Montaigne's project of self-realization as a possible engagement with his Jewish or Marrano belonging[83] as my point of departure, this chapter will try to understand Montaigne's text via his specific *écriture* rather than deliberate on the author's religious affiliation. This analytical perspective is intended to shift the focus away from the author and toward the *Essais*' authoredness. The most important point of reference in Montaigne's works and particularly in the *Essais* does not consist in classical or contemporary authors, but in the empirically ascertainable "I." The specific connection between writing and constitution of the self in Montaigne is central to this chapter.

The fifth and last chapter of text analysis examines the main work of João Pinto Delgado, the *Poema de la Reyna Ester, Lamentaciones del Propheta Ieremias y Historia de Rut*, published in Rouen in 1627 and dedicated to Cardinal Richelieu. Menéndez Pelayo counted João Pinto Delgado among the most eminent poets of biblical subjects and stories in the entire peninsula: "There hardly are better *quintillas* in the entire 17th century and certainly none so free of pomposity, so inspired, and so rich in sentiment."[84] In three subsections, I analyze the transformation of the three biblical stories of Esther, Ruth, and Jeremiah into poetic form. Delgado's work is considered the end point of the historical developments informing the works discussed in this study dating from between 1499 and 1627. All of the dimensions of writing between the religions carved out in the earlier analyses are present in his work.

The individual chapters are not intended as overall studies of the respective works but rather as attempts to understand the thought and writing of these authors outside of a line of interpretation explaining their distinctiveness exclusively as a result of religious or ethnic belonging. Nor shall the results of individual studies, such as the contextualization of works in their period, the demonstration of their references to classical sources, or the summary of the history of their reception, be repeated at this point. It is the specific engagement with Holy Scripture and the sphere of the sacred in each of the five texts that is illustrated instead.

In the following, the terms *converso* and *marrano* are not used as synonyms. The term *converso* evokes the particular historical experience central to this study. In medieval and early modern Spain, the word *converso* described people of faith who had converted from Judaism to Christianity. Until the beginning of the fourteenth century, the term was relatively neutral; it was only following the violent outbreaks against Jews and *conversos* in the fourteenth century, particularly in 1391, that it was transformed into a label for ancestry and origin, used not least by the Inquisition in order to mark a non–"Old Christian" affiliation. Up until the end of the 1420s it seemed as though the converts might gradually be integrated into the majority Christian society, for they gained access to areas from which they were previously barred as Jews. This situation changed massively in the fifteenth century, however, and attacks against converts, now increasingly imagined as Spanish society's main enemy, occurred repeatedly.

The term *Marranic* will be detached from its literal, highly pejorative meaning and transferred to a different semantic context in this study. The origins of this term insinuating a sham conversion and continued practicing of the ancestral faith are derived in various ways from different languages, for example, from the Aramaic-Hebrew *mar anus* ("forced convert"). In his study on the origins of the word, Arturo Farinelli has explained that the term in his opinion was derived from a Spanish curse word, namely, the word for "pig,"[85] while Yakov Malkiel believed that the etymology of the word was most likely to be explained as a contraction of the Arabic *barrān, barrānī* ("foreigner") and the Latin *verres* ("wild boar").[86] This study aims to update the term in the sense of a metaphor, as Elaine Marks has done in her study on the Jewish presence in French literature,[87] for example, or in the sense in which Yirmiyahu Yovel used it in his above-mentioned philosophical reflection on Jewish historical experience,[88] and not least in the manner in which Dan Diner has transferred the meaning of "Marranic" in order to characterize Hannah Arendt's writing.[89] The updates to the term made by this study are explained extensively in Chapter 5 and in the Conclusion. Finally, Chapter 5 also discusses the panorama of dual perspectives, which arises from the individual analyses, as one of the paradigms of the modern age.

My book examines 150 years of Romance literature in the early modern period. It tries to give the abiding question of its Jewish components a new direction in inquiry and to suggest an innovative way for literary studies to understand the contribution of Jewish experiences to the historical process of the crystallization of modernity.

One Skepticism and Irony

La Celestina (1499)

Few texts in Spanish literary history had such a lasting impact as the closet drama *Tragicomedia de Calixto y Melibea*. This "tragicomedy," which is considered a key literary work in Romance Europe's transition from the late Middle Ages to the early modern age, has become known under the title *La Celestina*, based on the name of the procuress who unites Calisto, the protagonist whose love is unrequited, with Melibea, who rejects him at first. To this day, hardly any other early modern text is edited and translated as often as this one. The history of its reception includes several film adaptations as well. For a text written in the year 1499, it is unusual in many respects. This is true of its form, which combines elements of both drama and the novel, yet even more so of its linguistic innovations, and not least with respect to its content. This explains why the peculiarities of this text, which in part cannot be explained immediately, have led to the most diverse attempts at explanation and interpretation in the course of Romance literary studies.

On Fernando de Rojas's Authorship

In 1902 the account of a trial mentioning a lawyer named Fernando de Rojas was found during research in the archives of the Inquisition tribunals.[1] According to the historical document, he had written *La Celestina* in his youth and had wanted to represent his father-in-law, Álvaro de Montalbán, in an Inquisition trial in 1525. Because of his status as a *converso*, however, he had been rejected as counsel by the tribunal. The author's name had been known to be Fernando de Rojas since *La Celestina*'s second edition of 1505, because he had revealed himself through an acrostic in a dedication poem. The dedication was prefaced by a letter in which the author described his work as the sequel to a literary discovery, the first act of *Celestina*, a text that according to the letter's author could only have been written by an author such as Juan de Mena or Rodrigo de Cota. It is not only because of this literary game regarding authorship—the first act does indeed differ from the rest of the piece—that, despite the archival discovery from the Inquisition files, it has not been decided to this day whether the text was written by one or several authors, nor has the identity of Fernando de Rojas, obscured by a play on words, been established beyond a doubt.[2]

Nevertheless, following the archival discovery, many studies have striven to complement the interpretation of this early modern text with a consideration of its historic origins as well as a focus on the author's identity. One of the first essays of this kind was an article by Louis G. Zelson titled "The *Celestina* and Its Jewish Authorship," which appeared in the journal *Jewish Forum* in December 1930. In it Zelson demands acknowledgment of *La Celestina* as a work of Jewish literature.[3] Rather than discussing the content of the literary text, he describes the discussion among scholars about the alleged author, which an article by Manuel Serrano y Sanz had triggered in 1902. Zelson also refers to a brief study by Julio Cejador presenting further archival finds on the ancestry and origin of Fernando de Rojas, which declared him a Hidalgo and thus a so-called Old Christian.[4] In the following decades, the archival-based discussion about the Jewish, *converso*, or Christian origin of *Celestina*'s author grew into a veritable research tradition.

Building upon the writings of his academic mentor, Américo Castro, Stephen Gilman has compiled essential studies that interpret *La Celestina* as a document of the author Fernando de Rojas's "Jewish-Christian split consciousness." While Gilman stresses overall that he does not want to unambiguously declare the literary text an inevitable result of the historical conditions of the author's existence, he interprets the tragicomedy's uniqueness from the "archivally imagined perspective of Spanish *conversos*,"[5] namely, the biographical experience suffered by Fernando de Rojas that was reflected in this text.[6] This and other attempts,[7] following Gilman, at a conjoined consideration of the author's affiliation and the extraordinariness of the text have led to a reading of *La Celestina* that recognizes in it a pessimism informed by true hardship as displayed by the *conversos*, whose only form of expression remained skeptical distance and irony. However, not one of the characters in the text is explicitly referred to as a *converso*, nor are questions of religious affiliation central to the plot in any way.

The passages analyzed in this chapter are taken mainly from the first and last acts of *La Celestina*, the latter of which has been perceived as that part of the text in which a "Jewish Skepticism" (Castro) finds its central expression in the above-mentioned interpretative tradition. My aim is to open up an alternative approach to *La Celestina* beyond the exclusively biographical one.

In 1499 the text of *La Celestina* first became available in print. This edition contained fourteen acts; in 1502 another edition with five additionally inserted acts was published, on which most editions are still based today. The text is difficult to categorize in terms of genre. Its division into acts and dialogical form point to the theater, yet, as Manfred Tietz has rightly pointed out, there was no such institution as the theater and no stage on which such a complex play could have been performed in Spain at that time:

> The piece . . . was probably meant for communal reading with assigned roles, yet not at court, in a mostly female dominated milieu, but instead at university, in a mostly male dominated context. This audience helps explain several stylistic traits of *Celestina*'s truly new literary language: the use of numerous elements of education . . . , but also the use of many sexual allusions as well as directness. Despite a connection to the theater, *La Celestina* is considered a *novela dialogada* today, and thus a precursor to the Spanish novel.[8]

The plot of this dialogical novel can be summarized as follows: While out hunting with his falcon, young nobleman Calisto finds himself in the garden of Pleberio's family and falls in love with his daughter Melibea. When she rejects him, Calisto, acting on the advice of his servant Sempronio, charges the old procuress Celestina with gaining him access to Melibea's heart and bedchamber. The plan succeeds, even though Calisto's second servant, Pármeno, warns him against accepting the procuress's services. Both servants know Celestina, and when she guarantees them regular relations with Elicia and Areusa, two girls in her charge, even Pármeno yields, not least because both servants hope to receive a share of the procuress's fee. Celestina manages to gain access to Melibea, and after having refused his advances at first, she confesses to the procuress that she is in love with Calisto. Celestina arranges a first meeting, for which the two lovers agree to a tryst through a half-open door. Calisto is so happy with Celestina's services that he gives her a gold necklace. On the night that Calisto enters Melibea's bedchamber with the help of a ladder, Pármeno and Sempronio demand a share of her generous fee from Celestina, but when she refuses to share with them, she is murdered by the two servants. They are executed for their crime. Meanwhile Calisto visits Melibea as often as possible, but one night he falls from the ladder leading to her chamber and dies from the fall. Melibea's despair over her lover's dying drives her to leap to her death.

The drama's ending, Melibea's suicide, was interpreted in pointed words as "deeply un-Spanish" by Marcelino Menéndez Pelayo as early as 1915.[9] In his introduction to an edition of *La Celestina* appearing in the series *Clásicos Castellanos*, its editor, Julio Cejador, stated: "Knowledge of the fact that the work's author was a converted Jew explains a lot. I doubt that such an ending would even have occurred to a Christian from the old Spain."[10]

How are we to judge such patterns of explanation? A comparative glance at Italian and French literary history of the same era shows the consequences that the archival discovery suggesting the experience of a *converso* with regard to the author's religious affiliation had: In Giovanni Boccaccio's *Decamerone* (1348), the character Ghismunda poisons herself out of love (first novella of the fourth day), yet thus far no interpreter of this work has ever suggested this to reveal "crypto-Judaism" on Boccaccio's part. The same is true for the story of the star-crossed lovers Pyramus and Thisbe in Christine de Pizan's *Livre de la Cité des Dames* (1405), in which the two lovers take their own lives because of a misunderstanding—Pyramus kills himself with a sword when he believes Thisbe to be dead; Thisbe, seeing her lover dead, then kills herself with the same sword. There have been no known attempts in this case, either, to understand this passage by way of speculation about Christine de Pizan's religious affiliation. The case is very different with the text discussed here, however: "The author is a converted Jew who has poured out those emotions in the entire work that the forced renunciation of the faith of his forefathers, and the failure to put down roots in his new motherland, has instilled in him."[11]

All of the distinctive features of *La Celestina*, which is indeed a singular document of literary innovation, have been ascribed to the author's religious affiliation in this interpretative tradition. The entire plot was interpreted as a coded portrayal of the impossibility of love between an "Old Christian" (Calisto) and the daughter (Melibea) of a "New Christian" (Pleberio), which represented the "spiritual reality in Spain at that time," the "complex society of converts and 'Old Christians' full of differences, hate, and incompatibilities."[12]

There have been several attempts to interpret individual protagonists of the text as representations of *conversos*, in one case with regard to Calisto's ancestry[13] and in another regarding Melibea's lineage.[14] In his study *The Evolution of Converso Literature*, Gregory Kaplan has rightly stated that a definite attribution of individual protagonists in *La Celestina* as representations of *conversos* is impossible and has further posited that the text mainly stages doubts about the ancestry, origin, and affiliation of all the characters in a virtuosic manner. Kaplan's study is one of the most interesting attempts to free the scholarly study of *La Celestina* from an exclusively biographical approach.[15] Kaplan analyzes the semantic signifiers in the text and identifies dominant, recurrent semes that belong to the semantic fields of ancestry, origin, and affiliation and that, most important, raise doubts about a clearly assignable religious identity for the novel's characters. Kaplan interprets this consciously employed ambiguity as de Rojas's reflection on his contemporary social reality and as evidence for the interpretation of the text as a *converso* allegory.[16]

Thus the archival find, which marked the religious affiliation of the alleged author Fernando de Rojas as *converso*, continues to dominate the text's interpretation, despite the focus on the autonomy of the literary text prevalent in reception aesthetics theory. In an allegorical reading, the dramatic novel's individual plot elements become symbols and metaphors of skepticism and despair. Marcel Bataillon, too, has interpreted *La Celestina* as a literary treatment of the converted Jews' distaste for the practices of procuring and prostitution widely accepted in the Christian world.[17]

This kind of reading of *La Celestina* might offer some clues for a more precise definition of what it is that distinguishes those literary texts whose peculiarity has thus far been explained by their author's ancestry from other texts of this epoch. In my thesis, it is less the author's origin but rather a specific kind of literary writing. In the view represented here, this kind of writing is characterized by a varying yet always specific literary treatment of the biblical text and Christian orthodoxy of the time, which will be described in its variations and shown in the textual analyses in the following sections. Thus any reference to the authors' religious affiliation will at most be an abstract dimension.

The Process of Narration

The prologue to the 1502 Seville edition of *La Celestina* points to the significance of its literary form:

> Unos les roen los huessos que no tienen virtud, que es la hystoria toda junta, no aprovechándose de las particularidades, haziéndola cuento de camino; otros pican los donayres y refranes comunes, loándolos con toda atención, dexando passar por alto lo que haze más al caso y utilidad suya. Pero aquellos para cuyo verdadero plazer es todo, desechan el cuento de la hystoria para contar, coligen la suma para su provecho, ríen lo donoso, las sentencias y dichos de philósophos guardan en su memoria para trasponer en lugares convenibles a sus autos y propósitos. Assí que quando diez personas se juntaren a oír esta comedia, en quien quepa esta differencia de condiciones, como suele acaescer, ¿quién negará que aya contienda en cosa que de tantas maneras se entienda? Que aun los impressores han dado sus punturas,

> poniendo rúbricas o sumarios al principio de cada auto, narrando en breve lo que dentro contenía: una cosa bien escusada segffln lo que los antiguos scriptores usaron.[18]

In contrast to a reading that considers the work a mere reflection of its author's biographical experience, the prologue treats the author in the sense of a textual implication: the reader who subordinates the story to the narrative process will find true pleasure in the text (Pero aquellos para cuyo verdadero plazer es todo, desechan el cuento de la hystoria para contar). The prologue directs the reader's attention to the specific order of plot elements and the process of narration. The dialogical form that the explicit author has chosen for creating his text is thus given an additional layer of meaning. According to the challenge offered here, the reader is to grasp this layer during the process of reading. It is only in the recognition of the narrative structure that the reader will be able to benefit from the book ("coligen la suma para su provecho, ríen lo donoso, las sentencias y dichos de philósophes guardan en su memoria para trasponer en lugares convenibles a sus autos y propósitos"). The prologue ascribes to the aesthetic process in *La Celestina* its own meaning.

In the above-mentioned research tradition, the ten listeners mentioned in this passage have been considered a numerical allegory of the *minyan*, the ten men required for a Jewish religious service.[19] Yet the prologue points less to a spiritual reading than to a highly variable perception and interpretation of the text by those ten imagined listeners to the closet drama, who are described as being very different from each other: "Assí que quando diez personas se juntaren a oír esta comedia, en quien quepa esta differencia de condiciones, como suele acaescer, ¿quién negará que aya contienda en cosa que de tantas maneras se entienda?" The diversity of the respective readers prompts the demand to pay attention less to the rendering of events but rather to the manner in which they are presented. The text points to the process of its creation and directs the reader's attention to its specific form in a manner that seems almost "modern."

The dedication poem, which has prefaced *La Celestina* ever since the 1502 edition, combines this demand from the prologue with an explicitly moral aim: in the stanza with the subheading "Amonesta a los que aman que siruan a Dios y dexen las malas cogitacion[e]s e vicios de amor" (He warns all who love to serve God and abandon vain thoughts and the vices of love), the intended purpose of this literary work is described as follows:

> Vosotros, los que amáys, tomad este enxemplo,
> este fino arnés con que os defendáys:
> bolved ya las riendas, porque n'os perdáys;
> load siempre a Dios visitando su templo.
> Andad sobre aviso; no seáys dexemplo
> de muertos e bivos y propios culpados; estando en el mundo
> yazéys sepultados;
> muy gran dolor siento quando esto contemplo. (75)[20]

Following the prologue's introductory words, this stanza of the dedication poem seems ambiguous, since the safeguarding hint, which the lover is supposed to derive from the tale and take as an example for his own, comparable constellations, cannot be identified without a doubt—after all, the reader has been asked to consider the narrative rather than its contents just a few lines above. The example as form is subordinated to the narrative as the place for potential moral insight. Considered from a different perspective, however, doubts are raised about the normative content of the plot, as conjured up in the dedication poem.

The literary game that starts with the prologue and the dedication poem, namely, the positing of a moral meaning contained within the narrative process rather than the rendered plot, characterizes the entire text. This can be shown in the following passage from the first act. It contains one of the passages that were expurgated when the book was put on the Index in 1640, and it is also one of the most commented-on passages from *La Celestina*, namely, Calisto's confession of faith:

> CALISTO: . . . Como de la aparencia a la existencia, como de lo bivo a lo pintado, como de la sombra a lo real, tanta diferencia ay del fuego que dizes al que me quema. Por cierto si el del purgatorio es tal, más querría que mi spíritu fuesse con los de los brutos animales que por medio de aquel yr a la gloria de los sanctos.

SEMPRONIO: (Algo es lo que digo; a más ha de yr este hecho. No basta loco, sino herege.)

CALISTO: ¿No te digo que hables alto, quando hablares? ¿Qué dizes?

SEMPRONIO: Digo que nunca Dios quiera tal, que es especie de heregía lo que agora dixiste.

CALISTO: ¿Por qué?

SEMPRONIO: Porque lo que dizes contradize la christiana religión.

CALISTO: ¿Qué a mí?

SEMPRONIO: ¿Tú no eres christiano?

CALISTO: ¿Yo? Melibeo só, y a Melibea adoro, y en Melibea creo, y a Melibea amo. (92–93)[21]

On the one hand, this passage has been interpreted as persiflage on the concept of courtly love; on the other hand—with emphasis on Calisto's profession of faith as a "Melibean"—as evidence for the non–Old Christian heritage of this character and thus the author.[22]

However, this passage is of a complexity that conflicts with a definite interpretation. The individual elements of each character's voice contradict each other, and with regard to the godlike elevation of Melibea, this contradiction is explicitly referred to ("contradize la christiana religión"). This is a purposely employed effect, which stands metonymically for the form and structure of the entire textual setting. Calisto's belief that his love has as much in common with other people's love as art has in common with all things living may point to one of the text's intentions. One of the main themes in *La Celestina* is the examination of reality through the literary text and the representation of varying, contradictory views of reality it enables. The triple rephrasing ("Como de la aparencia a la existencia, como de lo bivo a lo pintado, como de la sombra a lo real") suggests such an interpretation and creates awareness of the interaction between the familiar and the unexpected, the conceivable and the heretofore unimagined, thus extending the boundaries of previously experienced reality. The text's structure of a dialogue as "feigned orality staged in writing" (Klaus W. Hempfer) in itself creates a performative contradiction through its form.[23]

There are contradictions, gaps, and disruptions in the respective *Figurenrede* ("character voices," i.e., the speeches given by the characters in the play) as well, though, which point to ostracism, taboo, or appropriation beyond literary boundaries. It is remarkable that these chasms become apparent in the context of questions regarding Christian dogma. While medieval literature and art have often offered reliable and authoritative metaphorical imagery for the conception of reality, this text from 1499 delves deeply into paradigms of inevitability and points to a more diverse as well as contradictory reality. While other contemporary texts are centered on a belief in the universe as a coherent entity, and while, as attempts to represent this world, they are shaped accordingly, the pretense of representing the universal laws assumed to exist objectively no longer seems to exist in *La Celestina*. Art and artistic representation (referring initially to painting in this instance) is merely a shadow: this metaphor adapted from Platonic ontology and criticism of mimesis, which figures right at the beginning of the text, undermines the pretense of representing reality and most of all the moralizing claim, which the text seems to make so strikingly in the dedication poem, in the most effective manner. The seriousness of this denial in turn is made irritatingly ambiguous by putting it in the mouth of a character who frivolously inverts the hierarchy of the agony of purgatory and the agony of love.

The consciousness of the self no longer appears as a continuum to be narrated chronologically, but as a most contradictory matter. In order to do *La Celestina* justice, any reading of it must consider these elements of discontinuity.

Transformations of Biblical Semantics

Based on this underlying inner tension within the book, the following section will examine the status of the biblical quotations in the text. The inclusion and transformation of sacred texts and imagery are among the essential characteristics from which *La Celestina's* distinctiveness results. The following passage from the first act illustrates this point:

SEMPRONIO: (. . . ¡O soberano Dios, quán altos son tus misterios, quánta premia pusiste en el amor, que es necessaria turbación en el amante! . . . Paresce al amante que atrás queda; todos passan, todos rompen, pungidos y esgarrochados como ligeros toros, sin freno saltan por las barreras. Mandaste al hombre por la mujer dexar el padre y la madre. Agora no sólo aquello, mas a ti y a tu ley desamparan, como agora Calisto. Del qual no me maravillo, pues los sabios, los santos, los profetas por él te olvidaron.)

CALISTO: ¡Sempronio!

SEMPRONIO: ¿Señor?

CALISTO: No me dexes.

SEMPRONIO: (De otra temple está esta gayta.) (93–94)[24]

The servant Sempronio is the vehicle for two biblical quotations here, first from the Epistle to the Ephesians 5:30–32a ("For we are members of His body, of His flesh and of His bones. 'For this reason a man shall leave his father and mother and be joined to his wife, and the two shall become one flesh.' This is a great mystery") and second from Genesis 2:24 ("Therefore a man shall leave his father and mother and be joined to his wife, and they shall become one flesh").[25] In Sempronio's speech, the biblical passages are reformulated into an address to God. This transformation creates an ironic effect, which is characteristic of the entire text of *La Celestina*. In his study *Linguistik der Ironie* (Linguistics of irony), Ernst Lapp has described irony as a linguistic simulation of dishonesty: "Being ironic means expressing attitudes or emotions one doesn't have while simultaneously intimating that one doesn't have them."[26] According to Lapp, the emphasis on the recognition that honesty is being simulated is the constitutive element of irony. What the ironic speaker is saying is being recognized as a contradiction by the reader. An immediate, all-too-definite categorization, however, would destroy the effect of irony. Lapp states more precisely that the ironic speaker simulates being dishonest. This encompasses the ambiguity typical of ironic statements, the evasive recognizability of intended meaning, and the "necessity of listening repeatedly." In *La Celestina*, the characters' biblical quotations are subject to this discrepancy between what is said and what is meant. The ironic speech does not necessarily mean the opposite of what is said, however. As in the above quotation, it is not so much a completely opposite statement but rather a gradual dissolution of the sacred semantics that arises from the formal transformation of a biblical mandate into simulated speech. However, a subtle balance between retained dogmatic content and irony is maintained in *La Celestina*. This is particularly true for the following passage:

> Mandaste al hombre por la mujer dexar el padre y la madre. Agora no sólo aquello, mas a ti y a tu ley desamparan, como agora Calisto. Del qual no me maravillo, pues los sabios, los santos, los profetas por él te olvidaron. (94)

God himself had commanded man to leave his father and mother for woman's sake, yet today one doesn't leave only them behind but also God and his laws, without any protection. Sempronio is not surprised by this, since wise men, saints, and prophets, too, had forgotten God because of love. The ironic treatment of the biblical passage does not create new structures that might perform a transformation from contingency to meaning instead of the biblical text. The lover follows the biblical command when leaving his parental home for a woman. The problematic constellation arises when the lover puts the object of his love in God's place and no longer respects the law. The power of love appears like a symbol of a world no longer in order, the unraveling of which is beyond the individual.[27] Divine law is presented as inscrutable and incomprehensible ("O soberano Dios, quán altos son tus misterios, quanta premia pusiste en el amor, que es necessaria turbación en el amante!")—yet relinquishing this law is not put forth as an alternative despite the ironic treatment. This is true for the following passage from the first act as well:

> CALISTO: ¿Qué me repruevas?
>
> SEMPRONIO: Que sometes la dignidad del hombre a la imperfección de la flaca mujer.
>
> CALISTO: ¿Mujer? ¡O grossero! ¡Dios, Dios!
>
> SEMPRONIO: ¿E assí lo crees, o burlas?
>
> CALISTO: ¿Que burlo? Por Dios la creo, por Dios la confesso, y no creo que hay otro soberano en el cielo avnque entre nosotros mora.

SEMPRONIO: (¡Ha, ha, ha! ¿Oy´stes qué blasfemia? ¿Vistes qué ceguedad?)

CALISTO: ¿De qué te ríes?

SEMPRONIO: Ríome, que no pensava que havía peor invención de peccado que en Sodoma.

CALISTO: ¿Cómo?

SEMPRONIO: Porque aquéllos procuraron abbominable uso con los ángeles no conoscidos, y tú con el que confiessas ser Dios.

CALISTO: ¡Maldito seas! Que hecho me has reýr, lo que no pensé ogaño. (94–95)[28]

The comic effect in this highly ironic allusion to Genesis 18 and 19 is directed at the character Calisto. His blindness (*ceguedad*) and blasphemy (*blasfemia*), which become evident in his equation of Melibea with a deity, are exposed to ridicule by Sempronio's earthily comical comparison. The text continuously questions the story rendered and the individual characters' perspectives, and it is in this passage of *La Celestina* at the latest that it seems as though the text aims at a more elevated seriousness beyond its comic effect. The target of the ironic attack is not the sacred text at first, but humanity's "idolatry" of human love. In addition to a comic punchline, the comparison with the Sodomites evokes God's punishment of a sinful people and thus also the punishment for Calisto's blasphemy: in Genesis 19, the Sodomites who attack Lot are struck with blindness; Sempronio also calls Calisto's behavior "blind." It seems as if the ironic textual strategy of the tragicomedy were aimed at an aesthetic or even moral reflection on the reader's part—an unconsidered engagement with the text does not seem possible at all.

This interpretation may be expanded by another example of Sempronio's speech in the first act against the absolutization of love and Calisto's idolatry of woman:

SEMPRONIO: . . . Oye a Salomón do dize que las mujeres y el vino hazen a los hombres renegar. Conséjate con Séneca y verás en qué las tiene. Escucha al Aristóteles, mira a Bernardo. Gentiles, judíos, cristianos y moros, todos en esta concordia están. (96–97)[29]

Sempronio's first line is a quotation from Sirach 19:2. Several points can be made based on this short passage. The warning ascribed to the prophet Solomon that wine and women make man an apostate is linked to classical rhetoric (Seneca) and philosophy (Aristotle) as well as medieval moral doctrine (Bernard). The warning is eventually expanded to the knowledge of the dangers of woman, on which not only heathens, Jews, and Christians but also the Moors agreed. While Sempronio's warning is not rendered dogmatically false by the high level of exaggeration, it is clearly ironically marked as futile, since heathens, Jews, Christians, and Moors, despite their theoretical agreement on this point, have abstained neither from love nor wine. Owing to the irony in this passage, a morality regulated by philosophy or any religion appears as a futile endeavor that does not reflect the characters' respective realities.

This interpretation becomes evident in the discourse of Calisto's second servant. In the first act, Pármeno warns Calisto against availing himself of Celestina's services:

> PÁRMENO: . . . comunicava con las más encerradas . . . y aquestas en tiempo honesto, como estaciones, processiones de noche, missas del gallo, missas del alva, y otras secretas devociones. Muchas encubiertas vi entrar en su casa; tras ellas hombres descalços, contritos, y reboçados, desatacados, que entravan allí a llorar sus peccados. ¡Qué tráfagos, si piensas, traýa! . . . Con todos estos affanes, nunca passava sin missa ni bíspras ni dexava monasterios de frayles ni de monjas; esto porque allí hazía ella sus aleluyas y conciertos. (110–111)[30]

This description of Celestina, given in a gesture of warning, exceeds a mere portrayal of the procuress; it illustrates a deep interlacing of Celestina's practices with religious custom at the time. The procuress appears less as a destroyer of religious morals than as the product and beneficiary of degenerate religious morality. The language is highly ironic and does not spare sacred practice, either, in this example: both the circumscription of the plan, for the execution of which the gentlemen visit Celestina's house with the words "entravan allí a llorar sus peccados," and the circumscription of procuring between monks and nuns as "aleluyas y conciertos" show how the linguistic emblems of a religiously regulated everyday life have lost their original meaning. According to this passage, a value system of morality no longer exists in *La Celestina*. It is important to note, however, that the implied author of this text is not at all interested in promoting a morality "freed" from the laws of religion. Instead, the literary reflection creates the image of a universe in which definite knowledge and formalities are no longer valid and where the reflection itself is represented in the alternation between question and answer.

Later in the first act, Pármeno, who has warned his master about Celestina, speaks with the procuress herself. This dialogue is remarkable because of its complex reasoning:

> PÁRMENO: . . . Yaún más te digo, que no los que poco tienen son pobres; mas los que mucho desean. Y por esto, aunque más digas, no te creo en esta parte. Querría passer la vida sin embidia, los yermos y aspereza sin temor, el sueño sin sobresaltos, las injurias con respuesta, las fuerças sin denuesto, las premias con resistencia.
>
> CELESTINA: ¡O hijo!, bien dizen que la prudencia no puede ser sino en los viejos; y tú mucho moço eres. (123)[31]

Using a quotation from the book of Job 12:12, Celestina comments ironically on Pármeno's moral concepts, which are naïve from her point of view: "With the ancient is wisdom; and in length of days understanding." At this point it becomes clear what characterizes the inclusion of biblical quotations in *La Celestina* in many places: the quotations are freed from their biblical context and serve as instruments for the realization of the characters' own ambitions.

Later in the conversation, Celestina recommends excessive carnal pleasure to Pármeno and offers him a girl in exchange for his compliance:

> PÁRMENO: Todo me recelo, madre, de recebir dudoso consejo.
>
> CELESTINA: ¿No quieres? Pues dezirte he lo que dize el sabio: Al varón que con dura cerviz al que le castiga menosprecia, arrebatado quebrantamiento le verná, y sanidad ninguna le consiguirá. Y assí, Pármeno, me despido de ti y deste negocio.
>
> PÁRMENO: (Ensañada está mi madre, dubda tengo en su consejo; yerro es no creer y culpa creerlo todo. Más humano es confiar,

> mayormente en esta que interesse promete, a do provecho nos pueda allende de amor conseguir. Oýdo he que deve hombre a sus mayores creer. Ésta ¿qué me aconseja? Paz con Sempronio. La paz no se deve negar: que bienaventurados son los pacíficos, que hijos de Dios serán llamados. Amor no se deve rehuyr. Caridad a los hermanos; interesse pocos le apartan. Pues quiérola complazer y oýr.) (127–128)[32]

The irony in this passage is virtuosic. Celestina quotes Proverbs 29:1: "He, that being often reproved hardeneth his neck, shall suddenly be destroyed, and that without remedy." Again, this is the dialogue through which Celestina eventually turns Pármeno into one of her accomplices by offering him a girl's sexual services in return for his loyalty. The soliloquy in which Pármeno convinces himself of the lucrativeness of Celestina's offer culminates in a quotation from Matthew 5:9: "Blessed are the peacemakers: for they shall be called the children of God." In the composition of Pármeno's speech, Christ's formula for peace is used as a pretext for cooperation with the procuress because of the great advantages she can offer Pármeno. This is actually not an ironic treatment of the respective formulae of the sacred text, which would have been widely familiar at the time, for the effect of this passage is not to deny Christian virtues such as charity and peaceableness. The effect results from the decontextualization of the quoted statement and its recontextualization into contexts that conflict with the Christian value system on the whole (in this case, *luxuria*), but not with those values highlighted in the sacred formulae quoted ironically. This process might be described as an oblique use of irony, in which the effect is not to ridicule the sacred formula but to deprive it of meaning entirely. It appears in the shape of a disposable empty phrase. The intentionality is not aimed at a denial of Christian religion but at the undermining of the concept of the sacred word as such.

From one act to the next, the allusions to familiar formulae of religious discourse become more oblique and thus simultaneously more subtle. In the third act, there is a short conference about the state of business in the procuress's house, which includes the following dialogue between Celestina and her employee Elicia:

CELESTINA: Calla, bova, déxale, que otro pensamiento traemos en que más nos va. Dime, ¿está desocupada la casa? ¿Fuése la moça, que esperava al ministro?

ELICIA: Yaun después vino otra y se fue.

CELESTINA: ¿Sí, que no embalde?

ELICIA: No, en buena fe, ni Dios lo quiera, que aunque vino tarde, más vale a quien Dios ayuda, etc. (146)[33]

The laconic irony in this scene, which portrays the priest's visit to the brothel as a matter of course, aims at a no-longer-existent unity of reality and faith. The true effect, however, only emerges from Elicia's last reply. "[Q]ue aunque vino tarde, más vale a quien Dios ayuda" on the one hand hybridizes the reference to the allegory of the vineyard ("que aunque vinbo tarde, más vale a Dios") and the popular, ultimately antibiblical "belief" that those whom God helps are more valuable. This means that the mundane ideas of appreciation and support are being superimposed upon the divine logic transcending all human comprehension coded in the New Testament allegories. This "oblique" formula derived from a clash of contexts is then translated and embedded in a context with which it is connected solely and exclusively through the semantic vehicle of the sacred officiant, the priest—who is presented not in a serious manner, though, but according to the patterns of the anticlerical satire dating back to the Middle Ages, virtually as a "man of flesh and blood." In this case, too, the discursive effect lies less in a polemic against the quoted sacred phrases and stories but rather in a complete deprivation of meaning effected by repeated contextual clashes. If sacred language is *logos* with maximum density of meaning, then it is turned into vacuous speech without meaning in *La Celestina*.

An analogous constellation can be found in the following scene from the fourth act. It is an excerpt from a dialogue between Celestina and Melibea, in which Celestina wishes Melibea to hear her request:

MELIBEA: Celestina, amiga, yo he holgado mucho en verte y conoscerte; también hasme dado plazer con tus razones. Toma tu dinero y vete con Dios, que me parece que no deves aver comido.

CELESTINA: ¡O angélica ymagen, o perla preciosa, y cómo te lo dizes! Gozo me toma en verte hablar; ¿y no sabes que por la divina boca fue dicho contra aquel infernal tentador, que no de sólo pan biviriemos? Pues assí es, que no el sólo comer mantiene. (158)[34]

The quotation that Celestina uses to try to persuade Melibea harkens back to Matthew:

> Then was Jesus led up of the Spirit into the wilderness to be tempted of the devil. And when he had fasted forty days and forty nights, he afterward hungered. And the tempter came and said unto him, If thou art the Son of God, command that these stones become bread. But he answered and said, It is written, Man shall not live by bread alone, but by every word that proceedeth out of the mouth of God. (Matthew 4:1–4)

In the scene quoted above, the irony is created by the plot of the dramatic novel, since the reader knows that Celestina, too, will tempt Melibea. Celestina uses the shortened quotation in order to furnish Melibea's charity toward a hungry beggar woman with a level of meaning that will eventually aid her in making temptation palatable to Melibea and in making resistance seem almost "unchristian." The contextual clash, which almost reaches the level of carnivalesque inversion in this case, consists in the fact that in the sacred verse, what is referred to as that which man needs besides bread in order to live is the (divine) *logos*; the reference here, however, is to *luxuria*.

The extent of the discursive distortion that arises from Celestina's decontextualizing use of standardized religious formulae is noteworthy:

MELIBEA: Vieja honrrada, no te entiendo, si más no declaras tu demanda. Por una parte me alteras y provocas a enojo; por otra me mueves a compassión. No te sabría bolver respuesta conveniente, según lo poco, que he sentido de tu habla. Que yo soy dichosa, si de mi palabra ay necessidad para salud de algún christiano. Porque hazer beneficio es semejar a Dios, y más que el que haze beneficio le recibe cuando es a persona que le merece. Yel que puede sanar al que padece, no lo haziendo le mata, assí que no cesses tu petición por empacho ni temor.

CELESTINA: El temor perdí mirando, señora, tu beldad, que no puedo creer que embalde pintasse Dios unos gestos más perfetos que otros, más dotados de gracias, más hermosas faciones; sino que hazerlos almazén de virtudes, de misericordia, de compassión, ministros de sus mercedes y dádivas, como a ti. (159–160)[35]

In this passage, Melibea copies Celestina's rhetorical strategy, thus indicating that she is herself about to defect from the realm of chastity and sincerity to that of cynical hedonism devoid of meaning. The contextual clash in this instance is as striking as possible: without further expounding on the issue, formulae belonging to the Christian discourse of *agape* are being implanted into a discourse of *eros*, or rather of *fornicatio*.

The Depiction of the World of Faith

It is made evident in an *a parte* in the fifth act that this reasoning follows a logic that is meant to honor a lord other than the Christian God:

CELESTINA: . . . ¡O diablo a quien yo conjuré, cómo compliste tu palabra en todo lo que te pedí! En cargo te soy, assí amansaste la cruel hembra con tu poder y diste tan oportuno lugar a mi habla quanto quise, con la absencia de su madre. O vieja Celestina, ¿vas alegre? Sábete que la meytad está hecha quando tienen buen principio las cosas. ¡O serpentino azeyte, o blanco hilado, cómo os aparejastes todos en mi favor! ¡O yo rompiera todos mis atamientos hechos y por hazer, ni creyera en yervas ni piedras ni en palabras! Pues alégrate, vieja, que más sacarás deste pleyto que de quinze virgos que renovaras. (171)[36]

In a form structured analogously to a prayer, Celestina thanks the devil for keeping his word in leaving her alone with Melibea, thus giving her the opportunity to persuade the latter of her "Christian duties" during their conversation—namely, to hear Calisto's suit. Yet this "belief"' is also portrayed as merely functional rather than as a deep conviction. It becomes evident in the speech that Celestina's gratitude is linked to the fulfillment of her wish—had this not been the case, so

Celestina states, she would have dismissed her belief in the devil and sorcery as useless: "¡O yo rompiera todos mis atamientos hechos y por hazer, ni creyera en yervas ni piedras ni en palabras!" Thus it is inappropriate to describe Celestina as a devil worshipper after the fashion of a medieval witch character, as has been done in a great deal of the secondary literature. The "devil worship," too, is a decontextualized quotation devoid of meaning in this case. In the world of this text, there is no orthodox or blasphemous-satanic transcendence, for all the formulae originally filled with meaning have been reduced to cynically arranged, empty phrases, which operate above a reality "objectively" controlled by coincidence and "subjectively" by concupiscence.

Celestina's "world of faith" is described in more detail in another passage, in a scene in the seventh act in which Celestina speaks about Pármeno's mother:

> CELESTINA: . . . ¿Quién era todo mi bien y descanso, sino tu madre, más que mi hermana y comadre? ¡O qué graciosa era, o qué desembuelta, limpia, varonil! Tan sin pena ni temor se andava a media noche de cimiterio en cimiterio buscando aparejos para nuestro officio como de día. Ni dexava christianos ni moros ni judíos cuyos enterramientos no visitava. De día los acechava, de noche los desenterrava. Assí se holgava con la noche escura como tú con el día claro. Dezía que aquella era capa de pecadores. . . . Assí era tu madre, que Dios haya, la prima de nuestro officio, y por tal era de todo el mundo conoscida y querida, assí de cavalleros como de clérigos, casados, viejos, moços, y niños. (196–197)[37]

This passage clearly demonstrates that Celestina's "devil worship" is not an alternative religion but a profession, which may require unusual tasks but does not aim to replace the reality of the world regulated by the three religions ("Ni dexava christianos ni moros ni judíos"). Instead, it makes use of it for its own material benefit.

Celestina's speech also discloses the risks of this profession, however: Pármeno's mother had been arrested several times and charged with witchcraft as well. This passage is quoted at length here:

> CELESTINA: Hijo, digo que sin aquélla prendieron quatro vezes a tu madre, que Dios haya, sola. Yaun la una le levantaron que era

> bruxa, porque la hallaron de noche con unas candelillas cojendo tierra de una encruçijada, e la tovieron medio día en una escalera en la plaça puesta, uno como rocadero pintado en la cabeza. Pero cosas son que passan; no fue nada; algo han de sofrir los hombres en este triste mundo para sustentar sus vidas y honrras. . . . Assí que los que algo son como ella y saben y valen son los que más presto yerran. Verás quien fue Virgilio y qué tanto supo, mas ya avrás oydo cómo estovo en un cesto colgado de una torre mirándole toda Roma. Pero por esso no dexó de ser honrrado ni perdió el nombre de Virgilio. . . . Sabíalo mejor el cura, que Dios aya, que viniéndola a consolar dixo que la santa scritura tenía que bienaventurados eran los que padecían persecución por la justicia y que aquéllos poseerían el reyno de los cielos. Mira si es mucho passar algo en este mundo por gozar de la gloria del otro, y más que según todos dezían, a tuerto y sin razón y con falsos testigos y rezios tormentos la hizieron aquella vez confessar lo que no era. . . . Assí que todo esto passó tu buena madre acá, devemos creer que le dará Dios buen pago allá, si es verdad lo que nuestro cura nos dixo. Y con esto me consuelo. Pues seýme tú como ella, amigo verdadero, y trabaja por ser bueno, pues tienes a quien parezcas. (198–199)[38]

For Stephen Gilman (*The Spain of Fernando de Rojas*, 1972) this passage is an example of the fate of converted Jews in the Iberian Peninsula at that time. According to Gilman, the punishment of Pármeno's mother, Claudia, which Celestina describes here, evokes the sentences imposed during the Inquisition, which were mainly directed against the *conversos*. In his interpretation, Gilman particularly emphasizes Claudia's confession induced by torture and false witness statements, since it illustrates the dubiousness of all Inquisition trials.

This would be an interpretation that centers on the unarticulated, yet in the interpreter's view, "actually intended" statement. There are layers of meaning in what is actually articulated, however, that are not aimed at any particular religious group but attest to an emphatically ironic intention. The part of this overall highly complex passage that is directly accessible is the reference to the medieval legend of Virgil (which was ubiquitous in literary texts at that time).[39] The anecdote quoted here refers to one of the "sage's" amorous adventures, which had become public when the object of his admiration left him trapped in the basket or cage in which she was supposed to pull him up to her chamber, so that he was exposed to public ridicule the next morning. This passage mainly illustrates that the procedure of decontextualization and oblique recontextualization, which at first had only been applied to formulae of religious discourse, is increasingly extended to other discourses as well. After all, the point of this defense is to transpose the Inquisition trial that Pármeno's mother was subjected to—and thus the entire apparatus named "Inquisition"—to the realm of harmlessness and impunity: just as Virgil's public disgrace as rendered in the legend could not harm his renown as a sage, the Inquisition trial and public scorn had not shattered Pármeno's mother's reputation as an honorable woman, either.

In order to grasp the complexity of the semantic condensation in this example, one has to examine the diverse facets of this essentially oblique, subtle analogy: Virgil is an authentic sage, yet Pármeno's mother is not an honorable woman but a person who only calls herself honorable—as is transparent to anyone—to improve the performance of her "oficio." She is publicly scorned not because of a specific case of misconduct, but because of her perpetual transgression against official morals. Her pillorying is not carried out as carnivalesque ridicule but in the form of legally sanctioned disgrace.

Not only the implicit ridicule but also the discursive-rhetorical seriousness culminates in Celestina's eventually expressing an essential truth by her calumnious use of Virgil as an example: those who are without honor to begin with will not be affected by the Inquisition's public pillorying. As in the case of the formulae of sacred discourse, the precepts of the discourse of honor and popular heterodoxy monitored by the Inquisition are exposed as mere empty phrases, which only bear meaning and sense for those who believe in them. The "orthodox," biblically codified, sacred discourse is subsequently resumed in this long speech.

The priest sent to Pármeno's mother as minister had supposedly comforted her by telling her it was written in the Bible that those persecuted by justice were blessed, for theirs was the kingdom of Heaven. This transfer of the biblical saying to a context in which the deeds of Pármeno's mother are described as preconditions for blessedness in the afterlife by a priest legitimizes the deeds of this life not just as an opportunity but in fact as a specific prerequisite for reward in the afterlife: "Assí que todo esto passó tu Buena madre acá, devemos creer que le dará Dios buen pago allá, si es verdad lo que nuestro cura nos dixo." This reasoning of Celestina's is a straightforward example of the structure of decontextualization described repeatedly. The structure of events and the clear differentiation between religious law and human obedience increasingly dissolve during the narrative process, so that the aesthetic method and the concept of historical process eventually correspond. This approximation of historic event and fiction leads to a relativization of religious laws, not because they are considered wrong but because their capability of creating context is depicted as limited and arbitrarily interpretable.

There is a scene in the eighth act in which Calisto applies a similar functionalization to attending a church service:

> CALISTO: Agora lo creo, que tañen a missa. Dacá mis ropas; yré a la Madalena; rogaré a Dios aderece a Celestina y ponga en coraçon a Melibea mi remedio, o dé fin en breve a mis tristes días. (219)[40]

The ironic dig is again aimed at the logic of the exchange between God and humanity, which Calisto evokes in this short scene: in exchange for attending mass, he expects God's support, in this case the success of the procuring that so blatantly violates the divine commandment, or else an early death—in any case a divine intervention in exchange for a prayer.

Attending mass has an unwelcome side effect, however, that prompts Sempronio's caution in the eleventh act:

> SEMPRONIO: Señor, mira que tu estada es dar al todo el mundo qué dezir. Por Dios, que huygas que ser traýdo en lenguas, que al muy devote llaman ypócrita. ¿Qué dirán sino que andas royendo los santos? Si passion tienes, súfrela en tu casa; no te sienta la tierra. (249)[41]

Sempronio's admonition is obviously not based on concern about his master's salvation but on the effect of Calisto's behavior on fellow men. The irony is doubled in this case: the reader knows that Calisto attends mass not out of piety but as a precondition for the divine support of

Celestina's deeds. Yet this is nothing but an oblique quotation of a formula of lay piety, as has been described above. Calisto does not seriously hope for divine support for the satisfaction of his *luxuria*. The intention of his frequent attendance of church services is to create the impression of a "respectable" young man in public (presumably contrary to the impression created thus far) and to use this feigned respectability in order to convince Melibea to agree to a meeting—which in her view would not be jeopardizing her honor under these circumstances.

Sempronio points out that the deeply pious can easily seem like hypocrites if they demonstrate their faith too ostentatiously. His advice to Calisto, to act out his "pious" passion at home, indicates a religious life regulated not by faith but by comparison with one's peers and a concern with one's reputation. Piety is separated from its context and used in order to pursue profane and entirely irreligious interests everywhere. In the end, this undermines the efficacy of Calisto's strategy as well. What seems merely episodic at first eventually becomes explicit in Pleberio's lament at the end of the piece: the attitude that at first seems to be represented only by Celestina and Calisto has in fact long been universal. It is thus that the text gains its full dimension: the goal is a portrait not of the mores of frivolous young people but of a social cosmos in which nobody believes the words and formulae they constantly use to possess a coherent significance anymore. "Significance" merely is a fictitious category aimed at deceiving others. In a social fabric where deception has become a "universal" strategy, however, this strategy does not work (any longer). All that remains is purely animalistic interaction: crude sexuality and killing, *bestialitas* in the language of traditional moral philosophy.

The skeptical irony in *La Celestina* is a poetic reflection of a moral-theological nature. The drama contains a layer that makes the implied author as well as the conditions and principles of its creation and depiction explicit. Almost every character in the drama is deceived by someone else's functionalization of religion for his or her own benefit. Literary irony serves as the reflection of a universe in which definite knowledge and absolute faith are no longer valid. At the end this irony turns serious. The text continually questions the narration and all the characters' perspectives and—in the last act—possibly tends toward sincerity beyond comic effect.

The function of the literary text in this obscure world dominated by the human pursuit of personal benefit is not merely aesthetic. The purpose of the back reference to the act of artistic creation in *La Celestina* is not a playful relativization of an absolute worldview but rather an understanding of artistic creation in which the subject is given the opportunity for reflection—beyond actions recognizable as neither right nor wrong. In a constellation in which religion does not provide an orienting framework, the decision for literary irony is a decision for deviation. It attempts to see the included excluded and permits itself to anticipate the possibility of traversable boundaries and, depending on the situation, to play differing roles in order to maintain the balance between fundamentalism and occasionalism. The reality it "decides" on has a past requiring interpretation, a confusing present, and an uncertain future. The text's ironic aesthetics demonstrates by its contradictory relativizations to what extent the drama's characters are caught up in deception with regard to reality. The relativizations do include God's unquestionable existence and the unity of the reality of faith, however.

So what about the problem of ancestry, origin, and affiliation in a world thus described? Can it indeed be shown by means of the text that the "desperate worldview of a *converso*" has been preserved in *La Celestina*, as is presumed in the interpretations cited above? There are two passages in the drama that explicitly explore the question of ancestry and law. The first scene is to be found in the fourteenth act. Following the legally ordered execution of his servants Sempronio and Pármeno, who had murdered Celestina out of greed for her procuress's reward, Calisto is concerned about the consequences this scandal might have for his family's reputation. Calisto speaks by himself and accuses the absent judge to have done an injustice:

> CALISTO: . . . O cruel juez, y qué mal pago me has dado del pan que de mi padre comiste. . . . ¿Quién pensara que tú me havías de destruyr? No hay, cierto, cosa más empecible que el incogitado enemigo. . . . Tú eres público delinquente y mataste a los que son privados, y pues sabe que menor delicto es el privado que el

> público, menor su utilidad, según las leyes de Atenas disponen. Las quales no son scritas con sangre, antes muestran que es menos yerro no condennar los malhechores que punir los innocentes. ¡O quán peligroso es seguir justa causa delante injusto juez. . . . Pero, ¿qué digo; con quién hablo; . . . no vees que el offendedor no está presente? ¿Con quién lo has? Torna en ti; mira que nunca los absentes se hallaron justos; oye entrambas partes para sentenciar, ¿no ves que por executar justicia no havía de mirar amistad ni debdo ni criança; no miras que la ley tiene de ser ygual a todos? Mira que Rómulo, el primero çimentador de Roma, mató a su propio hermano, porque la ordenada ley traspassó. (289–290)[42]

The logic that Calisto wants to apply to the law in this monologue corresponds to the treatment of religious mandates by the drama's cast of characters. The moment they have to be applied to oneself, these mandates are perceived as hostile. The execution of the two murderers is described as a public crime against two people "merely" guilty of a private crime ("Tú eres público delinquente y mataste a los que son privados, y pues sabe que menor delicto es el privado que el público, menor su utilidad, según las leyes de Atenas disponen"). According to Calisto, the "privately" committed crime carries less weight than the publicly committed one owing to its limited effect on the general public. These were the laws of Athens—not "written in blood" but admonishing that it was more serious to punish an innocent person than to let a guilty one get away. Yet Calisto's soliloquy ends with his acceptance of judicial autonomy and the general validity of the law.

This soliloquy illustrates once more the particular role of skeptical irony in this text. Calisto, who at first demands a different judicial logic for himself, seems to be convinced of the justness of the law at the end of the soliloquy. Thus he leaves the sphere of oblique recontextualization, in which he usually consistently acts, for a moment (in this case the proclamation of a capital crime as a harmless misdemeanor and its punishment as a crime) and advances to the "right" view of things.

It becomes clear during the further course of the drama's plot, however, that this did not result from any true insight. Calisto continues his nightly visits to Melibea's chamber as if nothing had happened.

The servants guarding the ladder that he uses to climb the wall have changed, while his behavior remains the same. Word and deed, thus the résumé after reading the tragicomedy, are not necessarily linked for the drama's characters. As regards the drama as a whole, whether the portrayed world could be "healed" if all agents were to give up their cynical strategy of decontextualization and return to the original meaning of the words they use remains an open question. It is left up to each recipient how to answer this question. This fundamental openness is part of the text's aesthetic strategy as well.

Most importantly, there is no clear positioning on questions of origin and religion discernible in this passage referring to the "laws of the blood"—quite contrary to the claims made about Fernando de Rojas's *La Celestina* in a majority of the secondary literature "fixed on ancestry" since the discovery of the archival document. This reference is made with regard to the jurisdiction in Athens, which was more "humane" in comparison with older civilizations—Athens as a city is not a Christian emblem, however. With regard to "affiliation," this passage is rather vague. The second above-mentioned textual passage often quoted as relevant possibly contains one of the essential statements in the text overall. It appears in Areusa's speech in the ninth act:

> AREUSA: Ruyn sea quien por ruyn se tiene; las obras hacen linaje, que al fin todos somos hijos de Adán y Eva. Procure de ser cada uno bueno por sí, y no vaya a buscar en la nobleza de sus pasados la virtud. (229)[43]

La Celestina's author may have been a Christian, a *converso*, or a Jew—he has included a sentence in this passage that illustrates his conviction that a definition of affiliation was not essential. According to this sentence, it is a person's actions that determine his belonging, and only those who consider themselves low and act accordingly are of low origin. All people are descended from Adam and Eve and thus have in common the same initial conditions. All must make an effort to become decent rather than trying to derive their merit from the nobility of their ancestors. This is an obvious invective against the discourse of *limpieza de sangre*, of course. It is also no less obviously an invective against the belief in being a chosen people, however. Based on the biblically warranted idea of divine creation, this passage postulates a universalism that seems almost secular and modern in that it labels all categories of affiliation as defined by ancestry as absurd.

The Meaning of *La Celestina*'s Final Act

In the above-mentioned line of critical interpretation, the culmination of the *conversos*' worldview as preserved in the text has always been identified as the text's ending, namely the twenty-first act, in which Pleberio mourns the suicide of his daughter Melibea. In his reading of Pleberio's lament, Stephen Gilman identifies the back reference to the author's affiliation as the radical skepticism that showed itself in that funeral speech. Nonexistent hope for a reunion in the afterlife, decisive for a Christian worldview, and the lack of faith as a source of comfort in the face of loss are interpreted as ultimate evidence for the thesis that Fernando de Rojas had used the character of Pleberio as a "mouthpiece" for his own pessimistic convictions. These convictions had been imposed on him by the reality of life as a *converso*. Such a reading receives "external" support from the fact that, in comparison to later Christian ideas, the belief in life after death and an afterlife does indeed only exist in a vague form in Jewish tradition and has always caused controversy among scholars.

Wilhelm Dilthey claims in *Poetry and Experience* (*Das Erlebnis und die Dichtung* [1906]) that the author's experience shapes his or her specific relationship to reality and expresses itself in his or her oeuvre. Authorial intent is defined as the conscious or unconscious intention of the empirical author, which has to be reconstructed in order to understand his or her work. Yet the concept of authorial intent is quite problematic, particularly with regard to anonymously published texts. It is advisable to limit the role of the empirical author when analyzing texts of this kind, and possibly not just these, and to make specific the relevant concept of the author. The question as to what biographical information is relevant to an interpretation cannot be answered in the same way for every literary text. One needs to differentiate instead whether the text originates from a period in which text production was affected by a corresponding authorial concept and, accordingly, if this is a text in which the author has left any traces of self-dramatization. This is not the case for all texts.

This question could indeed be posed in a much more fundamental way: Why should it matter at all for the analysis of a literary text what the author "actually" meant to say? If the author managed to successfully realize his or her intention, it can be read from the text itself; if that attempt failed, it is irrelevant to the meaning of the text at hand. A literary text is not of interest as a biographical document of its author or a psychological substratum for the author's motives, but as an aesthetically shaped entity independent from the mental conditions that contributed to its creation. Thus the literary text itself becomes the only legitimate point of reference for scholarly interpretation.

Regardless of this limitation, literary texts do not originate in a space entirely disconnected from the world; they absorb the discourses of their time and transform them. The analysis of three passages below will demonstrate how Pleberio's lament could be interpreted as a document of the cultural constellation in the Iberian Peninsula of the Middle Ages and the early modern age without centering the analysis on the author.

The first passage refers to the radical skepticism toward the world, which Pleberio voices in view of his daughter's death:

> PLEBERIO: ¡O vida de congoxas llena, de miserias acompañada, o mundo, mundo! Muchos mucho de ti dixeron, muchos en tus qualidades metieron la mano, a diversas cosas por oýdas te compararon. Yo por triste experiencia lo contaré, como a quien las ventas y compras de tu engañosa feria no prósperamente sucedieron, como aquel que mucho ha hasta agora callado tus falsas propiedades por no encender con odio tu yra, por que no me secasses sin tiempo esta flor que este día echaste de tu poder. Pues agora sin temor, como quien no tiene qué perder, como aquel a quien tu compañía es ya enojosa, como caminante pobre que sin temor de los crueles salteadores va cantando en alta boz. Yo pensava en mi más tierna edad que eras y eran tus hechos regidos por alguna orden. Agora, visto el pro y la contra de tus bienandanças, me pareçes un laberinto de errores, un desierto spantable, una morada de fieras, juego

> de hombres que andan en corro, laguna llena de cieno, región llena de spinas, monte alto, campo pedregoso, prado lleno de serpientes, huerto florido y sin fruto, fuente de cuydados, río de lágrimas, mar de miserias, trabajo sin provecho, dulce ponçoña, vana esperança, falsa alegría, verdadero dolor. (338)[44]

Philosophical skepticism was one of the sixteenth century's intellectual movements not only because of a humanist interest in the authors of classical antiquity, but also as the result of changes experienced during this period: the discovery of America, the Reformation, and later, the end of the Ptolemaic system, brought about by the observations and hypotheses of Copernicus, followed by Galileo's proof and the eventual implementation of heliocentrism by Kepler. All these had decisively altered the valid categories for explaining the world—weakened and even inverted them. It was only with the earliest Latin translation of the *Outlines of Pyrrhonism* by Sextus Empiricus (second century CE) by Henri Estienne in 1562 and the Latin edition of his collected works by Gentian Hervet (1569), however, that the most important source of Pyrrhonism reentered European philosophy and could thus become the basis of a renaissance of classical skepticism in the sixteenth and seventeenth centuries. Michel de Montaigne's *Essais* later provided the basis for early modern and modern skepticism.

It is important to remember at this point that Pleberio's monologue appears in a text written in 1499. The diagnosis of *vanitas mundi* featured in it does not lead to praise of the afterlife but to despair about the "labyrinth of continuous misguidance" in this life. This is indeed a highly remarkable fact for a late medieval text, written long before the earliest translation of the fundamental text of classical skepticism. Does this mean it is a "Jewish skepticism" that is exhibited in Pleberio's monologue, however? This question reiterates the dilemma initially put forth. Intellectual developments that have yet to unfold as general bias are anticipated in literary form in *La Celestina*. In this sense the text is extraordinary. Does that make it "un-Spanish," though, and does it articulate the perspective of a *converso*?

The second passage to be considered is that part of Pleberio's funeral speech in which he accuses love in personified form:

> PLEBERIO: La leña que gasta tu llama son almas y vidas de humanas criaturas, las quales son tantas que de quien començar pueda apenas me ocurre; no sólo de christianos mas de gentiles y judíos y todo en pago de buenos servicios. ¿Qué me dirás de aquel Macías de nuestro tiempo, cómo acabó amando, cuyo triste fin tú fuiste la causa? ¿Qué hizo por ti Paris? ¿Qué Helena? ¿Qué hizo Ypermestra? ¿Qué Egisto? Todo el mundo lo sabe. Pues a Sapho, Ariadna, Leandro, ¿qué pago les diste? Hasta David y Salomón no quesiste dexar sin pena. Por tu amistad Sansón pagó lo que mereció por creerse de quien tú le forçaste a darle fe. Otros muchos que callo porque tengo harto que contar en mi mal. (342)[45]

There are several points that are remarkable in this short passage from Pleberio's monologue. First is the integrative view of "Christians, heathens, and Jews," who had all been love's loyal servants and were now ill rewarded for it. In 1499, seven years after the expulsion of those Jews who had refused forced conversion, this kind of view is anything but self-evident. Second is the choice of examples: Macías as representative of poetry written in popular speech, as well as figures from Greek culture and biblical heroes. Finally, what is remarkable in this text is the overall condemnation of love (without any distinction between *caritas*, *agape*, *eros*, and *cupiditas*). The belief in divine and fleshly love as the individual's opportunity for participation was a guarantee for the existence of a higher order and unity in both medieval Christian and Jewish thought. This order, however, no longer exists for Pleberio:

> PLEBERIO: Del mundo me quexo porque en sí me crió, porque no me dando vida no engendrara en él a Melibea; no nascida, no amara; no amando, cessara mi quexosa y desconsolada postremería. O mi compañera buena y mi hija despedaçada, ¿por qué no quesiste que estorvasse tu muerte? ¿Por qué no houiste lástima de tu querida e amada madre? ¿Por qué te mostraste tan cruel con tu viejo padre? ¿Por qué me dexaste, quando yo te havía de dexar? ¿Por qué me dexaste penado? ¿Por qué me dexaste triste y solo in hac lachrimarum valle? (343)[46]

The metaphor of *lachrimarum valle*, the "vale of tears," which ends the text, possibly illustrates the uniqueness of this text overall. At the same time, it contains a hint about detaching the interpretation of *La Celestina* from a biographical reading: the metaphor of the valley of Bakha, or tears, is not only to be found in Psalms (Ps. 83) and the *Salve regina*, but also in Solomon Ibn Verga's *Shebet Yehudah*, the great work that compiled stories of the suffering of the Jewish people from fifteenth-century chronicles and added an interpretation of the expulsion in 1492. The phrase "vale of tears" is the Christianized translation of Joseph ha-Cohen's title *Emeq ha-bakha*. The Latin translations of the Bible uniformly interpreted the valley of Bakha, which refers to a wasteland of barren soil inhabited by the bakha plant, metaphorically as a "vale of tears" or "vale of weeping." Thus the sacred aura surrounding this metaphor is a Christian as well as a Jewish one. In Pleberio's monologue it is rendered in Latin. Because of the choice of the language of Roman liturgy, the metaphor is charged accordingly, yet it has a different connotation than the Christian usage. Pleberio's vale of tears does not refer to this life in contrast to the eternal afterlife but to the despair of a father for whom no "higher" understanding of the world is valid any longer. The entity called upon at first is neither the God of the Old or the New Testament but his own daughter. At the same time, the text's discursive strategy, which ends with this sentence, suggests the final paradigmatic decontextualization with oblique recontextualization—the reference to the original context. In this sense, the lament about having been forsaken by his daughter simultaneously becomes a lament about having been forsaken by the biblical God.

Apart from a Christian or Jewish interpretation, Pleberio's own fate, irreconcilable with dogma, becomes the focus of attention. In Pleberio's monologue, a coherent explanation of the world has become impossible in the face of grief and pain. Relativism of this kind is more than unusual in 1499. Just as the origin of the "vale of tears" metaphor is hybrid given the finite nature of human existence, Pleberio's monologue is multilayered and ambiguous.

The author of this text may have been Jewish, a *converso*, or a Christian, and the "vale of tears" metaphor may have been interpreted differently in a contemporary Christian perspective than in a contemporary Jewish one. The decisive point, which made *La Celestina* part of world literature (a concept that arose only in the modern age), is the potential of the multiple contemporary contexts of application to connect to specifically modern ideas, in this case the notion of the absence of a "higher" order and the problematization of the idea of compensation in the afterlife.

Two An Aesthetics of Love

Leone Ebreo's *Dialoghi d'amore* (1505/1535)

Judah Abravanel, who is known under the name Leone Ebreo in Romance literature, was born the eldest son of the great theologian don Isaac Abravanel in Lisbon around 1460 and died after 1523. His father taught him Jewish and Arabic philosophy. In 1483 he was enrolled as a student of medicine in Lisbon, when his father was suspected of scheming against the Portuguese heir to the throne and had to leave the country, and he followed his father to Toledo. Father and son remained in Spain for nearly a decade serving the Catholic kings, the elder as financial adviser and the younger as royal physician at court. Several sources state that the father, Isaac Abravanel, had attempted to dissuade the kings from the Edict of Expulsion in 1492.[1] Rumors were spreading that his grandson was to be kidnapped in order to force this prominent Jewish family to convert, so Leone sent his one-year-old son to Portugal with his nurse. Once he had arrived there, however, King João II had the child arrested and baptized. This act of religious force is echoed in Leone Ebreo's oft-quoted poem *Telunah al ha-Zeman* (Lament against time), written in 1503. The Ebreo family initially settled in Naples. The French invasion of 1494 and the ensuing wars, however, forced them to leave Naples. Cecil Roth names Genoa, Venice, and Florence as further stations in the Ebreo family's life.[2] Leone Ebreo later returned to Naples, where he taught medicine at the university from 1501 on.[3] A document dating from 1520 confirms that Ebreo was in the service of the Spanish viceroy, don Gonsalvo de Córdoba, as a physician. The physician Amatus Lusitanus reports that in 1566 he had seen a work of philosophy in Thessaloniki that Ebreo had written for Pico della Mirandola.

This work does not survive, but the mention of it shows that contemporaries already considered Ebreo's connection with the Italian Neoplatonists to be a very close one.

In addition to the elegy about his son's kidnapping, Leone Ebreo wrote three shorter poems in Hebrew, in which he praised his father's works, as well as a poem in fifty-two stanzas commemorating his father.

Leone Ebreo has become known primarily for his *Dialoghi d'amore*, published posthumously in Rome in 1535. Publisher Mariano Lenzi rescued the work from oblivion and had it printed by Antonio Blado. The exact date of its composition is unknown, but the author mentions in the text that he had finished half of the third dialogue by 1502. A fourth dialogue is announced in the work but was never published. To this day, there is extensive scholarly discussion on the question as to what language this work was written in. The 1535 version still presumed to be the original text is written in Italian. The opposing point of view, that there is a Hebrew original or an original text written in the Judeo-Spanish language, however, cannot easily be dismissed.[4] A Judeo-Spanish manuscript survives in the British Museum in London, which many researchers, beginning with Cecil Roth, believe to be the original version. Owing to the current state of the source material, this is an extremely difficult question, which will not be pursued here.

Rabbinical Tradition, Biblical Exegesis, and Classical Myth

In his *Dialoghi*, Ebreo models the presentation of his philosophical concepts on Plato. Platonic lovers Filone and Sofia reflect Ebreo's belief that love can elevate human beings to the highest truth. The entire work's main subject is love, which Ebreo considers to be the source, the ruling force, and the most exalted purpose of the universe. In his work, he examines the nature of love and its effect in form and substance—in the four elements, the spheres, the constellations, and on earth. He explains what love means for human beings—their souls, their spirits, and their senses—but also for animals, plants, and inanimate objects. Step by step, Ebreo develops his thesis that the object of love is not possession but the lover's pleasure in uniting with the idea of beauty and goodness embodied by his or her beloved. The higher purpose of love is the unification of Creation and all creatures with the sublime beauty that exists in God. This unification is an act of will and of intellect for Ebreo—he calls this love "il amore intellettuale di Dio," desired and enjoyed by God as well. This obligation of reciprocal love between the universe and its creator forms a circle of love—literally, of "loves" (*il circulo degli amari*), which includes all parts of the cosmos in a vivid, blessed movement.[5] Starting from this central subject, Ebreo develops thoughts on diverse topics; thus reflections on religion, metaphysics, mysticism, ethics, aesthetics, cosmology, and astrology are combined into a vision encompassing the entire spiritual and material universe and its metaphysical object. His sources are selected from both the Jewish and Christian traditions, but most important, from that of antiquity as well. The author quotes Maimonides as well as Ibn Gabirol, author of the *Fons vitae*. There are references to an intensive study of the Gospel of John, particularly in the third dialogue.

The combination of rabbinical tradition, biblical exegesis, and the analysis of Greek myth is a distinctive feature of this work by Ebreo, who overall strives to reconcile Jewish and Greek philosophy in this text, in particular the much-admired Plato, on the one hand, and Aristotle and his Arabic commentators, on the other.[6] As a genuinely literary characteristic, this specific feature will be central to the thoughts developed here. Additionally, I will analyze the love poems of medieval Spanish-Hebrew poet Ibn Gabirol as another source for the *Dialoghi d'amore*, not without including back references to the entirely different concept of love in *La Celestina*.

Ebreo's *Dialoghi d'amore* is among the most important metaphysical works of its time;[7] it had a great influence on the philosophy, art, and particularly the literature of the sixteenth century. Twenty-five editions were published between 1535 and 1607, among them twelve in Italian and thirteen in various translations. Between 1551 and 1660, seven translations in four languages were completed: French, Latin, Spanish, and Hebrew. One of the Spanish translations was done by

Garcilaso de la Vega (El Inca). Later in the sixteenth century, a large number of essays and dialogues on love were written that adapted central ideas from Ebreo's work.[8] At the same time, Ebreo's concept of love informed lyrical poetry in Italy, Spain, and France, prominent examples of which are Michelangelo's sonnets and Torquato Tasso's *Minturno*.

What is surprising about *Dialoghi d'amore* is that it—in contrast to the anonymous *Lazarillo de Tormes* and the more or less anonymous *Celestina*—was written by an author whose Jewish origin and deeply felt Jewish belonging are undoubted. Nevertheless, it became one of the most influential treatises in a culture traditionally defining itself as Christian. This raises the question as to why. The answer will not be arrived at by merely emphasizing the importance of Platonism or Neoplatonism as a common denominator on which both Jewish and Christian contemporaries could agree. Ebreo's text is deeply steeped in Jewish philosophy; Jewish tradition did not see the kind of "overlap" with Platonism that Christianity had consciously developed since Augustine, at the latest. *Dialoghi d'amore* can make particularly visible the mechanisms and processes by which culturally specific concepts morph into universal ones in literary texts and thus become adaptable.

This line of reasoning focuses on the questions of knowledge and aesthetics, which are treated as principles of being and ethically religious norms in Ebreo's presentation of love. Understanding love as an ontological principle means that all things are connected to each other by love. As a consequence of this notion, differentiations originally considered stable become flexible. In this conception, love is also a dynamic principle that shifts the differences between the spheres of being.[9] The conception of love in Ebreo's dialogues itself contains a universalist trait, which was supposed to pave the way for a philosophy in which the human being becomes the starting point for all philosophical thinking. At the same time, this doctrine of love is the precondition for the ethical consequences Ebreo demands in his text based on classical, Jewish, and Christian sources. These consequences can best be illustrated by means of Ebreo's aesthetics. His theory of beauty links ethics and aesthetics in an unprecedented manner.

Content and Form of the Three Dialogues

As previously mentioned, the text is structured as a conversation between the lovers Filone and Sofia. Sofia's role is mostly to ask questions, while Filone comments and provides answers.

The first dialogue begins with a sentence by Filone addressed to Sofia: "Il conoscerti, o Sofia, causa in me amore e desiderio,"[10] which is followed by a discussion on the difference between love and desire. While Sofia believes love and desire to be mutually exclusive, Filone sees both emotions as connected, since both love and desire require knowledge of one's object of desire. Filone differentiates between desire as directed at the future and love as aimed at actual union with the beloved object. The conjunction of love and desire is presupposed by the character of the object at which the particular emotions are directed. To this end, three different categories are established: the useful, the pleasant, and the good. The useful is never desired and loved simultaneously, while the pleasant is always desired and loved simultaneously. Subsequently, Sofia embarks on an explanation of love between friends and love of God, resulting in the conclusion that God is the source, the way, and the end of all good as well as the highest purpose of all human actions, although love of God remains limited by the finite human mind.

Jacob Guttmann has commented on this passage of *Dialoghi d'amore* in *Die Philosophie des Salomon Ibn Gabirol* (The philosophy of Solomon Ibn Gabirol), since he believes it built upon Gabirol's thoughts while expanding them by an essential point:

> The question how love of God can be ascribed to human beings, considering that love has to be preceded by knowledge while God's essence can neither be discovered nor comprehended by human beings, is answered in the following manner in this book: Just as knowledge in general does not grasp the essence of the thing it desires to know, but only that part of it which is accessible to human beings according to their own cognitive capacity, and similarly to the mirror, which only shows the reflected image, but not the essence of an object, so it is with our knowledge of God's infinite essence and thus our love of

God; one has to imagine it in accordance with our human will and not with God's infinite benevolence.[11]

In the subsequent passages of the *Dialoghi*, there is a reflection on the nature of happiness. Placed in the first dialogue, this passage contains one of the book's essential theses: according to Filone, happiness does not consist in benefit or pleasure but in wisdom, which presupposes virtue. Wisdom is distinguished from omniscience, which he considers unattainable. At Sofia's request, Filone discusses the relationship between knowledge of God and love of God and arrives at the distinction between knowledge that creates and knowledge born from love. It is in this latter knowledge of God that human beatitude consists.

At this point Sofia asks Filone for a definition of love. Filone explains how, in his idea of perfect human love, a sensual element combines with a spiritual one and how this combination can even intensify love. Albeit born from reason, this love is not subject to it—at least not to simple reason aimed at one's own welfare, but at best to heroic reason, which knows no other object except one's beloved counterpart.

Following a passage in which Filone explains love's permeation of all things, the text's focus shifts for the first time to the specific nature of humanity:

SOFIA: Poi che siamo venuti a questo, vorria sapere in che modo consiste questa beatitudine umana.

FILONE: Diverse sono state l'opinioni degli uomini nel suggetto de la felicità. Molti l'hanno posta ne l'utile e possessione de' beni de la fortuna e abbundanzia di quelli fin che dura la vita. Ma la falsità di questa opinione è manifesta: perché simili beni esteriori sono causati per l'interiori; di modo che questi dependono da quelli, e la felicità debbe consistere ne li più eccellenti; e questa felicità è fine de l'altre e non per nessuno altro fine; ma tutti son per questo, massime che simili beni esteriori sono in potere de la fortuna, e la felicità debbe essere in potere de l'uomo. Alcuni altri hanno avuta diversa opinione, dicendo che la beatitudine consiste nel dilettabile; . . . E di sopra abbiamo detto che 'l fine del delettabile è l'onesto; e la felicità non è per altro fine, anzi è causa finale d'ogni altra cosa. Sì che senza dubbio la felicità consiste ne le cose oneste e negli atti e abiti de l'anima intellettiva; quali sono li più eccellenti e fine degli altri abiti umani; e son quelli mediante li quali l'uomo è uomo e di più eccellenzia che nissuno altro animale. (34)[12]

Filone answers Sofia's question, how he differentiated intellect, by naming five areas: art, reason, comprehension, science, and wisdom. In this constellation, knowledge has a special meaning, although in the sciences happiness does not lie in possessing knowledge but in applying it: "La felicità non consiste in abito di cognizione, ma ne l'atto di quello" (39).[13]

In Filone's perspective, happiness consists in the activity of the soul's most noble power, intellect ("Fra le proposizioni che sono vere e necessarie, l'una è che la felicità consiste ne l'ultimo atto de l'anima, come in vero fine; l'altra è che consista ne l'atto de la più nobile e spiritual potenzia de l'anima, e questa è l'intellettiva" [43]).[14]

Both knowledge and applying one's intellect require love—love toward other human beings but simultaneously love of God as well. Filone then transitions to the love he feels for Sofia, whose name implies both love of wisdom and love for a woman:

FILONE: Il perfetto e vero amore, che è quello ch'io ti porto, è padre del Desiderio e figlio de la ragione; e in me la retta ragione conoscitiva l'ha prodotto. Ché, conoscendo essere in te virtù, ingegno e grazia non manco di mirabile attraizione che di grande ammirazione, la volontà mia desiderando la tua persona, che rettamente è giudicata per la ragione in ogni cosa essere ottima e eccellente e degna di essere amata. (50)[15]

His love for Sofia is described as born from knowledge and thus as a way to reach the height of wisdom as well. Sofia's characteristics make her a worthy object of Filone's love, because she unites in herself all those elements of love that Filone considers important.

In Filone's view, love is not possession; its purpose is the joy emanating from union with the beloved object, which is full of beauty. This beauty is a sublime beauty composed of virtue and intellect and thus represents God's beauty.

The second dialogue opens with Sofia's reminder that Filone had promised to explain to her love's origin and universality. Filone comments on universality first. Love is common to all living things, humans and animals, and originates from bodily union, parenthood, mutual support, affection, and connection. Among humans, love can also grow from compatibility of character, as well as from moral and intellectual virtues. Filone continues to explain that love also extends to inanimate objects, for love and the knowledge presupposing it are to be found in three forms: as constitutional in inanimate objects, as sensation in animals, and as rational decision in humans:

> FILONE: . . . l'amor è di tre modi: naturale, sensitivo e razional volontario.
>
> SOFIA: Dichiarameli tutti tre.
>
> FILONE: Il natural conoscimento, appetito o amore, è quel che si truova ne li corpi non sensitivi, come son gli elementi . . . insensibili, come li metalli e spezie di pietre e ancor le piante, erbe o ver arbori; che tutti questi hanno conoscimento natural del suo fine e inclinazion naturale a quello. . . . Questa inclinazione si chiama, ed è veramente, appetito e amor naturale. Il conoscimiento e appetito, o vero amor sensitivo, è quel che si truova negli animali irrazionali, per seguir lor conveniente, fuggendo l'inconveniente. . . . Il conoscimento e amor razionale e volontario si truova solamente negli uomini, perché proviene ed è administrato da la ragione. (64–65)[16]

Filone explains how the elements were influenced by love, how the primordial matter forming the basis of the elements was shaped into form by love, and how nature was determined by connections through the degree of love between its constitutive elements: a low degree was enough to form inanimate objects, while a high degree enabled the union of soul and body.

Nor was love limited to the sublunar world. Heaven loved earth like a husband and her infants like his children. This analogy is complemented by a characterization of the planets' functions, which reflect the seven organs from which the human seed springs. This leads to a comparison of human beings and the universe.

Filone further explains that the celestial bodies loved each other with a love born from the harmony of the spheres and the two motives inherent in human love. Filone thus explains the erotic myths of classical antiquity, which he interprets as allegories. He illustrates their allegorical meaning with the help of classical poetry:

> Li poeti antichi, non una sola, ma molte intenzioni implicorno ne' suoi poemi, le quali chiamano sensi. Pongono prima di tutti per il senso litterale, come scorza esteriore, l'istoria d'alcune persone e de' suoi atti notabili degni di memoria. Di poi in quella medesima finzione pongono, come più intrinseca scorza più appresso a la medolla, il senso morale, utile alla vita attiva degli uomini, approvando gli atti virtuosi e vituperando i vizi. Oltre a questo, sotto quelle proprie parole significano qualche vera intelligenzia de le cose naturali o celesti, astrologali o ver teologali, e qualche volta li due o vero tutti li tre sensi scientifichi s'includeno dentro de la favola, come le medolle del frutto dentro le sue scorze. Questi sensi medullati si chiamano allegorici. (94–95)[17]

Filone begins with the hierarchy of the gods, with Zeus and then the celestial and the lower gods. He then relates and explains the myth of Demogorgon and his descendants; he speaks of Pan's love for the nymph Syrinx and of Uranus and Saturn. He speaks of Jupiter's battle against Saturn, his wedding with Juno and their children Mercury and Hebe, of Jupiter's love for Leto, the birth of Apollo and Diana, of Jupiter's other loves, of Venus, her origin and her love for Mercury, of the birth of her son Amor, of Hermaphroditus, and of Apollo's love for Daphne.

Subsequently, Filone moves on to a story about astrological love and hate. He explains the meaning of planetary aspects and conjunctions, the distribution of the signs of the zodiac, the opposition of planets and signs, and the additional reasons for celestial friendships and hostilities.

Filone locates love in the third, spiritual world. Not only does the inferior love the superior, but vice versa, for the deficiencies of the inferior also render visible the deficiencies of the superior, so that the latter must strive to perfect himself or herself through uniting with the inferior. This kind of love is also a path to union with all that lies beyond the superior. At this point, a problem arises in the discussion between Sofia and Filone. Who is the beloved object of the causative insight? The answer given is God, the original driving force and end of all being. The love of souls for those beneath them is necessary in order to execute God's plan for the universe and is consequently also a way to win God's love.

At the end of the second dialogue, Filone's image of a universe held together by love results in his lament about the hopelessness of his love for Sofia, the only one among God's creatures unwilling to be subject to love. Sofia insists on her refusal to surrender to Filone, and thus nightfall ends their conversation.

The third dialogue opens with an unexpected meeting between Filone and Sofia. Filone does not recognize Sofia at first and apologizes. So deeply had he been absorbed in his contemplation of Sofia's beauty that he had become oblivious to all perception of his actual surroundings. Deep thought, he explains, hinders sensual perception in the same manner as sleep does. This leads to a comparison of the soul and reason. Reason is purely intellectual, while the soul is only one part mental, its remaining part being of a physical nature. The soul moves continuously along the line between mind and body. Before Filone can lament his destiny, since Sofia still refuses him, she persuades him to tell her about the origins of love—when, where, by whom, and why love was born.

Filone defines the nature of love as the desire for something, and the object of this desire as pleasure. In Filone's view, love and desire are synonymous with deprivation, since the beloved object is either missing at present or will be in the future. This is true for divine love as well, since God, who himself is not subject to deficiency of any kind, does not strive for his own perfection but that of his creatures.

Desire for the beautiful is inadequate as a definition of universal love, since goodness and beauty are not the same. All beautiful things are good by nature or appearance, yet not all good things are beautiful. All-encompassing love depends on all-encompassing virtue, while human love depends on beauty. Beauty itself is a grace giving the mind pleasure and inducing it to love.

This passage has also been commented on by Jacob Guttmann, who understands it as an elaboration on Solomon Ibn Gabirol's ideas:

> The elucidation on love as permeating all of creation, from top to bottom and from bottom to top, and driving all beings, including inanimate ones, to strive for a higher level of being and to unite with the more complete, is entirely in the spirit of Gabirol's teachings. . . . God's infinite beauty does not manifest itself in the minds according to its own nature, but depending on the measure of receptiveness they hold for it. . . . The more immediate the effect of divine beauty is on a being, the more purely it takes shape in it. . . . In order to recognize the highest beauty, which is the original source of all things beautiful, the human being must . . . free himself of all earthly passions. . . . Once the human being has made a connection with the highest beauty, he is gripped by a love for it so powerful that he gladly renounces everything else in order to love only it, to unite with it completely, and, having become beautiful himself through his love for the beautiful, to experience the highest blessedness.[18]

Filone now addresses Sofia's first question and shows that love had to be created and was subject to birth, because it required both lovers and beloveds, in whom it has its origin. According to Filone, the answer to the question when love was first born depends on another question, namely, that of the earth's original creation. The first love and fertile creator of the universe was God himself as eternal lover and beloved, and hence love was born at the time the world was created. Filone assumes the place of love's origin to be the world of angels, which is the most perfect of all worlds.

In response to Sofia's query about the progenitors of love, Filone explains to her the allegorical meaning of the myth of the birth of Amor, of Hermaphroditus, of the creation of Adam and Eve, and of the fall of mankind. Love's all-encompassing father was beauty, while its all-encompassing mother was knowledge in conjunction with deprivation. Beauty was a primary condition of love, since it was nothing other than God's image itself, which he had impressed on the world. The highest beauty was God, his spirit and his wisdom, in whose image the entire world had been created. The beauty of both natural and artistically created objects originates from the form driving their substance and thus eventually from the divine spirit and the world soul (*anima mundi*), in which all forms or ideas preexist in eternal brightness. The circle of love is linked to the circle of all things, which is described as follows:

> Il circulo di tutte le cose è quello che principia gradualmente dal primo principio di quelle, e, circulando successivamente per tutte, volge in quello proprio principio come in ultimo fine, comprendendo tutti li gradi de le cose a modo circulare: del quale il punto che è principio ritorna fine. Questo circulo ha due mezzi: l'uno è dal principio, cioè il primo punto, al più distante da lui, che è il suo mezzo, e il secondo mezzo è da quel punto più distante fino al ritornare in lui. (353)[19]

The purpose of all love is pleasure, and this also means the lover's yearning for union with the beloved. The purpose of the universe's love is union with divine beauty, the highest perfection of all creation. At the end of the third dialogue, Filone emphasizes that his love holds only torment and grief, because Sofia has not fulfilled his desire nor reciprocated his love. Sofia insists on her refusal and emphasizes the spiritual love that exists between them, and she reminds Filone of his promise to speak about the effects of love. They part with an agreement to meet for a fourth conversation, which, as mentioned previously, has not been preserved. The question whether this is a "fragmentary" text or whether the author has purposely placed the "solution" to the open questions in a void, thus delegating it to the reader, must remain unanswered.

Ethics and Aesthetics

One of the distinctive features in Leone Ebreo's main work is the significance ascribed to rhetoric and poetics.[20] In this text, form and content are connected in a way that transforms aesthetics into a path to knowledge of divine presence. For example, in the universe that *Dialoghi d'amore* represents, physical beauty is a reflection of divine beauty and the human being an image of the universe. In this way, the intersection of the spiritual with the material can be experienced in one's own existence. The mental potential for the perception of these correspondences lies in the imagination, and its form is the literary text. The "rhetoricized" text facilitates the encounter with the beautiful and consequently the encounter with God. In this regard Ebreo transfers an essential prerequisite of Hebrew literature of the Spanish Middle Ages into philosophical reflection. This thesis is not aimed at an overall interpretation of the *Dialoghi* but refers to those text passages that include biblical passages, transform them, and transfer them into a separate aesthetics. This transformation is carried out in two steps. First, the allegoresis explicitly illustrated in the *Dialoghi* by means of the classical poets, and which is particularly evolved in the Hebrew poetry of the Spanish Middle Ages, is employed in the *Dialoghi* as well. Second, the form of the dialogue is functionalized in a particular manner; the form of the dialogue assigns an almost active role to the reader.

In recent decades, literary studies have identified essential criteria regarding the Renaissance dialogue that are relevant for the questions discussed here as well. First, the preconditions for Renaissance discourse structures were defined: accordingly, the "epistemological turn" of the Renaissance consisted in a "fundamental relativization of the concept of truth . . . which can be realized as a contextualization and/or pluralization of truth."[21] In these epistemological configurations, Renaissance literary dialogue is of particular interest, because it is a privileged form of either homogenizingly covering up these relativizing Renaissance questions as commanded by a "forced reconciliation" or exposing them in terms of a "staged plurality."[22] It is particularly in the latter case that the literary dialogue as genre seems predestined to stage a complexly structured interplay and thus to make the epoch's basic epistemological figure one of its own structural characteristics. This has been demonstrated in several studies of essential Renaissance dialogues such as Baldassare Castiglione's *Libro del cortegiano* (1528), Pietro Bembo's *De Guido Ubaldo Feretrio deque Elisabetha Gonzagia Urbini Ducibus* (1509/13), Pietro Aretino's *Sei giornate* (1534/36), and the same author's *Ragionamento delle corti* (1538). In this understanding, dialogue is a genuinely performative genre, a "written staging of a verbal communication."[23]

In *Dialoghi d'amore*, this strategy of staging a verbal communication can be observed in the conversation between Filone and Sofia. In Jewish tradition, the philosophical dialogue about religious themes has a long history: Solomon Ibn Gabirol's (ca. 1021–ca. 1058) Neoplatonic dialogue, which became known in its Latin translation under the title *Fons Vitae*, was structured similarly. Jehuda Halewi, too, chose the form of the dialogue for his work of philosophy of religion, *Kuzari* (ca. 1140). While this dialogue discussed the superiority of Jewish religion, the approach in Ibn Gabirol's *Fons Vitae* is much more universalist in nature. Leone Ebreo's intense study of this philosophical text has been discussed in various ways. Yet Ebreo's text activates an additional, genuinely literary-textual process in its intense examination of Ibn Gabirol's literary oeuvre. His best-known work, titled "Keter malkut" (Crown of the kingdom), informs those passages in the *Dialoghi d'amore* that discuss the planetary configurations and the relations between the signs of the zodiac. The aesthetic concept of love in the *Dialoghi d'amore* also makes reference to Ibn Gabirol's poetic reflections in several respects. Ebreo's text thus gains an added dimension—compared to the idea of beauty as a metaphysical principle, which is part of the basic inventory of Renaissance humanist thought.

In their works, Ficino and Pico della Mirandola adopted the ideas of Plotinus, who understood beauty as a cosmic principle guaranteeing humanity participation in the heavenly world. This universal principle also exists in the *Dialoghi d'amore*, but it is closely linked to the act of writing, which appears as an aesthetic path to experiencing God. This also explains the universal appeal of Ebreo's philosophy of love. The fusion of Jewish, Christian, and classical sources in the form of the dialogue and the horizon of all-encompassing love do not privilege one particular religious reading but instead appear as a universal allegory enabling an expression of love of God through the creative act.

In his poetry, Ibn Gabirol fused Arabic morphology with the Hebrew language and transferred this allegory of love from the sacred imagery of the canticle to the secular form of love poetry. The following poem is an example of this:

> I yearn for you in the morning and in the evening
> and reach out my hands and my countenance for you.
> My heart sighs with thirst for Thee, I am like
> the mendicant who begs at my threshold.

The heaven of heavens cannot contain thee,
and yet you have room in my heart.
Concealed in me is Thy glory, Thy name,
My love for you spills from my mouth.
Therefore I will praise the name of God,
as long as my breath lives in me.[24]

Ebreo transferred the merging of metaphors for desire with love of God and the longing for religious salvation to the ethical-aesthetic layout of *Dialoghi d'amore*. Earlier, this had been a characteristic of both medieval Hebrew poetry and Christian Marian poetry. Ibn Gabirol's poetry, whose imagery Ebreo evokes in the concept of love in the *Dialoghi*, formulates this merging in a particular manner and numerous variations:

You, my friends, I am sick with love!
My heart does not capitulate before passion.
Sweet is the bitter suffering of my soul—
Have you ever felt a sweeter suffering?
I'm so emaciated that with your eyes
You cannot see me, only with the mind.
And if you cannot find me, look for me there,
Where you weakly can hear a ghostly voice.
Voice of a man on the edge of an abyss,
Drowning in the sea of love.
I called you, my friends, that you saved me,
But I can neither see nor hear you answer.
I ride on the waters of your love
And cling to the One riding the clouds.
Friends, reveal me, how can I douse
The ardor which burns my heart?[25]

In *Dialoghi d'amore*, these images are incorporated into a concept of mimesis, which regulates the entire universe from the perspective of the text: not only are material objects representations of heavenly beauty, but our rational soul also becomes an image of the world soul. This earthly world is a mirror of the heavenly worlds, and this is rendered cognizable through language. Thus the aesthetically formed word becomes a path to knowledge of the divine presence.

For Ebreo, not only Ibn Gabirol's poetry but the figural language of the Thora as well is an example of this power of rhetoric. One of the final sections in the third dialogue on beauty and God's love contains the following passage:

> E per questo dice David: "Con la luce tua vediamo la luce"; e dice il profeta "Ritornane, Dio, in te, e tornaremo," e dice un altro: "Ritorname, e tornarò; ché tu sei il Signor mio Dio": però che, senza l'aiutorio suo a ritornare in Lui, saria impossibile noi soli retirarsi. E più precisamente l'esprime Salamone ne la sua Cantica, in nome de l'anima intellettiva innamorata de la divina bellezza, dicendo: "Ritirame, e dietro a te correremo; se 'l re mi traesse ne le sue camere, ci delettaremo e allegraremo in te, ricorderemo l'amori tuoi più che vino, le rettitudini t'amano." Mira come prima prega l'anima intellettuale che sia ritirata da l'amore de la divinità, e che allora ella col suo ardentissimo correrà dietro a quella; e dice che, essendo messa per mano del re ne le camere sue, cioè essendo unita per grazia divina bellezza regale; conseguirà la somma dilettazione in quella, quale è fine de l'amore suo in Dio; e dice che ricordaria gli amori suoi più che vino, cioè che l'amore divino gli saria altrimenti sempre presente, ricordato ne la mente, che l'amore de le cose mondane, che sono de la qualità de l'amore de vino, che imbriaca l'uomo e levalo de la rettitudine de la mente; e perciò finisce: "le rettitudini t'amano"; vuol dire: "Tu non sei amato per irrettitudine d'animo, come sono gli amori carnali, ma la propria drittezza de l'anima è quella che t'ama." Mira come principia a parlare in singulare, dicendo "ritirami," e incontinente dice in plurale: "dietro a te correremo"; e torna a dire in singulare: "se mi mena il re ne le sue camere," e torna in plurale a dire: "ci dilettaremo a allegraremo in te, ricorderemo gli amori tuoi più che vino," per mostrare che con l'unione de la parte intellettiva de l'uomo, o de l'universo prodotto, si felicita e diletta non solamente lei, ma tutte le parti di esso universo con lui; per le quali dice in plurali: "le rettitudini t'amano," perché tutte tendono ne l'amore divino mediante la parte intellettiva. (361–362)[26]

This passage from the *Dialoghi* demonstrates how Ebreo infers beauty as an aesthetic condition for experiencing God from the sacred text as well. First he cites three biblical aphorisms on the reversal toward God by David and the prophets. This is followed by the statement that the most precise explanation is to be found in the Song of Solomon ("E più precisamente l'esprime Salamone ne la sua Cantica"). The scene quoted from the Song is one of those passages in which a scene of human love stands allegorically for the love of the soul guided by reason, which is in love with divine beauty ("Ritirame, e dietro a te correremo; se 'l re mi traesse ne le sue camere, ci delettaremo e allegraremo in te, ricorderemo l'amori tuoi più che vino, le rettitudini t'amano"). Step by step, the speaking "I," in this case Filone, explains to his counterpart Sofia the logic of the allegorization, in which the lover's speech is explained as the soul's request to be pulled along by divine love, as it glowingly follows love and is granted union with divine love in the king's chamber. Filone analyzes the biblical rhetoricization in its alternation between the plural and the singular form and demonstrates that this transfer of imagery is not solely addressed to the part of the human being guided by reason, but rather to the entire universe with all its parts that experience bliss and pleasure in the union with the divine.

From the perspective of the *Dialoghi*, God and humanity become one through love. They supplement this meeting in faith and philosophical reflection with aesthetic experience. It is only through language that the contradictions in the human experience of love can find a theologically explicable place, that they can be represented in all their diversity through dialogue and thus become markers for the realities behind them. In the linguistic-literary realization of *Dialoghi d'amore*, a universal ethical claim arises from the diversity of Jewish, classical, and Christian sources.

Set against the historical events of his time, Ebreo's universal demand is a charged one indeed: in this constellation, God's love is an unconditional gift of grace bestowed on all of humanity rather than something human beings have to earn through any particular behavior. God's all-encompassing love unites all of humanity as God's creatures. Humanity's love for one another emphasizes its uniqueness and distinctiveness—in its unity with God. God is the true purpose of those who inquire about themselves and search for love. Contrary to the interlacing of the discourses of subject and love within Christian tradition, charity is not a means on the path to the afterlife but the crucial act of worship. *Dialoghi d'amore* conceives of love as the framework that makes humanity human. The aesthetic form of the three dialogues contains opportunities for reflection on the treatment of oneself and others, which eliminate the basis for tests of faith as carried out by the Inquisition, for example. As long as love as an active service to God is the rule regulating how human beings treat each other, interact, and share an ethos, this exchange, the encounter with the other before God, is right. This kind of amicably loving association means consummate being.

Dialoghi d'amore offers an aesthetic experience in which love permits human beings to get to know themselves reflexively, in amicable love, in loving friendship, and thus in recognition of the beloved. This idea of love as a process of reflection includes the world, the other, and the self. The lovers share a world whose possibilities appear through mutual encounter and thus become accessible. The nonlover, however, knows neither himself or herself, nor the other, nor the world—this is a consequence that follows implicitly from the aesthetics of love in Ebreo's *Dialoghi d'amore*. Despite the exclusivity of its aesthetic inquiry into the concept of love, the dialogue as realized in *Dialoghi d'amore* contains an ethical commentary on the religious situation at the time.

What is crucial for the question of affiliation and universalism examined in this book is this: Leone Ebreo's text refers to three related yet distinct lines of tradition, two of which are religions in a narrower sense (the Jewish and Christian traditions), the third a kind of philosophical religion (Neoplatonism). He hybridizes these traditions in such a way, however, that something new evolves, which cannot be absorbed completely within any of these traditions. Love as a universal principle pervading both the entire cosmos and all humanity is contrasted with the particularism of Jewish religious tradition. The integration of physical love as part of an all-encompassing love is unmistakably adopted from this tradition, however. This "integrative" view of *amore* suspends the Christian dichotomy of *eros* and *agape* and levels the Neoplatonic hierarchy of loves, in which love of physical beauty always ranks low—legitimate as a first step in the ascent to true love, yet always involving the duty to fulfill the ascent and transcend physical love. The universalism of Ebreo's concept of love is unmistakably extracted from the two latter traditions.

Meanwhile, the inclusion of God in the chain of those who require love is foreign to Christianity in its questioning of divine absoluteness and stems from a Neoplatonic context. The idea of the reciprocity of love between "higher" and "lower" spheres of being, though, is a genuinely Christian rather than a Neoplatonic one—emanation is a "top-down" process.

Placing Ebreo's thoughts on the nature of love in the larger context of the Italian discussion of this phenomenon would facilitate a more precise characterization of the peculiar position presented in *Dialoghi d'amore*. The pressing question about the ontological significance of love inherent in it has been on the agenda since Dante's *Commedia*. In the *Dialoghi*, the question of the relation between *amor* and *desiderium* also discussed by Dante not only leads to a marked deviation from Christian orthodoxy as defined by Thomas Aquinas, for example, but also serves as an essential subject for Pietro Bembo's *Asolani*, which is composed as a dialogue as well. The hybridization of different religious positions, too, corresponds to a religious syncretism, or rather, relativism, as characteristic of Pico della Mirandola. In this respect, a contextualization of Ebreo's *Dialoghi d'amore* would enable a more precise examination of that form of hybridity which can be linked to specifically Jewish patterns of experience.

Hybridity in this case is not a reality or a postulated reality, but an aesthetically staged possibility. The question whether and to what extent the deliberate perception of such new possibilities has prompted the establishment of new (spiritual) realities is of a speculative nature and will not be addressed here.

Based on an emphatic notion of love, which initially appears very premodern in its formulation, the hybridization in Ebreo's text causes a semantic transgression of boundaries with regard to the distinctive ideological positions that had shaped occidental intellectual history in the early modern age. The discursive territory thus created is a purely aesthetic one at first—as literary text and feigned dialogue. It proposes an emphatic-universalist concept of love as a possibility of conceiving the world outside the narrow frame of the three above-mentioned traditions, albeit it not in direct opposition to their traditions.

Three Inquisition and Conversion

El Lazarillo de Tormes (1554)

Few texts in sixteenth-century Spanish and perhaps even European literature have been as much in the focus of academic interest to this day as *Lazarillo de Tormes*, published anonymously in 1554 in Burgos, Antwerp, Medina del Campo,[1] and Alcalá de Henares. In this short text, the first-person narrator, Lazarillo, reports with complete naïveté and free of any moral considerations on the state of the social order in the Spain of his time. He does this from the perspective of a penniless servant to changing masters. Owing to his ability to deal with any given reality, which he has acquired along the way, Lazarillo eventually manages to set himself up in relatively opulent, albeit morally precarious, circumstances: he assumes the office of town crier of Toledo and marries a maidservant whom he shares with the town's archpriest, as it is phrased ironically at the end of the novel.

In 1559, the Inquisition put the text on the *Index Librorum Prohibitorum*, and in 1573, an expurgated version was published, the so-called *Lazarillo castigado*, from which censorship had removed passages about the clergy. The degree of religious satire in *Lazarillo de Tormes*, even in its censored version, is still astonishing today, as Ilse Nolting-Hauff has pointed out.[2] Both the text's anticlerical passages, presented in the tenor of mock naïveté and cutting in their substance, and the fact that its author remained anonymous have opened up a broad field of conjecture and speculation with regard to the author's affiliation. In this case, too, Américo Castro may be considered the initiator of an interpretive tradition that regards the anonymous author as being a forcibly converted Jew:

> El estilo autobiográfico resulta así inseparable del mismo intento de sacar a la luz del arte un tema hasta entonces inexistente o desdeñado. La persona del autor (de ascendencia judía) se retrajo tanto, que ni siquiera quiso revelar su nombre. El autobiografismo del Lazarillo es solidario de su anonimato.[3]

In 1966, Stephen Gilman reinforced Américo Castro's thesis that the anonymous author of *Lazarillo de Tormes* had to be a *converso* and interpreted the novel's first three chapters as a parody of the Christian dogma of death and resurrection.[4] Others have speculated that an Erasmist had cloaked his convictions in the form of a fictional autobiography in this short but very dense text.[5]

Analyzing the picaresque novel in light of the author's descent grew into a *topos* of academic inquiry in the wake of these studies. In 1994, a volume on the genre of the picaresque novel summarized:

> It is assumed of many authors who wrote a *novela picaresca* that they were Jews converted to Christianity—this is certainly the case for Alemán, and it is presumed for the anonymous author of *Lazarillo de Tormes* and for López de Úbeda. . . . It is hardly surprising under these circumstances that disappointment with the world is very prominent in the literature of that time.[6]

The material political conditions in the *Siglo de Oro* had been especially painful for the group known as the New Christians, the *conversos*; and this has been interpreted as the genre's crucial impulse.[7] The following discussion tries to render the thesis of authorship more precisely by means of an approach that reconciles historicity with literariness.

A Satire on Christian Dogma

Bernhard König has demonstrated the level of irony with which the text refers to the Christian idea of God. In particular, he has pointed out the numerous moments in which Lazarillo, as if animated "by the Holy Spirit himself," finds a way out of a seemingly hopeless situation: "In this situation (as in other passages) God has become a phrase for success, for the lucky rescue from a difficult situation by means of shrewdness and dexterousness, regardless of how the rescue strategy may be judged morally."[8] Hans Robert Jauss has even gone so far as to claim that as a result of his constant verbal inclusion, God appeared as "quasi-accomplice to the rogue."[9] This can be observed in the second *tratado* in particular. Lazarillo describes the escape from his first master, the blind man, to his second master, the *clérigo*, as a way out of the frying pan into the fire, for in comparison to this man of the church, the blind man had been a paragon of generosity:

> Escapé del trueno y di en el relámpago, porque era el ciego para con éste un Alejandre Magno, con ser la mesma avaricia, como he contado. No digo más, sino que toda la laceria del mundo estaba encerrada en éste: no sé si de su cosecha era o lo había anejado con el hábito de clerecía.[10]

The first-person narrator complains he did not find a single piece of food in the *clérigo*'s house; there had merely been a carefully locked container of onions, of which he had been given one every few days, accompanied by the remark that he must not indulge in the sin of *gula* by enjoying the onion. Where his own behavior was concerned, however, the *clérigo* was less strict. And when he left the gnawed-on bones of a meat dish for Lázaro, he did this with the following words: "Toma, come, triunfa, que para ti es el mundo" (50; Take! Eat! Triumph! for you is the world).[11]

This modification of Jesus' words during the Last Supper begins a literary travesty of the Holy Communion in the *tratado* that Castro and Gilman have interpreted as an ironically rendered reckoning of a forced convert with one of the central mysteries of Christianity. Had God and he himself not found a solution for his exigency, Lazarillo continues, he would certainly have died of hunger: "Vime claramente ir a la sepultura, si Dios y mi saber no me remediaran" (51).[12] The *clérigo* had kept the only bread supply in a lockable cupboard, the key to which he guarded carefully, and he had explained to Lazarillo: "Mira, mozo, los sacerdotes han de ser muy templados en su comer y beber, y por esto yo no me desmando como otros" (52).[13] To this and other similar statements of his master, Lazarillo immediately adds a remark that uncovers the true circumstances behind the pious words: "Mas el lacerado mentía falsamente, porque en cofradías y mortuorios que rezamos, a costa ajena comía como lobo y bebía más que un saludador" (52).[14] According to Lazarillo, it was the hospitality at funerals that alone had saved him from starvation, so that when he accompanied the *clérigo* on his calls on the sick, he had begun to wish not for the recovery of those suffering but instead for their death, only in order to see another funeral feast as soon as possible. He then, however, prayed to God to deliver him from his plight: "Pues estando en tal aflición, cual plega al Señor librar della a todo fiel cristiano, . . . llegóse acaso a mi puerta un calderero, el cual yo creo que fue ángel enviado a mí por la mano de Dios en aquel hábito" (54–55).[15]

The tinker who coincidentally (*acaso*) appears immediately afterward is described as God's messenger, as an angel, who enables a minor theft on the part of Lazarillo by means of his trade and is therefore presented as Lazarillo's liberation from his un-Christian wishes prompted by God himself. The virtuosic irony in this passage results from the fact that the theft of bread now regularly committed is a sin, yet from the perspective of Christian orthodoxy it presents a less severe problem morally than wishing the death of one's neighbor, even for the most understandable reasons. Thus it is simultaneously the unlimited naïveté of someone familiar only with the external formulae of faith owing to his own limits and lack of education, biting antireligious ridicule, and finally also a sentence "backed up" by moral theology with which Lazarillo continues to say that the moment he encountered the tinker he was "enlightened as if by the Holy Spirit" (*alumbrado por el Spíritu Sancto*) and had a copy of the key to the cupboard for the Holy Communion bread made for himself. It is his lack of familiarity with the subtleties of dogma owing to his low social rank that then legitimizes the sentence "Cuando no me cato, veo en figura de panes, como dicen, la cara de Dios" (55–56).[16] From the perspective of the reader, the notion of transubstantiation is exposed to ridicule, and the description of Lazarillo's breadwinning as access to his "paraíso panal"[17] follows the same line.

The episode reaches the peak of its satire directed against the dominant faith with the report that when the *clérigo* noticed his servant's raids, Lazarillo had begun to worship the bread in order to assuage his hunger: "Yo, por consolarme, abro el arca, y como vi el pan, comencélo de adorer, no osando rescebillo. . . . Lo más que yo pude hacer fue dar en ellos mil besos" (58).[18] It is not the belief in the idea of transubstantiation but sheer hunger that drives Lazarillo to worship (*adorar*) the bread—and yet he does not dare to take any, that is, to receive it (*recibir*). Dogma, interpreted naïvely and therefore incorrectly in a simultaneously blasphemous and satirical manner, thus indeed prevents Lázaro from continuing to commit the sin of theft. That there is no religiously orthodox notion behind this constellation—for example, that God sometimes prevents the faithful from sin in mysterious and at times unusual ways—is assured by the fact that the initial impulse for Lázaro's "timidity" is nothing other than the banal fear of being discovered.

It becomes clear how justified this fear is when the *clérigo* finally finds out who, or rather what, is behind the "inexplicable" disappearance of the bread. He takes revenge with such brute force that Lazarillo remains unconscious for more than three days: "De lo que sucedió en aquellos tres días siguientes ninguna fe daré, porque los tuve en el vientre de la ballena" (69).[19] The three days of unconsciousness after the beating has been correctly interpreted as an ironic allusion to the resurrection of Christ. The biblical story of Jonah and the whale to which Lazarillo alludes—in complete ignorance of the contexts and implications—in order to describe his almost miraculous return to life is regularly interpreted as a prefiguration of the Resurrection in typological biblical exegesis.[20]

One thing becomes evident even in this cursory reading of the second *tratado*: the multiply graduated, complex, ironic linguistic form of *Lazarillo de Tormes* is the text's greatest fascination. This certainly is one reason for the attempts to identify an author of whom it can be believed that he "anticipates a level of development in novelistic technique that will only become common in Europe in the 18th century."[21] The text's artistry was particularly evident in its hybridization of everyday discourse and religious imagery.[22] The above-mentioned representatives of the *converso* thesis concluded that Lazarillo's "adoración del pan" was a clear indicator that, on the one hand, the text's anonymous author was familiar with the subtleties of Christian dogma in great detail, but on the other hand, that he considered the corresponding beliefs as abstruse, or rather, that he wanted to suggest such an evaluation to his readers.

Historical Context

The following section focuses more closely on the historical contexts of what has been discussed so far in order possibly to gain new insights, if not directly with regard to the question of authorship, at least with regard to a question connected to it and no less intricate, namely, that of the origin of this genre that suddenly appeared virtually without precursor in sixteenth-century Spain.

The majority of those Jews who had remained in the country after the violent outbreaks of 1391 in Seville, Córdoba, Ciudad Real, Toledo, and Logroño, in Orihuela, Alicante, Valencia, Barcelona, and Jaca, had converted to Christianity. Until the first third of the fifteenth century, it seemed as if the integration of the converts into Spanish Christian society might succeed. Following a riot in Toledo in 1449, during which an angry mob stormed the house of the hated tax collector Alonso de Cota, a *converso*, and subsequently attacked the entire large community of the city's *conversos*, the situation changed radically. The leaders of this riot issued a so-called penal statute stipulating that *conversos* were to be excluded from all public offices because of their Jewish origin. The Crown restored public order, though, and Pope Nicholas V initially condemned the statute. During the reign of Henry IV of Castile (1454–1474), there were renewed attacks against the converts (1467 in Ciudad Real; 1473 and 1474 in Córdoba), who were the target of more severe hostilities than the Jews who had remained in the country. When the king approved a statute promulgated by the city of Ciudad Real according to which the local *conversos* could be excluded from all public offices in July 1468, the ramparts erected against distinguishing among various groups of different origin within the Christian population fell. The exclusion laws, initially limited to the local level, quickly spread across the entire peninsula.

Thus one of the main goals of the Spanish Inquisition, enacted in 1478 through a papal bull by Sixtus IV (1471–1484) under the reign of Isabella I of Castile and Ferdinand II of Aragon, was to test whether forced baptism indeed led to true conversion. In his work *Fortalitium Fidei*, the Franciscan Alonso de Espina argued as early as 1460 that the belief in Judaism, Islam, and Christian heresies was "transferred as in a biological way" and that therefore a serious adoption of the "true" Christian faith by conversion was impossible. Such a view, that eventually only an "Old Christian descent" guaranteed this faith, led ultimately to the enactment of the *estatuos de limpieza de sangre* by inquisitor Tomás de Torquemada in 1483. These statutes prevented Christians from having access to both secular and religious offices if so-called Jewish blood could be proven in their family. Regardless of a test of faith carried out *ad personam*, converted Jews were thus deprived of all possibility of social mobility and were considered "of impure blood"—contrary to the "Old Christians" (allegedly) descended from the Goths.

Benzion Netanyahu has pointed out the role that the constellations of realpolitik and power politics played in the development of this early form of "racial laws." The number of Jews who converted after the assaults of 1391 was considerable. Because of their conversion, they were equal to the "Old Christians" before the Crown. The *conversos* seemed more threatening to the majority Christian society than before because they could now obtain offices that had been previously denied them. The solution was to rob the *conversos* of their initially attained equality by means of a "de-Christianization" invoking descent and thus to portray their conversion and their Christianity as impossible.[23]

Consequently, in the first hundred years following its enactment, the Inquisition mainly targeted so-called *judaizantes*, "Judaizing New Christians." Sixtus IV's papal bull came into effect in 1480, when the first Dominicans were appointed as inquisitors. According to Andrés Bernáldez (1450–1513), who wrote a chronicle of the era of the Catholic kings, seven hundred *judaizantes* were burned between 1481 and 1488 alone, while more than five thousand recanted and were "reconciled" with the church in elaborate public procedures:

> Quemaron mas de setencias personas, y reconciliaron mas de cinco mil y echaron en cárceles perpétuas, que ovo tales y estuvieron en ellas quatro ó cinco años ó mas y sacáronles y echáronles cruces é unos San Benitillos colorados atrás y adelante, y ansí anduvieron mucho tiempo, é después se los quitaron porque no creciese el disfame en la tierra viendo aquello.[24]

The public was excluded from the interrogations during the tribunal. One of the inquisitors asked the questions, and a clerk recorded the trial in writing. The prosecutor had to present witnesses, but witnesses and the accused rarely faced each other. Instead, every witness had to answer a standardized catalogue of forty to fifty questions. The prisoner was questioned next. The inquisitors then passed their judgment, which was handed to a group of assessors, mostly priests, monks, or scholars. Once the representatives of church and secular jurisdiction had agreed on a sentence, it was either carried out, usually in the form of death by burning alive, or—in cases considered less severe—the prisoner was given probation. In the latter case, the accused had to do penance by submitting to an act of faith (*auto da fe*), a de facto act of gross public humiliation, which by no means involved the regaining of civil rights.[25]

In today's view, the statutes of *limpieza de sangre* are often seen as an instrument of political unification in the political system of Spain, which only began to develop under the Catholic kings. While the Iberian Peninsula was still characterized by a strong internal heterogeneity in the late Middle Ages, the concept of "pure blood" served as the means for a complete restructuring of society on the part of the early absolutist, centralist state. The principle of "inherited" and thus incorrigible otherness, which the state controlled by means of "proof of descent," was not only an effective means of homogenization but also an early modern state directive symbolizing the state as the authority that exercises power through bureaucratic inclusion and exclusion. Along with the concept of *limpieza de sangre*, it was the concept of honor (*honor*) that became a regulatory factor for social interaction in the Spain of that time.

The decisive point is that *Lazarillo de Tormes* deals not only with the religiously based apparatus of exclusion described above but also with its secular equivalent, and in an indissoluble connection. The third *tratado*, in which Lazarillo serves an impoverished nobleman, deals explicitly with the sense of honor.

After his parting from the *clérigo*, Lazarillo ends up with the *escudero*. The manner in which the encounter is conceived of linguistically refers once more to a parody of the formulae of religious discourse: "Mochacho, ¿buscas amo? Yo le dije: Sí, señor. Pues vente tras mí—me respondió—, que Dios te ha hecho merced en topar comigo; alguna buena oración rezaste hoy" (72–73).[26] The call to Lazarillo—"Then come along with me"—is a direct quotation of words by the founder of Christianity himself, and the *escudero*'s entire discourse is so strongly permeated with religious formulae that both his character and discourse are exposed to ridicule by means of exaggeration alone. The number of the nobleman's exclamations of "By God!" can hardly be counted, and daily attendance of mass is part of his everyday accomplishments. Lazarillo accompanies his master to church and then recounts his impressions.

In hitherto existing studies, there are prominent examples of an all-too-cursory reading of this episode as well. Américo Castro has interpreted the first-person narrator's comments on the *escudero*'s attendance of mass as another piece of evidence that the character of Lazarillo, and thus the anonymous author, could not have been a devoted Christian: "Entonces se entró en la iglesia mayor, y yo tras él, y muy devotamente le vi oír misa y los otros oficios divinos" (73).[27] According to Castro, the phrasing "Lazaro *saw* the *escudero* listen to mass very devoutly" implies that he did not follow mass "muy devotamente" himself. The example of this interpretation serves to illustrate the central problem of this understanding of *Lazarillo de Tormes*: such an interpretation assumes—without articulating it but in accordance with the basic presumption of the Inquisition—that the conversions of the so-called New Christians from Judaism to Christianity had in fact only been a pretense.[28] First and foremost, this and similar interpretations are based on a vague idea of what significance the identification of a possible Jewish or *converso* origin for a text's author actually has for the study of literature. Is there—outside the realm of the religious—a specifically "Jewish discourse"? We know nothing about the factual origin of the author of *Lazarillo de Tormes*, and it is not likely that documents solving the mystery of its authorship will appear one day.

The text extensively and repeatedly broaches the topic of affiliation, but it does so in an indirect—specifically literary—manner, so that one might also call the corresponding textual context an emblematics of affiliation. In *Lazarillo de Tormes*, descent and origin become central themes and receive literary treatment in a very particular manner: they are consistently subjected to an ironic perspective, at times to the point of parody.

Seeing the *escudero*'s moral conduct, Lazarillo addresses God directly in a gesture of righteous horror. While the nobleman does everything possible in order to appear outwardly to be an honorable nobleman and devout Christian, despite almost starving at home and only surviving by the food Lazarillo obtains by questionable means, Lazarillo notes:

> ¡Grandes secretos son, Señor, los que Vós hacéis y las gentes ignoran! ¿A quién no engañará aquella buena disposición y razonable capa y sayo? ¿Y quién pensará que aquel gentil hombre se pasó ayer todo el día sin comer . . . ? Nadie, por cierto, lo sospechará. ¡Oh, Señor, y cuántos de aquestos debéis Vós tener por el mundo derramados, que padescen por la negra que llaman honra lo que por Vós no sufrirán! (83–84)[29]

Lazarillo claims he has felt empathy with noblemen ever since, because he has always feared that a similarly miserable fate as that of his third master was disguised behind their demeanor: "Dios es testigo que hoy día, cuando topo con alguno de su hábito con aquel paso y pompa, le he lástima con pensar si padece lo que aquél le vi sufrir" (92).[30]

It is of particular interest that another episode ridicules not only the *escudero*'s concept of honor but also his inclusion of himself in a "linaje castiza": after his master escapes, when Lazarillo is interrogated by the judiciary—collecting his master's debts—he states where the wanted man can be found, in his opinion:

> Señores—dije yo—, lo que este mi amo tiene, según él me dijo, es un muy buen solar de casas y un palomar derribado.—Bien está—dicen ellos—. Por poco que eso valga, hay para nos entregar de la deuda. ¿Y a qué parte de la ciudad tiene eso?—me preguntaron.—En su tierra—les respondí.—Por Dios, que está bueno el negocio—dijeron ellos—. ¿Y adónde es su tierra?—De Castilla la Vieja me dijo él que era—le dije yo. Riéronse mucho el alguacil y el escribano, diciendo:—Bastante relación es ésta para cobrar vuestra deuda, aunque mejor fuese. (108–109)[31]

The laughter at Lazarillo's reference to the *escudero*'s claim that he hailed from Old Castile shows what this character stands for in the text. While the debt collectors had initially hoped for the existence of actual property, after hearing Lazarillo's statement they consider the *escudero* as someone whose pretensions are nothing but discursive schemata backed up by no reliable, material realities of any kind. Similarly, the *escudero*'s attempt at being gallant as a true nobleman ends very quickly when the two ladies he approaches ask him to pay for their breakfast:

> [É]l estaba entre ellas, . . . diciéndoles más dulzuras que Ovidio escribió. Pero como sintieron dél que estaba bien enternecido, no se les hizo de vergüenza pedirle de almorzar, con el acostumbrado pago. Él sintiéndose tan frío de bolsa cuanto estaba caliente del estómago, tomóle tal calofrío, que le robó la color del gesto, y comenzó a turbarse en la plática y a poner excusas no validas. Ellas, que debían ser bien instituidas, como le sintieron la enfermedad, dejáronle para el que era. (85–86)[32]

The above-mentioned satirical treatment of the topics of origin and descent in the novel has certainly directed attention toward the anonymous author's affiliation. One essential reason for this is the novel's first-person narrator, which brings up the question about the identity of the narrating "I" and the author. Furthermore, the autobiographical mode of speech had "a truly precarious status in the communicative milieu of the Counter-Reformation," since "such a discourse was only to be legitimized by its function as encouragement for *imitatio*," as Hans Ulrich Gumbrecht has emphasized.[33]

The first-person narrator is hardly an early modern invention but can already be found in epic poetry, for example, in Odysseus's first-person narrative (of the Cyclops, Circe, the souls of the dead, and his encounter with Scylla and Charybdis) or in Aeneas's narration of the events of the Trojan War as told to Dido. Lucian of Samosata at times used the first person in his satires as well, and extensive use of first-person narration is made in both Apuleius's *The Golden Ass* and Petronius's *Satyricon*. Yet, as Bernhard König first pointed out, in the case of *Lazarillo de Tormes*, "both its greatness and the difficulties regarding its interpretation result from the narrative focus on the perspective of the fictitious first-person narrator."[34]

The Ironic Treatment of Descent and Origin

In this context the opening sequence has always been interpreted as one of the novel's key passages, particularly the address to "Vuestra Merced."[35] The satirical functionalizing of the confessional genre, especially in *Lazarillo de Tormes*, has been discussed extensively in the course of Romance studies.[36]

It is of particular interest for the present context that the account opens with a detailed review of the hero's descent, in which the protagonist explains how his last name, "de Tormes" ("from the river Tormes"), had come to be:

> Pues sepa Vuestra Merced, ante todas cosas, que a mí llaman Lázaro de Tormes, hijo de Tomé González y de Antona Pérez, naturales de Tejares, aldea de Salamanca. Mi nascimiento fue dentro del río Tormes, por la cual causa tomé el sobrenombre; y fue desta manera: mi padre, que Dios perdone, tenía cargo de proveer una molienda de una aceña que está ribera de aquel río, en la cual fue molinero más de quince años; y estando mi madre una noche en la aceña, preñada de mí, tomóle el parto y parióme allí. De manera que con verdad me puedo decir nascido en el río. (12–14)[37]

In a text from sixteenth-century Spain, such an account has a dimension far beyond the anecdotal. In light of the religious discourses and stories still generally familiar at the time, the story of the protagonist's birth appears multiply coded. Sixteenth-century Spanish Lazarus shares the birth from water with biblical Moses, about whom is written in Exodus 2:10: "And the child grew, and she brought him unto Pharaoh's daughter, and he became her son. And she called his name Moses [that is, Drawn out], and she said, Because I drew him out of the water." The structural similarity of these two birth stories has another dimension: Moses eventually had two mothers, one from the house of Levi who had abandoned him, and the pharaoh's daughter who took him in. In the biblical story, it is the Egyptian who gives him his name. Thus Moses is an Israelite who also has a—virtually adoptive—element of Egyptian descent. The story of Lazarillo's descent evokes a dual affiliation to begin with, while both the water alluding to the baptismal sacrament and the name Lázaro may be considered to be references to the

Christian dimension. Additionally, the characterization of the parents points to an origin outside the norms of the system of inclusion.

The account of the protagonist's descent at the beginning of *Lazarillo de Tormes* seems to make reference to a historic foil from the repertoire of the judicial procedures of the Sanctum Officium to which previous studies of the text have not paid attention. The usual instruments of the tribunals of the Spanish Inquisition of the time did not only consist in interrogations during the trial as outlined above. The interrogations were recorded by a scribe, who phrased the statements in the third person: "he/she said" (*dixo*); this was the pattern of those texts from the Inquisition archives newly edited in the past four decades.[38]

There was an additional procedure of investigation, differing in terms of genre, thatt demanded a written personal *confessio*, consequently an account written in the first person. The resulting texts were documents that could decide the fate of the interrogated. These were the so-called *informaciones genealógicas*, which in the Spain of that time were not only demanded of those under suspicion of secretly adhering to Mosaic law after their conversion but of anyone wishing to hold public office. It is quite possible that the opening of all picaresque novels, which became a *topos*—the detailed description of the protagonist's origin—refers to the discursive pattern of the Inquisition's proof of descent. The central question the genre of the picaresque novel has provoked ever since its inception is this: How did it come about historically that the genre of autobiography, existing for centuries yet reserved for the upper classes, all of a sudden is transferred to voices from marginalized milieus in the guise of literary fiction? This question needs to be asked especially with regard to the opening accounts of lineage featured in all the texts under discussion: members of the lower classes had no "lineage," or put differently, the very fact that they have no genealogy or none worth recording positively identifies them as members of the lower classes and marginal groups.

It was the religiously based racism in the Spain of that time briefly described above that altered the differentiation between relevant (and thus potentially noteworthy) and irrelevant lineage that had existed up till then. Under the suspicion of their secretly acting against state religion, it was particularly the genealogy of those members of society with regard to whom one previously did not even speak of a *genealogía* that suddenly became a subject of interest.

Hence Lazarillo's fictitious autobiography is only at first sight a mere justification of the course of his life up until his happy marriage to the mistress of the archpriest. Beyond that, it is first and foremost the satirical accusation of a widespread genre in sixteenth-century Spain[39] and thus also a mocking attempt at a revolt against the apparatuses of exclusion associated with the corresponding juridical text genre.

To this day, the relevant documents have essentially not been printed. The image reproduced in figure 1 contains one such report, which the physician Ledesma addressed to the Sanctum Officium on May 4, 1565. Introduced by the words "Illustres y muy estimados senores, esta es la memoria de mi Ascendencia que vuestras mercedes me mandaron que diese" (Illustrious and highly esteemed Lords, this is the memory of my descent, which Your Graces have demanded of me), the physician sheds light on his father and his paternal grandparents as well as his mother and maternal grandparents.[40] The transcript is below.

(apostil date) Illustres (sic) y muy Honrados Señores (apostil date and registry)

Esta es la memoria de mi Ascendencia que vuestras mercedes me mandaron que diese

A mi padre llaman Pedro de Ledesma

Mi abuelo de partes de mi padre se llamo Andrés Bcormniego de la Bibda

Mi abuela se llamo Ioanna de dios la guarde el evejero mujer única del dicho Andres Bcormniego naturales entreambos de Pereira tierra de Ledesma

A mi madre llaman Anna Fernandez

Mi abuelo se partes de la dicha mi madre se llama Bartholme Sanchez Ortalano vezino del Arrabal de Sanctiago

Mi abuela de partes de la dicha mi madre se llamo Maria Gomez mujer única del dicho Bartholme Sanchez vezina assi mesmo del Arrabal de Santiago desta dicha cibdad

(signature): El licenciado de Ledesma

(apostil official comments)[41]

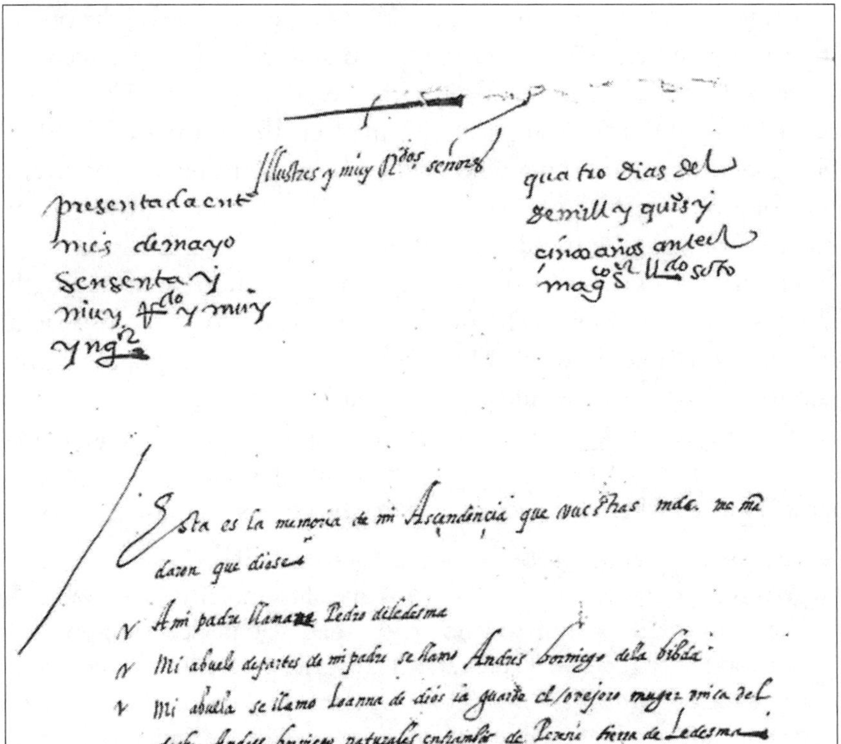

Figure 1. Informaciones genealógicas del Tribunal de la Inquisición de Toledo sobre Pedro de Ledesma. His *limpieza de sangre* was investigated in 1565 (Archivo Histórico Nacional, Inquisición, *legajo 360, expediente* 7).

These historical documents open up a new perspective on the opening passage of *Lazarillo de Tormes*. One possible reading of the account given by the first-person narrator at the beginning of *Lazarillo* is that of a parody of the "genealogical information" that those suspected of being *judaizante* and those who applied for appointment to or retention of a public office (which also included the office of town crier) had to submit to the Inquisition authorities.

The narrator's account of his origin is by no means finished with the passage cited above. The most striking aspect of his subsequent statements is that Lazarillo does not relate anything praiseworthy about his origin—as would be expected in an account of one's descent—but instead gives only compromising details, yet he does this in a tone intended to play down, or rather trivialize, the objective facts, some of which are even known to the courts:

> Pues siendo yo niño de ocho años, achacaron a mi padre ciertas sangrías mal hechas en los costales de los que allí a moler venían, por lo cual fue preso, y confesó y no negó, y padesció persecución por justicia. Espero en Dioas que está en la gloria, pues el Evangelio los llama bienaventurados. . . . Mi viuda madre . . . y un hombre moreno de aquellos que las bestias curaban vinieron en conoscimiento. Éste algunas veces se venía a nuestra casa y se iba a la mañana. . . . Yo, al principio de su entrada, pesábame con él y habíale miedo, viendo el color y mal gesto que tenía; mas de que vi que su venida mejoraba el comer, fuile queriendo bien, porque siempre traía pan, pedazos de carne y en el invierno leños, a que nos calentábamos. De manera que, continuando la posada y conversación, mi madre vino a darme un negrito muy bonito, el cual yo brincaba y ayudaba a calentar. Y acuérdome que estando el negro de mi padrastro trebajando con el mozuelo, como el niño vía a mi madre y a mí blancos y a él no, huía dél, con miedo, para mi madre, y, señalando con el dedo, decía:—¡Madre, coco![42] Respondió él riendo:—¡Hideputa! Yo, aunque bien mochacho, noté aquella palabra de mi hermanico y dije entre mí: "¡Cuántos debe de haber en el mundo que huyen de otros porque no se veen a sí mesmos!" (14–18)[43]

The difference between royal, that is, secular courts and the Inquisition trials consisted mainly in the secrecy of all inquisitorial trials. None of the involved were ever allowed to speak publicly about the tribunals and the tribunal case files:

> Upon either their release or the beginning of their sentence, the accused had to sign a document in which they declared under oath and threat of punishment not to tell anyone about what they had heard in prison and during the trial.[44]

From the perspective of this imperative of secrecy, the intention to publish Lazarillo's life story formulated in the prologue seems doubly satirical:

> Yo por bien tengo que cosas tan señaladas, y por ventura nunca oídas ni vistas, vengan a noticia de muchos y no se entierren en la sepultura del olvido, pues podría ser que alguno que las lea halle algo que le agrade, y a los que no ahondaren tanto los deleite. Y a este propósito dice Plinio que "no hay libro, por malo que sea, que no tenga alguna cosa buena." . . . Y esto para que ninguna cosa se debría romper ni echa a mal, si muy detestable no fuese, sino que a todos se comunicase, mayormente siendo sin perjuicio y pudiendo sacar della algún fructo. Porque, si así no fuese, muy pocos escribirían para uno solo, pues no se hace sin trabajo, y quieren, ya que lo pasan, ser recompensados, no con dineros, mas con que vean y lean sus obras y, si hay de qué, se las alaben. (3–6)[45]

On the one hand, this is an ironic rendering of the common *topos* of usefulness. After all, the following text presents the autobiography of a man whose various misdeeds (and the more serious misdeeds of his noble and clergyman masters) remain unpunished. On the other hand, this passage demonstrates the particular possibilities of the literary treatment of history. It is evident that authors of literary texts can make use of aesthetic means of composition much more radically than historians—the liberty of literary depictions of history consists in the texts' very literariness. History always addresses events and their depiction simultaneously, for not only does every depiction imply a depicted event, but historical events also only become manifest through the medium of their depiction. The judicial processes of the Inquisition were linked to the oath of discretion. The anonymous author of *Lazarillo*, however, considers it "to be good that such remarkable things" as have happened to him "should not be buried in the tomb of oblivion." Finally, Pliny the Elder is quoted as saying that "no book was so bad but some good might be got out of it" (recorded by Pliny the Younger, *Epistulae* 3.5, 10).

This strategy of legitimization for narrative episodes in *Lazarillo*, which could hardly be reconciled with the moral code of the Counter-Reformation, reinforces—albeit with a different emphasis from our perspective—Bernhard König's analysis of the novel, according to which its meaning is all in its form.[46] This suggested interpretation of the first-person narration in *Lazarillo de Tormes* as a satire on the bureaucratic procedure for proving *limpieza de sangre*, however, does not result in another argument for the empirical author's affiliation. Converts naturally were at the center of inquisitorial attention, but they were not the only ones affected. In the argument I am making, it is this very fact that demonstrates the distinctiveness of those worlds of memory that can be identified through a textual analysis of *Lazarillo de Tormes*: since literary memory is in itself structurally ambiguous and cannot be tailored to any one cultural identity,[47] layers of memory of a converted Jew's life exist in *Lazarillo* not exclusively but among others. At the same time, other perspectives diverging from the dogmatic spirit of the time are preserved in the text, for example, that of an Erasmist, a liberal Christian, or even a position one would have to call Protestant in regard to other European cultures.[48]

Another, short excerpt from the prologue of *Lazarillo* will elucidate the suggested perspective once more:

> Suplico a Vuestra Merced reciba el pobre servicio de mano de quien lo hiciera más rico, si su poder y deseo se conformaran. Y pues Vuestra Merced escribe se le escriba y relate el caso muy por extenso, parescióme no tomalle por el medio, sino del principio, *porque se tenga entera noticia de mi persona; y también porque consideren los que heredaron nobles estados cuán poco se les debe, pues Fortuna fue con ellos parcial, y cuánto más hicieron los que, siéndoles contraria, con fuerza y maña remando salieron a buen puerto*. (9–10; author's emphasis)[49]

The fictitious addressee "Vuestra Merced" is supposed to receive a detailed report on the person writing. The same or similar phrasing can be found in the documentations of the *informaciones genealógicas*. The second sentence, however—that "Vuestra Merced" may consider how little those who had inherited a noble estate or rank had contributed to it themselves, since Fortuna had been partial to them, and how much more those had done to whom Fortuna had been hostile and who had nevertheless achieved relative happiness through courage and dexterity—encodes *in nuce* the text's meaning as suggested here. The analysis of this sixteenth-century novel makes it evident that in a situation of externally imposed marginalization irreversible for the individual, a representative language for historical reality is found that effects a change of literary genres in a very unique way.[50]

One conclusion from what has been discussed above is that the origin of the picaresque novel is mainly to be found in its link with Spanish history of the *Siglo de Oro*.[51] Seen from this perspective, *Lazarillo* also demonstrates the specific character of early modern processes of individualization: through the "telling of things never heard before" from the perspective of a first-person narrator who might be construing his own experiences and ideas in the medium of the text against the backdrop of the Inquisition tribunals, a modern opening of the text to individual experience takes place—mostly where it is no longer in accordance with the premises of the traditional realm of experience.

The anonymous author of *Lazarillo de Tormes* has transformed the pseudobiography of a marginalized historical existence into a satirical textual game. Perhaps it is in this very approach, namely, the ironic look at the end of a culturally heterogeneous society, that the genre's distinctiveness lies overall.

A synthesis of the historical foil and the first picaresque novel shows the specifics of the literary use of language in relation to the pragmatic text, whether in the form of an authentic historical document or in the form of an expository text making an argument. Literary texts, taken out of precisely definable real contexts, are rendered unpragmatic and thus are always more or less plurivalent in their communicative dimension. They don't argue, they narrate; and they leave the condensation of the narrated into an argument, into what is called the message, to the reader. What might at first appear as a deficit subsequently becomes an enormous resource: owing to their ambiguity and multiple possibilities for coding, texts by one specific author with one specific cultural and ethnic affiliation can be read by readers of entirely different cultural and ethnic horizons, who can even identify with them. Literature is the place where the walls of ethnic-cultural boundaries become permeable. It produces a symbolic hybridity that can become a real cultural hybridity—not necessarily, but possibly. It can also become an instrument of disciplinary action and partition. Its "noncommittal" character seems, however, to tend to facilitate experimentation with the boundaries of different discourses.

Four Marranism and Modernity

The Meaning of Form in Michel de Montaigne's *Essais* (1580–1588)

The entry on French literature in the second edition of the *Encyclopedia Judaica*[1] written by Denise R. Goitstein and Anne Grynberg contains the following explanatory passage on the early modern age:

> After a gap of nearly 200 years, writers of Jewish origin again made their appearance on the French literary scene. Outstanding among them were the celebrated astrologer and physician Nostradamus (Michel de Nostre-Dame) and the great essayist Michel de Montaigne (1533–1592). The latter's mother, Antoinette de Louppes de Villeneuve, was a Christian descendant of Mayer Paçagon (Pazagón) of Calatayud who, after his forcible conversion at the beginning of the 15th century, took the baptismal name of Juan López de Villanueva. A skeptical humanist, more deistic than Christian, Montaigne in his Essays reveals a tolerant abhorrence of the Inquisition in Portugal, but only an outsider's interest in Jewish survival.[2]

The *Encyclopedia Judaica* also features an entry on Montaigne himself, in which his ancestry is reconstructed. Reference is made to his education at the Collège de Guyennes, an institution run by Portuguese "New Christians," and to his subsequent studies at the University of Toulouse, a "center of New Christian heterodoxy."[3] The most interesting passage in this encyclopedia entry refers to the role Jews played in Montaigne's oeuvre. This passage is quoted at length below because it succinctly illustrates the fundamental problems of all research arguing on the basis of ancestry and origin:

> It is difficult to know what Montaigne actually thought of the Jews, for this was a dangerous subject in those days of religious intolerance. Almost all his references to the Jews, however, show a sympathetic

> attitude. In the Essais he mentions disapprovingly the persecutions in Portugal, as well as the Jews' stubborn loyalty to their religion (Book I, chap. 14). But it is in the Travel Diary (Journal de Voyage), not intended for publication (it saw the light for the first time in 1774), that numerous references are found to Jewish life and customs, as Montaigne saw them first hand during his Italian journey. There is no doubt that he went out of his way to visit synagogues, attend Jewish ceremonies, and converse with Jews. Montaigne gives a detailed, accurate, and sympathetic account of Sabbath services and a circumcision ceremony. He comments on the communal participation in prayer, study, and discussion, and on the widespread knowledge of Hebrew, even among children. . . . In all these instances his tone is objective, detached, and completely free from the accepted prejudices of the time. But two facts remain puzzling: Montaigne's obvious interest in Jewish life and his refraining from any mention of his mother in the Essais, a largely autobiographical work. Some critics interpret this as proof that Montaigne was deeply preoccupied with his Jewish identity, and for reasons of caution deliberately avoided any reference to it. This may be so, but one basic fact is unknown, whether Montaigne even knew of his mother's Jewish ancestry. It seems doubtful, as her ancestors had been Christian for several generations, and no one, in those intolerant days, would have gone out of his way to unearth his Jewish ancestry.[4]

According to the logic of this study's overall argument, Montaigne represents an early modern author prominent in world literature who had neither a consciously Jewish identity, as Leone Ebreo did, nor an untraceable ancestry and identity, as did the authors of *La Celestina* and *Lazarillo de Tormes*, but a Marranic affiliation, which he might not have been aware of or which was of no particular significance to him. Thus the delicate question of origin on the one hand and effect on the other meets a particularly complex case in this instance.

This complexity can also be demonstrated by means of a position from an earlier period of Romance studies, which is diametrically opposed to the endeavor of the *Encyclopedia Judaica*: in his epilogue to Hugo Friedrich's study of Montaigne, Frank-Rutger Hausmann has pointed out that Friedrich's study of the French author was by no means a matter of course in the 1940s and was thus in need of an explanation—in 1938, Walter Mönch had stated in his *Nationalpolitische Geistesgeschichte der französischen Renaissance* that Montaigne lacked "heroic passion" and "commitment to the religious and national political interests of the fatherland," and in 1942, one of Hugo Friedrich's friends teaching in Berlin, Swiss privatdozent Gerhard Hess, had "Aryanized" Montaigne in what today can only be considered a grotesque essay, and using Nazi terminology, had concluded that Montaigne's "portion of Jewish blood" probably was "less than a quarter."[5]

In light of these constellations, the problems regarding studies of the specifics of sixteenth-century Romance literature based on an author's origin, which have been repeatedly diagnosed in this book, again become particularly evident.[6]

Marranism as Metaphor—Contingent Selfhood and Literary Writing

The linguistic realizations of various areas of intellectual history in Montaigne's *Essais* are being analyzed irrespective of biographical considerations in this study. The astonishing modernity of this author, who construes an "I" that unremittingly observes and describes itself, will be explained as a potential way of confronting the forced disclosure of descent and origin.

Montaigne's oeuvre, and particularly the *Essais*, is unusual in multiple respects. It is neither the authority of the classical authors nor that of the great theologians of the time but instead the internal dimension of the empirical "I" that serves as the text's central point of reference: "Je n'ai pas plus faict mon livre, que mon livre m'a faict. Livre consubstantial à son autheur: D'une occupation propre: Membre de ma vie: Non d'une occupation et fin, tierce et estrangere, comme tous autres livres."[7] Montaigne also transfers classical Pyrrhonian skepticism into the modern age in his *Essais*. As nearly every interpretation of his texts points out, Montaigne's singular act seems almost mysterious, particularly with regard to the genealogy of its genesis. For the result of his literary consciousness reads with virtually no distance due to the passage of time and is remarkably modern. Montaigne focuses the attention on the act of writing and the process of thought, not on the result:

> Ce fagotage de tant de diverses pieces, se faict en ceste condition, que je n'y mets la main, que lors qu'une trop lasche oysiveté me presse, et non ailleurs que chez moy. Ainsin il s'est basty à diverses poses et intervalles, comme les occasions me detiennent ailleurs par fois plusieurs moys. Au demeurant, je ne corrige point mes premieres imaginations par les secondes, ouy à l'aventure quelque mot: mais pour diversifier, non pour oster. Je veux representer le progrez de mes humeurs, et qu'on voye chasque piece en sa naissance. . . . Un valet qui me servoit à les escrire soubs moy, pensa faire un grand butin de m'en desrober plusieurs pieces choisies à sa poste. Cela me console, qu'il n'y fera pas plus de gain, que j'y ay fait de perte. (2.37, 796)[8]

This passage contains two levels of meaning that characterize Montaigne's entire writing in the *Essais* and are inextricably linked to each other: the virtuosic irony of the writing "I" and the energetic self-assertion of the subject. The ironized discourse when talking about himself requires a skepticism extending even to his own person, which forms the basis for argumentation in all of the *Essais*. Skeptical thinking means a radical rejection of any possibility of knowing the absolute truth of a judgment. As a consequence of this mode of thinking, antagonistic, contradictory opinions must be recognized as equally valid. The Greek physician Sextus Empiricus, to whom we owe our knowledge of Pyrrhonian skepticism, wrote in the second century CE that this suspension of judgment resulted from the insight that "we find that undecidable dissension about the matter proposed has come about both in ordinary life and among philosophers. Because of this we are not able either to choose or to rule out anything, and we end up with suspension of judgment."[9]

Montaigne makes his reference to skepticism explicit throughout the text. The following excerpt is among the numerous passages in which Sextus Empiricus is quoted almost literally:

> Finalement, il n'y a aucune constante existence, ny de nostre estre, ny de celuy des objects: Et nous, et nostre jugement, et toutes choses mortelles, vont coulant et roulant sans cesse: Ainsin il ne se peut establir rien de certain de l'un à l'autre, et le jugeant, et le

> jugé, estans en continuelle mutation et branle. Nous n'avons aucune communication à l'estre, par ce que toute humaine nature est tousjours au milieu, entre le naistre et le mourir, ne baillant de soy qu'une obscure apparence et ombre, et une incertaine et debile opinion. Et si de fortune vous fichez vostre pensée à vouloir prendre son estre, ce sera ne plus ne moins que qui voudroit empoigner l'eau. (2.12, 639)[10]

Verena Lobsien has pointed out that there are basically two paradigms dominating the present debate on "subjectivity" in the early modern age and has noted laconically: "Both sink to the level of cliché at times."[11] The first paradigm implies the notion of the subject's autonomy, which virtually "seized" Renaissance people like an "awakening" after the "sleep" of the Middle Ages. The school of New Historicism has formulated a contrary paradigm of heteronomy, according to which it is not self-awareness and self-presence but an "irreversible being divested of oneself and differing from oneself" (Lobsien) that characterized the human condition in the early modern age. Stephen Greenblatt has suggested the term "self-fashioning" for the individual's constantly variable processes of negotiation within cultural meanings, regulations of conduct, and forms of representation.[12]

Including the mental consequences of the procedures of the Inquisition might prove a critical expansion in the attempt to get a better grasp of the sources of self in the sixteenth century. The previous chapter has shown that the Sanctum Officium's documents for proving the ancestry of *judaizante* suspects have possibly been parodied by the genre of the picaresque novel, which might answer the question about the genesis of this novelistic genre.

Montaigne began work on the *Essais* in 1572, the year of the so-called St. Bartholomew's Day Massacre, which would aggravate the French Wars of Religion. Julia Kristeva has attributed the invention of the unstable and fragmented "I" in autobiographical discourse to Montaigne.[13] The self Montaigne construes in the *Essais* is not a stable entity giving the sort of clear statement regarding origin and ancestry that would have been expected at the time:

> Si je parle diversement de moy, c'est que je me regarde diversement. Toutes les contrarietez s'y trouvent . . . : Honteux, insolent, chaste, luxurieux, bavard, taciturne, laborieux, delicat, ingenieux, hebeté,

> chagrin, debonnaire, menteur, veritable, sçavant, ignorant, et liberal et avare et prodigue: tout cela je le vois en moy aucunement, selon que je me vire: et quiconque s'estudie bien attentivement, trouve en soy, voire et en son jugement mesme, ceste volubilité et discordance. (2.1, 355)[14]

There are frequent references to the father in the *Essais*, while the mother is not mentioned at all in this three-volume work. This does not necessarily mean that Montaigne thus mainly intended to avoid inquiries about her origin. After all, we cannot reconstruct with absolute certainty whether Montaigne knew about the origin of his mother's family, as has been explained above. Yet it seems that—after the judicially forced *confessio* of one's ancestry paradoxically induced the first-person narration of the picaresque novel—twenty years after the publication of *Lazarillo de Tormes*, a subject exploring itself perspectively is created in the act of speaking about the "I" for whom biological ancestors have been replaced by the act of writing itself: "I have not made my book any more than it has made me—a book of one substance with its author, proper to me and a limb of my life."[15]

Hence the first-person form of the *Essais* does not have its basis in the logic of ancestry and origin but inverts it in the process of writing. The "I" constitutes itself in the act of writing and in the text. Thus "Marranic writing" should not be understood as a reference to Montaigne's origins in this instance, but as a metaphor for an *écriture* that transforms the speaking about the "I" so steeped in designations of affiliation into a skeptical self-reflection at the beginning of the early modern age. The latter eventually was to guarantee the freedom of the modern self. From the resistance against the legitimacy of a "genealogical" discourse of basically unquestioned validity for a man of his class at that time would arise in Montaigne the strikingly modern-seeming conception of a subject that has its origin in itself as writer:

> Le monde regarde tousjours vis à vis: moy, je replie ma veue au dedans, je la plante, je l'amuse là. Chacun regarde devant soy, moy je regarde dedans moy: Je n'ay affaire qu'à moy, je me considere sans cesse, je me contrerolle, je me gouste . . . moy, je me roulle en moy-mesme. (2.17: 697)[16]

The following selection of text analyses will show whether this interpretive perspective leads to results with regard to the work as a whole. The initial assumption that Montaigne arrives at a literary mode of writing by way of philosophical skepticism can be proven comprehensibly:

> Et d'avantage, je le puis dire pour l'avoir essayé, ayant autrefois usé de cette liberté de mon chois et triage particulier, mettant à nonchaloir certains points de l'observance de nostre Église, qui semblent avoir un visage ou plus vain, ou plus estrange, venant à en communiquer aux homes sçavans, j'ay trouvé que ces choses là ont un fondement massif et tressolide: et que ce n'est que bestise et ignorance, qui nous fait les recevoir avec moindre reverence que le reste. Que ne nous souvient il combine nous sentons de contradiction en nostre jugement mesmes? Combien de choses nous servoyent hyer d'articles de foy, qui nous sont fables aujourd'hui? La gloire et la curiosité, sont les fleaux de nostre ame. Cette cy nous conduit à mettre le nez par tout, et celle là nous defend de rien laisser irresolu et indecis. (1.26, 189)[17]

Montaigne arrives at the skeptical suspension of judgment in several steps. Contrary to the aforementioned quotes from the *Outlines of Pyrrhonism*, this excerpt exemplifies the aesthetic-productive transformation of the philosophical reference text that characterizes Montaigne's particular writing and the specifics of the essay form, as well as the semantic layer reminiscent of the juridical dimension of the first-person account. At the beginning of the passage, the narrating "I" confesses that he had committed several sins regarding the exact observance of the Church Order in the past. Only through conversation with scholars had he realized that these supposedly meaningless things, too, rested on a solid foundation, and that it was owing only to our stupidity and ignorance that these were shown less reverence. Up to this point the text evokes standardized formulae of church doctrine. The following sentences reveal the distinctiveness of Montaigne's writing, however: two questions—"Why do we not remember how much contradiction we sense even in our own judgment? How many things were articles of faith to us yesterday, which are fables to us today?"—lead to the final, aphoristic formula calling vainglory and curiosity the scourges of the soul. The transformation into a question and the resulting rhetoricization of the statement mark the shift from pragmatic to literary text. The ambiguity immanent in the literary text has far-reaching consequences in this instance, for the skeptical "we" includes those learned men who had previously enlightened the narrating "I" about questions of dogma with great certainty. Thus, irony appears as the fundamentally modern device of subjective-aesthetic perspectivism in the *Essais*. In this text passage, it refers to a real historical context that was part of the conditions of early modern existence beyond the boundaries of the literary: dogmatic certainty in matters of doctrine.

L'*Apologie de Raimond Sebond*—Consequences of Skeptical Writing

The passage analyzed above is taken from the twenty-sixth essay of the first book, titled *It is Folly to Measure Truth and Error by Our Own Capacity*. This shorter text seems like a prelude to the much longer and consequently much more radical essay of the second book containing the *Apology for Raymond Sebond* (2.12). This essay is one of the central texts in the entire work. At the opening of this long essay, the narrating "I" recounts that he had translated Raymond Sebond's *Theologia naturalis* (first printed in 1484) from Spanish into French at the request of his father. A friend of his father's, a certain Pierre Bunel, had given his father the book in the hope that the recipient might, with a little help, gain something from reading it, since he himself had considered it a very useful and timely work. The *Theologia naturalis* is one of those fifteenth-century Christian theological texts written in reaction to Averroism.

In his text, Sebond had attempted to restore the unity of faith by describing the human mind as naturally capable of recognizing the truth of dogma and the constitutional orientation toward God of all being with complete clarity. To the narrating "I" of the *Essais*, Sebond's thoughts appear beautiful, his work coherently structured, and his intent full of piety; and the rhetorical gesture at the beginning of this essay is that of a defense of Sebond against his critics as well. In its execution of this apologetic intent, however, the text turns into a scathing rebuttal of Sebond's attempt to prove the mysteries of revelation by means of reason.

The opposing trend in the argumentation of the essay in question can be observed in the first reply given by the narrating "I" to the objections against Sebond's work:

> La premiere reprehension qu'on fait de son ouvrage; c'est que les Chrestiens se font tort de vouloir appuyer leur creance, par des raisons humaines, qui ne se conçoit que par foy, et par une inspiration particuliere de la grace divine. En cette objection, il semble qu'il y ait quelque zele de pieté: et à cette cause nous faut-il avec autant plus de douceur et de respect essayer de satisfaire à ceux qui la mettent en avant. Ce seroit mieux la charge d'un homme versé en la Theologie, que de moy, qui n'y sçay rien. Toutefois je juge ainsi, . . . comparez nos moeurs à un Mahometan, à un Payen, vous demeurez tousjours au dessoubs: Là où au regard de l'avantage de nostre religion, nous devrions luire en excellence, d'une extreme et incomparable distance: et devroit on dire, sont ils si justes, si charitables, si bons? Ils sont donq Chrestiens. Toutes autres apparences sont communes à toutes religions. . . . La merque peculiere de nostre verité devroit estre nostre vertu. . . . Il n'est point d'hostilité excellente comme la Chrestienne. Nostre zele fait merveilles, quand il va secondant nostre pente vers la haine, la cruauté, l'ambition, l'avarice, la detraction, la rebellion. À contrepoil, vers la bonté, la benignité, la temperance, si, comme par miracle, quelque rare complexion ne l'y porte, il ne va ny de pied, ny d'aile. Nostre religion est faicte pour extirper les vices: elle les couvre, les nourrit, les incite. (2.12, 460–464)[18]

This passage serves to illustrate that there are always at least two layers of meaning contained in Montaigne's writing. The chastisement of believers is initially backed up theologically. Propelled by the dynamic inherent to skeptical irony, it subsequently goes beyond the boundaries of dogmatic discourse, however. The problem of representation raised in Montaigne's text reflects the dialectics of a self attempting to reproduce itself for posterity as identical with itself and simultaneously escaping itself continuously in the process. There are no exceptions to this experience of heteronomy up to the moment when the defense of a position guaranteeing certain belief through incorruptible reason reveals a previously hidden view of the Christian faith. While it is described as our religion—*nostre religion*—it is also portrayed as inferior to the customs of Muslims and pagans. One could summarize that the disavowals of early modern existence are imprinted on Montaigne's dialectical writing. The essay in defense of Raymond Sebond steers toward the philosophical self-discovery of its author, a skeptical confession. The *Essais* are fundamentally different from St. Augustine's *Confessiones*, however, as a follow-up to which they have often been understood. The latter's confessions describe Augustine's spiritual development toward peace in God. Montaigne's self-examination not only results in a secularization of the literary form of the confessional autobiography; the first-person account also voids possible components of Marranic history extending to the universal in the process of writing.

It is by no means a coincidence that general works on Montaigne—from Hugo Friedrich in 1949 to Martin Gessmann in 1997—have taken the essay in defense of Sebond as an essential source for their discussion of Montaigne's philosophical thinking. The long piece on Sebond invariably seems to be one of the fundamental texts in the entire *Essais*—and in light of this chapter's hypothesis, one of the essential texts with regard to the exploration of the self in the process of writing.[19]

The crucial point is that the essay's criticism of attempts to "prove" the reality of Christian dogma by using reason and of the endeavor to justify Christianity's moral superiority by means of a reference to theological virtues and their significance does not culminate in a rejection of traditional Christianity. Regardless of the problems associated with Christian religion demonstrated in the text, the writing "I" appears as a Christian and a Catholic. However, this decision does not result from (ethnic) affiliation or a pre-rational clinging to tradition, but rather from the lack of a rationally based alternative option, which becomes evident in the process of writing. The textual "I" in the *Essais* is based on neither "truth" nor "origin" but on the impossibility of a decision for anything other than the given.

The "I" in Writing: *De la solitude* (1.38), *Que nostre desir s'accroist par la malaisance* (2.15), and *Du repentir* (3.2)

In his essay on repentance (*Du repentir*, 3.2), Montaigne states that his work is not about spreading a doctrine. He does not teach, he narrates: "Je n'enseigne point, je raconte" (3.2, 846).[20] This differentiation not only enables an examination through the lens of literary studies—without discounting the enormous value of philosophical readings of the text—but also points to the importance of the writing "I" constantly emphasized in the *Essais*. The following analyses of passages from three essays—from the above-cited *Du repentir*, *De la solitude* (1.38), and *Que nostre desir s'accroist par la malaisance* (2.15)—will illustrate the specific manner in which the "I" defines itself through the process of writing in Montaigne's *Essais*.

In his study on Montaigne's oeuvre, Jean Starobinski has emphasized the importance of the essay *De la solitude* and has highlighted the particular character of the confinement to the self described by Montaigne in this text. What Montaigne seeks in the *Essais* is a place in the world truly his alone, contrary to others who, in letting themselves be carried away by external things, relinquish the self in order to obtain an imaginary rank or riches. The return to the self that Montaigne advocated, however, was fundamentally different from Christian self-communion. While the latter confinement to the self, demanded not least by the Augustinian annunciation, was to serve the purpose of listening to God's voice and accepting his judgment, the self-communion sought by Montaigne was aimed at finding a mirror-image interlocutor in order to enable the individual to fully pass his own judgment again. The solitude Montaigne sought in his essay was not to be compared with the traditional *vita contemplativa*, which religion opposes to the *vita activa*. According to Starobinski, this differentiation was essential, for the religious calling for an "internal conversation" was only a first step, followed by obedience to the divine voice and hope for salvation, while in Montaigne's essay the accomplishment of self-contemplation was an end in itself.[21]

In the *Essais* this self-reference is a result of the recourse to writing. Both classical and contemporary authorities and in some cases even biblical aphorisms are included in the process of writing, although not in the sense of a reassuring repetition but in the form of a dialogue sounding out the truth of those doctrines, not as absolute but rather as "right" only when transferred to one's own situation: "Il y a dequoy bien et mal faire par tout: Toutesfois si le mot de Bias est vray, que la pire part c'est la plus grande, ou ce que dit l'Ecclesiastique, que de mille il n'en est pas un bon . . . " (1.38, 241).[22]

In this quotation, doctrine turns into a justification for introspection in solitude. The moral question of good and bad is omitted—and marked as nonessential by the qualifying phrase "toutesfois si le mot est vray." It is not the externally imposed decision on morally right or wrong conduct but inner truthfulness that Montaigne seeks in his solitary writing:

> La solitude me semble avoir plus d'apparence, et de raison, à ceux qui ont donné au monde leur aage plus actif et fleurissant, à l'exemple de Thales. C'est assez vescu pour autruy, vivons pour nous au moins ce bout de vie: ramenons à nous, et à nostre aise nos pensées et nos intentions. Ce n'est pas une legere partie que de faire seurement sa retraicte; elle nous empesche assez sans y mesler d'autres entreprinses. Puis que Dieu nous donne loisir de disposer de nostre deslogement; preparons nous y; plions bagage; prenons de bon'heure congé de la compagnie; despétrons nous de ces violentes prinses, qui nous engagent ailleurs, et esloignent de nous. Il faut desnouer ces obligations si fortes: et meshuy aymer cecy et cela, mais n'espouser rien que soy: C'est à dire, le reste soit à nous: mais non pas joint et colé en façon, qu'on ne le puisse desprendre sans nous escorcher, et arracher ensemble quelque piece du nostre. La plus grande chose du monde c'est de sçavoir estre à soy. Il est temps de nous desnouer de la societé, puis que nous n'y pouvons rien apporter. Et qui ne peut prester, qu'il se deffende d'emprunter. Noz forces nous faillent: retirons les, et resserons en nous. Qui peut renverser et confondre en soy les offices de tant d'amitiez, et de la compagnie, qu'il le face. En cette cheute, qui le rend inutile, poisant, et importun aux autres, qu'il se garde d'estre importun à soy mesme, et poisant et inutile. Qu'il se flatte et caresse, et sur tout se regente, respectant et craignant sa raison et sa conscience: si qu'il ne puisse sans honte, broncher en leur presence. (1.38, 246)[23]

This passage does indeed illustrate that the solitude the writing "I" considers essential for human insight is not a solitude human beings seek in order to hear God or expect his intervention. God figures in a different way in this passage: he allows human beings time for introspection after an active life ("Puis que Dieu nous donne loisir de disposer de nostre deslogement; preparons nous y; plions bagage"), and they can and should seize this opportunity for self-care. This deferred time is characterized by doubt and reflection, however, not certainty in faith. This applies to relationships with other people as well. The bonds one has become fond of in the course of a lifetime must be broken in favor of a consciousness for which, in a world rich in deception, the only means of having a presence in the world is self-reference in writing. Among these deceptions Montaigne casually mentions the assumption that ancestry and origin and the opinions of others could provide existential certainty:

> Il nous eschoit à nous mesme, qui ne sommes qu'avortons d'hommes, d'eslancer par fois nostre ame, esveillée par les discours, ou exemples d'autruy, bien loing au delà de son ordinaire: Mais c'est une espece de passion, qui la pousse et agite, et qui la ravit aucunement hors de soy: car ce tourbillion franchi, nous voyons, que sans y penser elle se desbande et relasche d'elle mesme, sinon jusques à la derniere touché; au moins jusques à n'estre plus celle-là. (2.29, 741)[24]

Depending on others appears miserable, and it is one object of the *solitude* recommended in this text to liberate oneself from commitments and the public eye. All human beings are "qu'avortons d'hommes"—and thus nobody is privileged by his or her origin to judge another. The inner life of the "I" alone is to determine one's being in the world.

The essay *De la solitude* contains a contrast that adds another aspect to what has been demonstrated so far:

> L'imagination de ceux qui par devotion, cerchent la solitude; remplissants leur courage, de la certitude des promesses divines, en l'autre vie, est bien plus sainement assortie. Ils se proposent Dieu, object infini en bonté et en puissance. L'ame a dequoy y rassasier ses desirs, en toute liberté. Les afflictions, les douleurs, leur viennent à

> profit, employées à l'acquest d'une santé et resjouyssance eternelle. La mort, à souhait: passage à un si parfaict estat. L'aspreté de leurs regles est incontinent applanie par l'accoustumance: et les appetits charnel, rebutez et endormis par leur refus: car rien ne les entretient que l'usage et l'exercise. Cette seule fin, d'une autre vie heureusement immortelle, merite loyalement que nous abandonnions les commoditez et douceurs de cette vie nostre. Et qui peut embraser son ame de l'ardeur de cette vive foy et esperance, reellement et constammant, il se bastit en sa solitude, une vie voluptueuse et delicieuse, au delà de toute autre sorte de vie. (1.38, 249)[25]

By means of linguistic composition, the writing "I" once more directly and explicitly differentiates its own endeavor from the solitude sought out of pious devotion and in preparation for the afterlife, the eternal life. As clearly as the advantages of such a belief are mentioned, it is phrased just as clearly that this is not the writer's belief ("Et qui peut embraser son ame de l'ardeur de cette vive foy et Esperance, reellement et constamment, il se bastit en la solitude, une vie voluptueuse et delicieuse, au delà de toute autre sorte de vie" [Whoever can, in reality and constancy, set his soul ablaze with the fire of this lively faith and hope, builds in his solitude a life of choicest pleasures, beyond any other mode of life]). This is not evidence for Montaigne's knowledge of his possible Marranic belonging but a clear indicator of the awareness of an "I" not defining itself in a manner associated with the Christian hope for salvation. The advantages of this belief are characterized as desirable, yet not definitive for the mental world of the writer. For him the primacy of the reflected relationship to himself applies: "Notre mal nous tient en l'ame: or elle ne se peut eschapper à elle mesme. . . . Ainsin il la faut ramener et retirer en soy: C'est la vraye solitude, et qui se peut jouir au milieu des villes et des cours des Roys; mais elle se jouyt plus commodément à part" (1.38, 244).[26] The object of this relationship is the inner regaining of the soul beyond all claims of a political or religious nature.

The fifteenth chapter of the second book of the *Essais* is titled *Que nostre desir s'accroist par la malaisance* (2.15, 649)[27] and opens by quoting the basic principle of philosophical skepticism: "Il n'y a raison qui n'en aye une contraire, dit le plus sage party des philosophes" (2.15,

649).[28] How closely Montaigne's self-reflection follows the insights of philosophical skepticism has been discussed above. There is a previously unseen facet in this essay, however, which I am now going to discuss in the relevant context.

The argument in this shorter essay is directed at the paradoxical anthropological constant that the will to achieve something grows with the difficulties one meets with:

> Il en va ainsi par tout: la difficulté donne prix aux choses. Ceux de la Marque d'Ancone font plus volontiers leurs voeuz à Sainct Jaques, et ceux de Galice à nostre Dame de Lorete: on fait au Liege grande feste des bains de Luques, et en la Toscane de ceux d'Aspa: il ne se voit guere de Romains en l'escole de l'escrime à Rome, qui est pleine de François. Ce grand Caton de trouva aussi bien que nous, desgousté de sa femme tant qu'elle fut sienne, et la desira quand elle fut à un autre. . . . Nostre appetit mesprise et outrepasse ce qui luy est en main, pour courir après ce qu'il n'a pas. (2.15, 651)[29]

In the course of the argument, this insight is not only applied to human endeavor but also to the institution of the church, and in a rather remarkable manner:

> C'est un effect de la providence divine, de permettre sa saincte Église estre agitée, comme nous la voyons de tant de troubles et d'orages, pour esveiller par ce contraste les ames pies, et les r'avoir de l'oisiveté et du sommeil, où les avoit plongées une si longue tranquillité. Si nous contrepoisons la perte que nous avons faicte, par le nombre de ceux qui se sont desvoyez, au gain qui nous vient pour nous estre remis en haleine, resuscité nostre zele et nos forces, à l'occasion de ce combat, je ne sçay si l'utilité ne surmonte point le dommage. (2.15, 653)[30]

The insight contained in the essay's first part, that obstacles often only serve to fuel the desire for something, is linked to a momentous argument. The writing "I" explains it as an effect of divine providence that the Holy Church had to weather through turbulent times, since those pious souls who had previously been carelessly asleep were now awakened in the face of the Church's battle for its rights ("pour esveiller par ce contraste les ames pies, et les r'avoir de l'oisiveté et du sommeil, où les avoit plongees une si longue tranquillité" [in order by this opposition to awaken the souls of the pious and to bring them back from the idleness and torpor in which so long a period of calm had immersed them]). These newly awakened souls compensated for the loss of those souls gone astray on the path of error. This argument seems harmless at first but is by no means so: this is a skeptical suspension of judgment—nowhere in this passage is it clear which battle, which party, and which losses in the religious conflict are meant. Seen against the background of the Religious Wars, such a relativist phrasing has ample consequences, especially since it contains criticism of a conviction inherent in all the competing religions of that time. Using the particularly delicate question of religious schism, a prime example of skeptical equipollence [*isostheneia*] is demonstrated: the religious schism (or the diversity of religions existing ever since) is bad from the perspective of any given denomination, at least under universalist premises. Yet it is also a good thing, since it counteracts the weakening of religious zeal. Which of both alternatives is better or worse remains undecided. Not a positioning, not even a negative one, but the questioning of the gesture of positioning itself provides the essay's semantic axis. This also automatically dissolves all (ethnic, political, national, etc.) affiliations in favor of a figure of broad relativity.

In the line of studies described above, the date of Montaigne's preface to the reader has been read as a coded reference to his dual affiliation. The date signed under the preface, March 1, 1580, corresponds to 14 Adar 5340 in the Jewish calendar. This was the day Purim was celebrated that year. In her study of Montaigne, Sophie Jama has tried to link the tradition of Purim to the date of Montaigne's preface. In the Jewish tradition, Purim commemorates the deliverance of the Jewish people from the kingdom of Ahasuerus as told in the biblical book of Esther. The celebration is held in masks and costumes, and Jama believes the Hebrew word for "masquerade," *lehithapes*, to be the source of the search for the "I" in Montaigne's *Essais*. According to Jama, the Hebrew word can be translated literally as "inquiring into oneself," and this was exactly what Montaigne did in the entire *Essais*.[31] This interpretation seems plausible at first, yet the question as to what consequences this show of evidence has for the meaning of the *Essais* remains unanswered. Montaigne is not interested in granting privilege to any one religion or in calling for a clear declaration with regard to ancestry and origin in these texts. On the contrary—as a result of skeptical introspection, ethnic, religious, or political designations are rejected by the act of writing about himself:

> Au Lecteur. C'est icy un Livre de bonne foy, Lecteur. Il t'advertit dès l'entrée, que je ne m'y suis proposé aucune fin, que domestique et privée: je n'y ay eu nulle consideration de ton service, ny de ma gloire: mes forces ne sont pas capables d'un tel dessein. Je l'ay voué à la commodité particuliere de mes parens et amis: à ce que m'ayans perdu (ce qu'ils ont à faire bien tost) ils y puissent retrouver aucuns traicts de mes conditions et humeurs, et que par ce moyen ils nourissent plus entiere et plus vifve, la connoissance qu'ils ont eu de moy. Si c'eust esté pour rechercher la faveur du monde, je me fusse paré de beautez empruntées. Je veux qu'on m'y voye en ma façon simple, naturelle et ordinaire, sans estude et artifice: car c'est moy que je peins. Mes defauts s'y liront au vif, mes imperfections et ma forme naïfve, autant que la reverence publique me l'a permis. Que si j'eusse esté parmy ces nations qu'on dit vivre encore souz la douce liberté des premieres loix de nature, je t'asseure que je m'y fusse trèsvolontiers peint tout entier, et tout nud. Ainsi, Lecteur, je suis moy-mesme la matiere de mon livre: ce n'est pas raison que tu employes ton loisir en un subject si frivole et si vain. À Dieu donq. De Montaigne, ce 12 de juin 1580. ("Au Lecteur," 27)[32]

Introspection, thus the obvious consequence, interferes with traditional self-conceptions—previously established emblems and symbols of collective origin are of no relevance to this inquiry into the self. Montaigne goes as far as a playfully conceived affiliation with the "savages," who in his era were not considered human in the literal sense in the opinion of the majority of even educated people. The preordained and defining attribution of affiliation is replaced by the "I" originating in itself alone, not allowing any criterion of attribution other than itself and mentioning affiliation only playfully and self-ironically.

Both the preface and the *Essais* themselves in their respective ways argue against a closed definition of the individual sanctioned by religious law or ascribing a collective ethnicity. The individual presents himself as alienated from any religious or political collective and its sacred components. The search for one's own self derives from this detachment. It is in this very aspect that the modern impetus of Montaigne's *Essais* consists. The pursuit of insight born from this detachment and its form of thinking find their privileged place in the literarily composed text. It is especially in the literary text that this very search finds its artistic expression.

The last essay to be examined in this chapter is from the last book of the *Essais*, the second chapter of the third volume titled *Du repentir*. Despite its title, which evokes the Christian practice of repentance and penance, this essay discusses an ethics referring strictly to the self:

> Je propose une vie basse, et sans lustre: C'est tout un. On attache aussi bien toute la philosophie morale, à une vie populaire et privée, qu'à une vie de plus riche estoffe: Chaque homme porte la forme entiere, de l'humaine condition. Les autheurs se communiquent au peuple par quelque marque speciale et estrangere: moy le premier, par mon estre universal: comme, Michel de Montaigne: non comme Grammairien ou Poëte, ou Jurisconsulte. Si le monde se plaint dequoy je parle trop de moy, je me plains dequoy il ne pense seulement pas à soy. (3.2, 845)[33]

In this passage, it becomes evident once more that the first-person form is the essential condition of all reflections contained in these texts. Not only does it simultaneously identify Montaigne as author, writing "I," and remembered "I"; the author furthermore continually reinvents himself by means of writing and in the act of writing. In this process, the writing "I" is concerned with essential questions characteristic of all human beings. Since each human being bears the entire form of man's estate ("Chaque homme porte la forme entiere, de l'humaine condition" [Every man bears the whole form of the human condition]), self-reflection seems the best version of moral reflection.

In all three volumes of his *Essais*, Montaigne is concerned with the development of his speech as the history of the self, as well as with his seeing in this world and thus the establishment of an authorship for his texts: "Icy nous allons conformément, et tout d'un train, mon livre et moy. Ailleurs, on peut recommender et accuser l'ouvrage, à part de l'ouvrier: icy non: qui touche l'un, touche l'autre" (3.2, 846).[34]

The continual recording, the seamless fabric of language apparent in the form of the *Essais*, results in the complete absorption of the book as part of the self. There is no authority except that of his own writing, and the quoted texts from classical philosophy and the biblical book of Wisdom do not become orienting authorities by means of being quoted, but their reading and inclusion in his own process of writing means a capturing, a winning of power over the foreign texts. In this way the book Montaigne equals to the self in this instance is not an attempt just to compensate for the absence of an interpretive worldview on the part of the authorities by means of an aesthetic composition, but to replace them with the latter. The precondition for this objective is honest self-reflection:

> Ce n'est pas un leger plaisir, de se sentir preservé de la contagion d'un siecle si gasté, et de dire en soy: Qui me verroit jusques dans l'ame, encore ne me trouveroit-il coupable, ny de l'affliction et ruyne de personne: ny de vengeance ou d'envie, ny d'offence publique des loix: ny de nouvelleté et de trouble: ny de faute à ma parole: et quoy que la licence du temps permist et apprinst à chacun, si n'ay-je mis la main ny ès biens, ny en la bourse d'homme François, et n'ay vescu que sur la mienne, non plus en guerre qu'en paix: ny ne me suis servy du travail de personne, sans loyer. Ces tesmoignages de la conscience, plaisent, et nous est grand benefice que cette esjouyssance naturelle: et le seul payement qui jamais ne nous manque. De fonder la recompense des actions vertueuses, sur l'approbation d'autruy, c'est prendre un trop incertain et trouble fondement, signamment en un siecle corrompu et ignorant, comme cettuy cy la bonne estime du peuple est injurieuse. À qui vous fiez vous, de veoir ce qui est louable? Dieu me garde d'estre homme de bien, selon la description que je voy faire tous les jours par honneur, à chacun de soy. (3.2, 847)[35]

Neither religious rituals of confession nor the law but the honest relation to oneself regulates the self in this essay: "J'ay mes loix et ma cour, pour juger de moy, et m'y adresse plus qu'ailleurs" (3.2, 848).[36] As the "I" repeatedly enters into a mirror relation with the self, the definition of the subject—no longer adequate for the contemporary identity of the "I" as determined by descent, religious affiliation, and political inclusion—is put into question. In this constellation, it is remarkable that Montaigne avails himself of the term "conscience" so essential to religiously coded penance, yet he—contrary to Catholic doctrine—understands it as a concept opposite to public estimation by others, specifically, by the "community" of believers:

> C'est une vie exquise, celle qui se maintient en ordre jusques en son privé. Chacun peut avoir part au battelage, et representer un honneste personnage en l'eschaffaut: mais au dedans, et en sa poictrine, où tout est caché, d'y estre reglé, c'est le poinct. (3.2, 848)[37]

Finally, I would like to examine one of the very few explicit references to contemporary Jewish history in the *Essais*. The fortieth essay of the first book (*Que le goust des biens et des maux despend en bonne partie de l'opinion que nous en avons*) contains the following passage:

> Les Roys de Castille ayants banni de leur terre, les Juifs, le Roy Jehan de Portugal leur vendit à huict escus pour teste, la retraicte aux siennes pour un certain temps: à condition, que iceluy venu, ils auroient à les vuider: et leur promettoit fournir de vaisseaux à les trajecter en Afrique. Le jour arrive, lequel passé il estoit dit, que ceux qui n'auroient obeï, demeureroient esclaves: les vaisseaux leur furent fournis escharcement: et ceux qui s'y embarquerent, rudement et villainement traittez par les passagers: qui outre plusieurs autres indignitez les amuserent sur mer, tantost avant, tantost arriere, jusques à ce qu'ils eussent consumé leurs victuailles, et contreints d'en acheter d'eux si cherement et si longuement, qu'on ne les mit à bord, qu'ils ne fussent du tout en chemise. La nouvelle de cette inhumanité, rapportée à ceux qui estoient en terre, la plus part se resolurent à la servitude: aucuns firent contenance de changer de religion. Emmanuel successeur de Jehan, venu à la couronne, les meit premierement en liberté, et changeant d'advis depuis, leur ordonna de sortir de ses païs, assignant trois ports à leur passage. Il esperoit, dit l'Évesque Osorius, non mesprisable historien Latin, de noz siecles: que la faveur de la liberté, qu'il leur avoit rendue, aiant failli de les convertir au Christianisme, la difficulté de se commetre à la volerie des mariniers; d'abandonner un païs, où ils estoient habituez, avec grandes richesses, pour s'aller jetter en región incognue et estrangere, les y rameineroit. Mais se voyant decheu de son esperance, et eux tous deliberez au passage: il retranca deux des

> ports, qu'il leur avoit promis: affin que la longueur et incommodité du traject en reduisist aucuns: ou qu'il eust moien de les amonceller tous à un lieu, pour une plus grande commodité de l'execution qu'il avoit destinée. Ce fut, qu'il ordonna qu'on arrachast d'entre les mains des peres et des meres, tous les enfans au dessous de quatorze ans, pour les transporter hors de leur veue et conversation, en lieu où ils fussent instruits à nostre religion. Il dit que cet effect produisit un horrible spectacle: la naturelle affection d'entre les peres et enfants, et de plus, le zele à leur ancienne creance, combattant à l'encontre de cette violente ordonnance. Il fut veu communement des peres et meres se deffaisants eux mesmes: et d'un plus rude exemple encore, precipitants par amour et compassion, leurs jeunes enfans dans des puits, pour fuir à la loy. Au-demeurant le terme qu'il leur avoit prefix expiré, par faute de moiens, ils se remirent en servitude. Quelques uns se feirent Chrestiens: de la foy desquels, ou de leur race, encore aujourd'huy, cent ans après, peu de Portugais s'asseurent: quoy que la coustume et la longueur du temps, soient bien plus fortes conseilleres à telles mutations, que toute autre contreinte. (1.40, 261–262)[38]

No direct evidence for Montaigne's Jewish identity can be inferred from this passage. One could point to a similar, unemotionally phrased empathy and simultaneous denunciation of the "Christian" position in the essay *Des cannibales* (1.30), referring to the indigenous societies of the New World, without feeling compelled to make the somewhat bold claim that Montaigne placed himself not just ironically—as cited above—in the tradition of these "native peoples."

Most important, Montaigne's skeptical writing affects the reflection on the fate of the Spanish Jews. Their forced conversion is considered just as matter-of-factly as their brutal economic exploitation by the Portuguese king. In such a constellation, however, the skeptical suspension of judgment has serious consequences. Against the background Montaigne draws in the *Essais*, which only accepts self-reflection through writing as a regulating authority, the Portuguese king's behavior seems like barbarism pure and simple without the necessity of a qualifying evaluation. This reported historical anecdote also reflects the fate of Leone Ebreo. It is related along with the actions of the desperate Jewish parents, however. These are without question acts of religious zeal that—following the mechanisms explained in essay 1.40—have only been stimulated by the attempt to deprive the believers of their faith. Yet the fact remains that innocent children whose opinion had not been asked are killed in the name of holding on to the one, true faith; from the perspective of a concept of religion emancipated from zeal, fervor, and activism as developed in the *Essais*, this action of the pressured parents may be understandable psychologically, however problematic it remains morally and intellectually. The often-formulated attempt to explain this much-quoted passage as a more or less veiled Jewish *confessio* of the "I" of the *Essais* is foiled by the report of the children killed by their parents.

A metaphorical understanding of the attribute "Marranic" for Montaigne's texts places the *Essais* more firmly in the framework of textual theory. The interpretive focus on ancestry, *converso* identity, or origin limited mainly to external phenomena in the line of studies outlined above can be significantly extended by such an understanding. Transformations of emblems of the sacred, the liturgical, and the ritual, as well as other codings of religiosity, can thus be traced in the *Essais*. Hence this text represents the transformation of the sacred and thus supposedly immutable components of self-conception. A metaphorical understanding of the "Marranic" labeling of the *Essais* would therefore contribute to overriding those readings that perpetuate an unnecessary ethnic designation. It is only through detachment that the parallel to questions of Jewish affiliation evoked by the uncertainty regarding the attribution of affiliation in Montaigne's *Essais* can become evident. Skeptical uncertainty is first of all a general diagnosis, and certainly not an exclusively Jewish phenomenon but rather an expression of the modern age that no longer offers a defining determination of affiliation. As metaphor, "Marranic" would mean an attitude deriving first-person speech from an authority other than—only supposedly objective yet in fact dogmatically determined—affiliation. This would result from insight into the—at times enforced—availability of religious denominations and affiliations.

Historically, the "I" constituting itself in dialogue with itself outside of all tradition and religious denominations is a "product" of the early modern age. It may be that the source for Montaigne's relativist-skeptic questioning of the paradigm of "affiliation" was his reflection on the history of his maternal family; it is just as possible, however, that the impulse came from the experience of the religious civil war between Christians in France at the time. And finally, there are the effects of the Age of Discovery, namely, the new knowledge that there were people who existed outside of all affiliations heretofore considered possible by the European mind.

The staged hybridity we saw in *La Celestina* and *Lazarillo de Tormes* was dissolved in an emphatic-metaphysical, speculative, all-encompassing concept of unity in *Dialoghi d'amore*. Montaigne's *Essais* are a complement to this concept, explicitly rejecting all metaphysical speculation. These diametrical positions are represented by the Neoplatonic *hen* summoned by Ebreo, on the one hand, and by the "I" as reference point for the monologue in the *Essais, on the other*. This "I" relativizes all traditions and affiliations.

Five Sacred Text and Poetic Form

The Poetry of João Pinto Delgado (1627)

João Pinto Delgado was born in the mid-1580s in Vila Nova de Portimão and died in 1653. His grandfather bore the same name and was employed in the governmental administration of the Algarve. From the few sources on João Pinto Delgado's life, we know that his parents, who were persecuted as so-called Judaizing New Christians, escaped from Portugal, going first to Antwerp and from there to Rouen, where they settled in 1609. When some of the New Christians from Portugal were also suspected of "Judaizing" there in 1633, João Pinto Delgado and his father sought refuge in Antwerp. In 1634, João Pinto Delgado moved to Amsterdam, where he renounced Christianity and joined the Jewish community. From that point on he called himself Moshe Pinto.[1] Delgado was a poet who consciously absorbed the signature events of his time and incorporated them into his work. His autobiographical texts,[2] published in excerpts by Israël S. Révah in 1961, provide an example of this. In one of these texts, Delgado attacked the Inquisition and ridiculed those among Rouen's New Christians who had denounced supposed "Judaizers" to the Inquisition.

In 1627, before his turn to Judaism, João Pinto Delgado published a collection of poems in Rouen that is the focus of the analyses in this chapter: *Poema de la Reyna Ester, Lamentaciones del Propheta Jeremias y Historia de Rut y varias poesías*. Delgado dedicated this volume to Cardinal Richelieu (fig. 2). These poems are highly remarkable, for according to the hypothesis of this chapter, they present a self-confident interpretation of the history of the Jewish converts and Jews of that time in the form of a poetic paraphrase of the Bible.

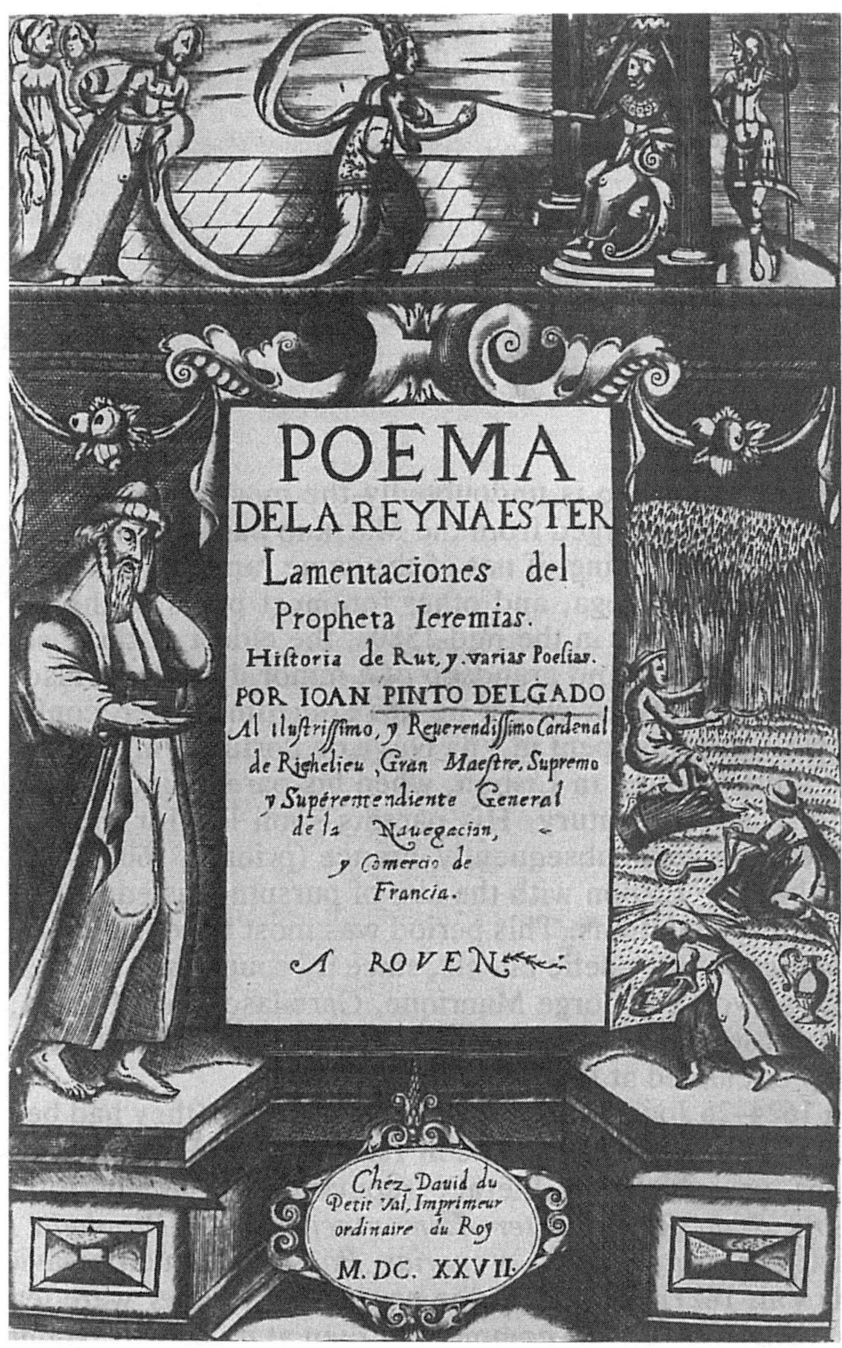

POEMA
DELA REYNA ESTER
Lamentaciones del
Propheta Ieremias.
Hiſtoria de Rut, y varias Poeſias.
POR IOAN PINTO DELGADO
Al iluſtriſſimo, y Reuerendiſſimo Cardenal
de Richelieu, Gran Maeſtre, Supremo
y Superentendiente General
de la Nauegacion,
y Comercio de
Francia.
A ROVEN
Chez David du
Petit Val, Imprimeur
ordinaire du Roy
M.DC.XXVII.

Figure 2. Title page of the first edition of João Pinto Delgado's volume, printed in 1627 by David du Petit Val. The dedication to Cardinal Richelieu is visible on the title page. The woodcuts show emblems of the biblical scenes referred to in Delgado's poems.

At first glance, the *Poema de la Reyna Ester*, composed of nine *cantos* of roughly two hundred lines each, is a paraphrase of the biblical narrative of Esther closely following the sacred text. The volume's second section is made up of a series of poetic reflections on the first two parts of the book of Lamentations. These *Lamentaciones del Propheta Jeremias* contain a brief introduction and forty-four poetic units corresponding to the forty-four verses of the biblical text.

The third text is the *Historia de la Rut Moabita*, in which the story of Ruth is transformed in 648 lines grouped as *redondillas*. This is followed by a poem on the Jewish exodus from Egypt. In this part, Delgado's interpretive claim is evident in the work's title itself: *Canción, aplicando misericordias divinas, y defetos proprios a la salida de Egipto asta la tierra santa*. In stanzas comprised of 8 lines each, the following allegorical text of 111 lines titled *A la sabiduría* refers to the book of Wisdom. The volume closes with the *Cántico de la salida de Egipto*, a second, yet shorter, lyrical text (126 lines) about the exodus narrative that mainly focuses on Exodus 15.

The few very commendable studies of this lyrical oeuvre mainly concentrate on Delgado's life[3] and sometimes on the question whether Delgado used the Septuagint or the Hebrew original as the source for his paraphrases of the sacred text.[4] A groundbreaking study by A. D. H. Fishlock on the rabbinical sources for the poetry of João Pinto Delgado was published in 1952.[5]

The following subsections, structured in correspondence to the individual texts, deal mainly with the interpretation of history in Pinto Delgado's texts, which not only is deduced from the sacred texts but also results from the critical study of Spanish (Christian) poetic texts of that period. Aside from individual poems, Delgado's poetry also makes reference to authors such as Lope de Vega and his play *La Hermosa Esther* of 1610, and possibly Francisco de Quevedo y Villegas and his *Lágrimas de Hieremías castellanas* (1613), a text whose manuscript Delgado might have seen, according to Edward Wilson.[6] Delgado was not the only writer of this period who made poetic reference to the Hebrew bible—the Old Testament in Christian terminology. Among the familiar texts written by contemporary Catholic authors of the Counter-Reformation are, for example, an *auto sacramental* on the story of Ruth by Pedro Calderón de la Barca (*Las espigas de Ruth*) from 1663 and Tirso de Molina's drama *La major espigadera* (1634).

Delgado's texts are particularly interesting in this regard because—read against the background of Christian biblical writing—they seek to grasp a specifically Marranic understanding of history documented in the literary transformation of the biblical history books. On the one hand, Delgado uses a mode of argumentation making universal claims and a verbalization in his rendition that aims at generality. On the other hand, components displaying the peculiarity of the Marranic experience of history are inscribed into this universally minded text: it is precisely in their multiple references that João Pinto Delgado's texts reveal a virtually epistemic interest in the Jewish fate in the early modern age, so that this last chapter will hone the overall hypothesis of this study once more.

Poema de la Reyna Ester

In the theme of the first poem, Delgado chose a subject quite prominent in early modern poetry. There are two early, anonymous literary treatments of the Esther motif in the Romance languages, the Italian verse drama *La rappresentazione della Reina Hester* (1500), published in several editions in the sixteenth century, and a mystery play treatment in *Le mistère du Viel Testament*. In the German-speaking territories, Hans Sachs's *Gantze Hystori der Hester* was published in 1530 and Valentin Voith's *Spiel von der Heiligen Schrift und dem Buch Esther* in 1537. In 1561, the English verse drama *A New Enterlude of Godly Queene Hester* was published anonymously. In the mid-sixteenth century, Salomon Usque, the translator of Petrarch's *Canzoniere* into Spanish, dramatized the book of Esther in Italian for the Purim celebration. Usque's *Ester* premiered in Venice in 1558 and was later revised by Leone Modena. Antoine de Montchrétien dedicated three tragedies to the subject, *Esther* (1585), *Vashti* (1589), and *Aman* (1601). The most prominent French-language treatment of the subject, Racine's *Esther*, was published in 1689. Lope de Vega's aforementioned dramatization of the material that Pinto Delgado refers to, the play *La hermosa Ester*, dates from 1610.

Before I begin the analysis of Pinto Delgado's literary transformation, I will briefly summarize the biblical narrative. In the Hebrew bible, the book of Esther (Hebr. אֶסְתֵּר מְגִלָּה, *Megillat Ester*), the book of Ruth, the Song of Songs, Ecclesiastes, and the book of Lamentations compose the five Megillot (scrolls). The Megillot are part of the Writings (Hebr. כְּתוּבִים, *Ketuvim*; Greek *Hagiographia*), the third section of the Tanakh. The Purim celebration is based on the book of Esther.

The story of Esther, divided into ten chapters, does not focus on a singular historical event but relates exemplary episodes of hostility toward the Jews and of the victorious overcoming of the enemies of the Jewish people. In the first two chapters, the dramatis personae, Persian king Ahasuerus and his wife Vashti, together with Esther and her guardian Mordecai, are introduced. The main part (Esther 3–9) contains the nucleus of the Esther narrative, namely, the tale of the rescue of the Jews from Haman's despotic rule through Esther's intervention. Following these events, the origins of the Purim celebration are explained in the final part (Esther 9:20–10:3).

The biblical narrative begins with a celebration at the court of the Persian king Ahasuerus. At the height of the festivities, Ahasuerus orders his wife Vashti to appear before the guests so that they may delight in her beauty. When she refuses, he expels her and (after having been procured young women from his entire realm for twelve months in order to find a new queen) chooses the Jewish maid Esther as his new queen. Esther hides her religion on the advice of her foster father, the court official Mordecai. Mordecai discovers an assassination plot by chamberlains Bigtan and Teresch and thus prevents an attack on the king. The events are entered into the records of the kingdom. At the same time, a dynastic decision is made: the king promotes ambitious Haman to second-in-command. Haman demands a show of public subordination from all subjects. Mordecai alone refuses to pay public homage to Haman on the grounds that he is not willing to grant to a human being what is due only to God. Consequently, Haman decides not only to take Mordecai's life but also to murder all the Jews in the Persian Empire in revenge for his disobedience. Haman justifies his plan to the king by claiming that the Jewish faith is irreconcilable with the interests of Persian rule. In addition, he offers the king ten thousand silver talents, so that the latter eventually grants him permission to execute his murderous plans. Haman casts lots in order to decide when to carry out his plan against the empire's Jewish population. When Mordecai finds out about the plan, he tells Esther to go to the king and ask for mercy for the Jewish people. Initially, Esther is too afraid, since she is not allowed to approach the king without having been summoned first. Mordecai confronts Esther with a choice between aiding the Jewish people and risking her life or saving her life by silently surrendering her people to their doom.

Esther accepts the dangerous task, fasts for three days, and approaches the king, who forgives her for doing so. She invites the king and Haman to a banquet feast. During this feast, she announces another one, which she is going to hold for Haman and the king and to which she again invites both men. With this invitation she honors Haman in equal measure with the king, leading Haman to celebrate the great honor with his family, and in his exuberance he orders the gallows from which he wants Mordecai to be hanged. The king, disconcerted that his wife honors another man equally with him, has a sleepless night, during which he reads through the empire's records. In them he reads that Mordecai recently protected him from an assassination plot and never received an appropriate reward. He seeks Haman's advice on how to properly reward a man who has served the king well without disclosing the man's name. Assuming that this man is himself, Haman suggests the highest honors, which the king then grants to Mordecai. During the second banquet, Esther accuses Haman of plotting an attack against her, the queen, and her people. She reveals to the king that she, too, shares a Jewish belonging. At the same time, she expands the threat posed by Haman in that she makes the king feel as if the threat was directed not just against her but against him as king and thus the empire as well. When Haman prostrates himself before Esther, the king misinterprets the scene as an assault and has Haman executed. The king replaces Haman with Mordecai, but the menace to the empire's Jews has not been averted yet. According to the laws of the Persian Empire, a royal decree cannot simply be reneged on. Mordecai responds with a second writ, which he has the king authorize: the Jews are given the right to defend themselves against their assailants, and they emerge victorious from the fight. Queen Esther decides that in the future the victory of the Jews will be commemorated by the newly established annual celebration of Purim.

Jewish interpretations of this biblical text can be distinguished as either historical or paradigmatic.[7] The latter have understood the book of Esther as a reflection of the situation of the Jews in a non-Jewish environment. From our perspective, Delgado transfers this impetus very artfully to the literary form. The poem picks up the biblical narrative at the point when Vashti refuses to obey her husband. King Ahasuerus's speech is delivered in the first person. He is portrayed as a ruler forced by law, not personal decision, to leave his wife because of her irregular behavior.[8]

In the following stanza, the lamenting ruler is given lines expressing the subject with which this very special literary treatment of the Esther story is concerned: the free will of the individual. Delgado's virtuosic composition becomes evident in the fact that he lets the Persian ruler himself and not one of history's actual subordinates formulate the praise of free will:

> Dichoso aquél que, humilde en libre estado,
> No le oprime violente señorío,
> Su misma ejecución es su cuidado,
> Y el deseo sujeto a su alvedrío,
> Ni le detiene, entre su gloria, el freno
> De fiera obstinación de gusto ajeno. (17)[9]

This lament of a ruler as a gesture of representative humanity is a poetic strategy describing the curtailing of free will not only by the demands of rule but as a restriction in general. Thus, the king's suffering has a dual function: first, a connection between ruler and subjects is established by the lament, and second, the ubiquitous subject of free will not limited to aspects of rule is introduced in a completely innocuous manner.

Delgado's poem continues with the king's choice of a bride. In this passage, Esther, who at this point is referred to as Mordecai's niece, is described in verses evoking the poetic vocabulary of Luis de Góngora:

Criando Ester, que de sus padres llora
De tránsito común última pena,
Cuadal de sus virtudes atesora
Entre los rayos de su luz serena;
Belleza honrosa es inocencia bella,
El sol el alma y su hermosura estrella.

Los ojos, que modestos representan
De piedad interior divino indicio,
Vueltos al cielo, en humildad frecuentan,
En ardiente oración, santo ejercicio;
Y es el humor, que de su centro exhala,
Cual el rocío que la flor regala.

El dulce labio, que a la rosa enseña
De su viva color la imagen viva,
Perlas señala en majestad risueña,
De cuyo acento alta razón deriva. (19)[10]

The similarities with the first quatrain from Góngora's sonnet *El beso* are unmistakable.[11] There is another textual layer, though. Esther's outward appearance is described as a reflection of her inner, morally perfect beauty. Delgado employs the imagery of Marian poetry for this description. This includes dew or the dewdrop (Spanish *rocío*) as a symbol of the Immaculate Conception, as well as the invocation of the rose as Mary's traditional symbol. The development of Marian rose symbolism is part of biblical allegoresis. Biblical sources of this image include the rose planted in Jericho (Vulgate: Sir. 24:18, "plantatio rosae in Hiericho") read as a symbol of eternal wisdom and compared to Mary, as well as a prophecy by the prophet Isaiah according to which a shoot was to grow from the stump of Jesse (Vulgate: Isa. 11:1, "Et egreditur virga de stirpe Iesse, et flos de radice eius ascendet"). As a rose without thorns, Mary was represented as *immaculata*, free from original sin, whereas thorns were considered symbols of sin. The white rose was a symbol of Mary's purity and virginity, while the red rose was associated with Mary's commiseration with her son's passion, but also with the passion and blood of Christ themselves. In this context, the five roses might refer to the Savior's five wounds.[12]

Delgado's quoting of the imagery of Marian poetry in his description of the figure of Esther evokes Lope de Vega's treatment of the Esther story.[13] The latter had altered the source material from the Hebrew bible considerably in his drama *La hermosa Ester*, among other things by a Marianization of Esther's features of beauty, thus putting her in figural relation to the Mary of the New Testament. Delgado's description of Esther situates her simultaneously within and outside of this iconography, for the repetition of the word "viva" has the effect that the two lines in which the image of the rose appears in relation to Esther ("El dulce labio, que la rosa enseña / De su viva color la imagen viva") may be read as if the live image of Esther's lips not only shared the color of natural roses but exceeded them in intensity of color. This rhetorical praise of Esther's lips as redder than the red of the rose bespeaks the specific character of Delgado's poetry. In comparison with Lope de Vega's poetry, the figural meaning in his texts is omitted, or more precisely, Delgado's texts defy the figural dimension. This can be illustrated by means of the image of dew as well: the latter has a nonsymbolic, literal meaning, namely "manna." What Delgado says about Esther is limited to a conventional praise of beauty or symbolic references confined to the symbolism of the Old Testament, while the imagery of the Hebrew bible is systematically applied in a figural manner in the biblical writings of Catholic authors of the Counter-Reformation. This includes the reduction of the meaning of the Old Testament to that of an adumbration of the New Testament. Delgado rejects this interpretation in his poetry by means of imagery that consequently eludes a figural interpretation.

It is the combination of internal and external beauty displayed by Esther that leads to the king's choosing her as a bride and to his and his people's exceeding admiration of her as queen soon after. The poem's next section describes everyday life at the court of the Persian king, and Mordecai stands out as an especially loyal courtier because his faith demands loyalty of him especially, more than anyone else. When Haman commands the subjects to pay homage to himself in a manner due only to a god, however, Mordecai refuses to obey. He considers himself beholden to God's power alone:

Siervos del Rey, obedeciendo, inclinan
(Fiero precepto) su rodilla as suelo,
Que entre su engaño, ciegos, no imaginan
Que al hombre dan lo que se debe al cielo,
Y si el deseo lo aparente obliga,
El tiempo es vara que su error castiga.

No es Mardochay, a quien temor mundano,
Ni su lisonja, a idolatrar le obliga,
Que, justo corazón, ídolo humano
No lo pertuba, aunque con él litiga;
Y, aunque los ramos tempestad quebranta,
Siempre es el fruto ejemplo de su planta. (30)[14]

Delgado's literary text makes a particularly astute argument in citing the Baroque theme of *engaño/desengaño* as justification for this refusal to obey orders. Volker Roloff has interpreted the tension between illusion and disillusion, *engaño/desengaño*, in the Baroque era as an "aesthetic space for artificiality, masks and costumes, for social and imaginary roles and games of deception and thus a polyphonic *theatrum mundi*."[15] This Baroque rhetorical technique aims at portraying a world in the state of illusion (*engaño*) and hinting at a hidden "true being" beneath the surface untouched by the insignificance of worldly reality, wealth, and vanity.[16] In Delgado's poetic logic, Mordecai's behavior thus becomes the expression of an ideal of his time that seems to collapse the boundaries between the monotheistic religions of his time.

Haman's reaction is portrayed not as a dynastic decision but as mere personal revenge for his humiliation by Mordecai. Face to face with the king, however, Haman does argue politically:

¿Cómo, Señor, tu majestad consiente
Un pueblo (dice) al mundo licencioso,
Si a nuestra ley la suya diferente
Miras opuesta a general reposo?
Y en fiera obstinación de su alvedrío
Sacude el yugo, niega el señorío.
...

Soberbio, en tus provincias dividido,
El justo fuero del tributo niega,
Si poco el útil miras que ha siguido,
El daño inmenso a tu corona llega;
Y nueva causa tu piedad no aguarde,
Siendo mi queja y tu remedio tarde. (35–36)[17]

The following twenty stanzas, in which Mordecai laments the fate of his people, feature one of the largest textual additions in comparison with the biblical source. This lament refers to the threat to the Jews in Susa, and in some passages it also becomes a general lament on the fate of the Jewish people. The first stanzas recount a dream of Mordecai's not found in the Hebrew bible text but in the apocryphal Greek version of a later date. A. D. H. Fishlock has shown that Pinto Delgado most likely also used a Midrashic anthology of biblical passages, the *Yalkut Shimoni*, as the basis for his additions. The interpretation of the punishment of the Jews as divine punishment for their idolatry in the age of Nebuchadnezzar contained in Mordecai's dream dates back to Rashi's biblical commentary.[18] In a piece of biblical poetry written in 1627, however, this interpretation is of particular virulence.

The interpretation that the tortures the Jewish people must suffer are inflicted upon them for having renounced the true faith, as highlighted in Pinto Delgado's lyrical text, makes reference to the historic Christian behavior toward the Jews in the form of biblical poetry. Forced conversion was not followed by smooth integration into the Christian community but by persecution in the shape of the permanent suspicion of "Judaizing," which in itself was irrefutable—as all allegations are. According to the logic of the Inquisition, the absence of evidence was proof of particularly clever hypocrisy. Delgado here seems to conceive persecution as a consequence of conversion (possibly ordered by God himself), even in the form of forced conversion, or at least to suggest the thought.

In Mordecai's apparently divinely inspired dream as rendered in Delgado's literary biblical adaptation, it is the exact opposite, however, that poses a threat to the Jews. At the same time, Mordecai's lament evokes the biblical text following the Esther story in Delgado's volume: the book of Lamentations. The latter also contains the interpretation that Zion was punished for the sins of its people by the destruction of the temple.

Mordecai's speech following his dream features a lament on the fate of the Jewish people that reinforces the aforementioned dimension. Mordecai describes the Jews' precarious situation as a consequence of losing the temple:

> Agora ausente del sagrado muro,
> Del santo culto, muertos nostros Reyes,
> Cual hoja al viento el pueblo no seguro,
> Sujeto al fuero de diversas leyes,
> En el profundo de tristeza y miedo,
> La voz le ofende y señala el dedo.
>
> ¿Cuál más humilde calla nuestro agravio?
> ¿Quién no se alegra oyendo nuestra pena?
> Y al inocente, ¿cuál compuesto labio
> En la opinión del mundo no condena?
> Que en odio tanto, alegre en la mudanza,
> De nuestro mal su proprio bien alcanza. (45)[19]

This lament embedded in Mordecai's prayer evokes Ibn Verga's *Shevet Yehudah* (Rod of Judah), written in the early sixteenth century. This historiographical text was begun by Solomon Ibn Verga and continued by his son Joseph Ibn Verga after his father's death. Solomon Ibn Verga's life and work were influenced significantly by the Jews' expulsion from Spain in 1492: in 1489, the author negotiated the ransom for the Jewish prisoners held by the Catholic kings; in 1492 he fled to Portugal, where he was forced to convert to Christianity in 1497. With these experiences in mind, he traced the reasons why the Jewish people were a particular target of persecution. As Sina Rauschenberg, the editor of the German translation, has noted, Ibn Verga seeks the cause mainly in the hatred among peoples: "Ibn Verga finds an answer in religious hatred, envy, and jealousy, all of which oppose reason in human beings and bear great destructive potential when they get out of control."[20]

In the last three stanzas of his lament, Mordecai addresses God directly:

¿Cómo, Señor, la fuerza del delito
Te obliga así, que en nuestro mal te agrades?
Siendo la nube a un Sol, que es infinito,
Y un monte opuesto al mar de tus piedades:
Si nuestro error, aunque mayor condene,
Tu luz no encubre, ni tu mar detiene.

Mira, Señor, que un breve santuario
Al pueblo fuiste, que tu ausencia llora,
Y, aunque su error se ha vuelto su contrario,
Amaste un tiempo y no olvidaste agora;
En tanto mal la voz de sus gemidos
Los aires rompa y suba a tus oídos.

Cuando tu espada desnudar quisiste,
En la venganza del mayor pecado,
Piedoso el celo de tu siervo oíste. (45–46)[21]

The rhetorical strategy of this dialogue with God aims at emphasizing compassion, which is mentioned at the beginning of the last line quoted above. In Judaism, compassion is one of God's distinctive features, for he forgives human beings their sins and faithfully maintains the bond with his people. In Deuteronomy 6:5 ("And thou shalt love the Lord thy God with all thine heart, and with all thy soul, and with all thy might"), compassion is linked to fear of God and transferred to the behavior toward one's fellow people.

In Christianity, compassion is a cardinal virtue. The central narrative of compassion in the New Testament is the parable of the Good Samaritan (Luke 10:25–37), which Jesus tells in order to illustrate the above-mentioned passage from Deuteronomy. The priest and the Levite obey religious law in not helping the severely wounded man in order to preserve their ritual purity. Only the Samaritan, who belongs to a related population group yet not one of the most religiously influential Jewish groups, helps the wounded man. The message of the parable is that neither religious law nor one's origin is a reason not to help someone.

Through the particular poetic speech in which the lyrical voice addresses his counterpart, a lyrical "You," Mordecai's prayer also contains a demand for human compassion. What was illustrated above on the level of linguistic symbolism in Delgado's consistently nonfigural interpretation here finds its correspondence on the level of religious-moral concepts. Compassion is a value of primary importance in Christianity as well. The concept is applied differently in Delgado's poetry than in the biblical text, however. Of course Judaism and Christianity have certain things in common with regard to their understanding of *misericordia*. Yet Delgado's text contains an obvious hint against one of the New Testament's fundamental rhetorical strategies in its specific embedding of the concept of compassion, interpreted universally in Judaism as well, in the poetic form: Christian theology pursued the strategy of exaggerating an "ethnic fixation" of Judaism in the interest of promoting universalism as an exclusive feature of the "new" religion. Delgado demonstrates, however, that compassion is a universal concept in the Jewish tradition as well, and that actions derived from a mere fixation on ancestry are more likely to be expected from the enemies of the Jews.

The literary adaptation of the biblical narrative continues to follow the stations of its source. In comparison with the biblical source, Mordecai does not have to work very hard to persuade Esther, who quickly decides to approach the king despite the potential dangers involved. The dialogue between Esther and the king is remarkable. The king, fascinated and captivated by Esther's beauty, offers his wife half of his kingdom. When she, in a gesture of modesty, merely invites him to the banquet, he becomes even more enamored. The contrast with Haman's reaction could not be more extreme. The latter is completely beside himself and informs his wife about the immense honor his family is being paid. Following this lack of self-control, Delgado has Haman's family formulate an indirect warning to the enemies of the Jews:

> Ay! (le responden) si verdad recela
> Lo que en bosquejo el corazón imprime,
> No en vano el alma en el temor se hiela,
> Aunque el vigor de tu poder le anime;
> Que es la fortuna, en sus regalos fiera,
> Al bien difícil, pero al mal ligera.

Si de Judá te procedió la guerra,
Justo el dolor y justo el recelo,
Que cuando caye, caye humilde a tierra,
Y cuando sube, sube altivo al cielo;
Que polvo iguala, iguala a las estrellas,
Postrado en él o levantado en ellas. (76)[22]

The warning contained herein corresponds to the Midrashic tradition of exegesis, which describes Haman's intentions as a doomed endeavor. The English translation of the Midrash to the book of Esther reads as follows:

> R. Aibu said: It is written, *For the kingdom is the Lord's; and He is the ruler over the nations* (Ps. XXII, 29), and yet you say here [that Ahasuerus sat] ON THE THRONE OF HIS KINGDOM? The truth is that formerly sovereignty was vested in Israel, but when they sinned it was taken from them and given to the other nations, as it says, *And I will give the land over into the hand of evil men* (Ezek. XXX, 12), which R. Isaac explained to mean, "Into the hand of evil stewards." But to-morrow when Israel repent God will take it from the idolaters and restore it to them. When will this be? *When saviours shall come up on Mount Zion* (Obad. I, 21).[23]

Mordecai's prayer structurally corresponds to a prayer spoken by Esther before the banquet. Both prayers are literary additions by Pinto Delgado. The expansions on the Esther story in the Septuagint do contain prayers later moved to the Apocrypha, but those prayers provide inspiration rather than a direct source for Delgado's own poetic creation. In Delgado's adaptation, the stanzas of Esther's prayer are composed as an answer to those questions that in Mordecai's prayer were formulated as pleas to God. Esther lists the situations in which God had rescued his chosen people from great misery. She quotes the biblical legend of the young woman named Yael, who killed Sisera, commander of the Canaanite army, with a wooden tent peg (Judg. 4:17–22). In traditional exegesis, the story has been interpreted as evidence for the fact that God may sometimes send his rescue in the form of a seemingly weak instrument. Esther—humbly, yet clearly—projects this example onto herself.[24] Thus Esther's lyrical "I" joins a tradition of Jewish heroines symbolizing the irrevocability of the bond God forged with Israel. In the reference to Yael, Esther's diplomatic and careful behavior is also implicitly given the character of a repeated threat to the enemies of Israel: using whatever "instrument" is available, God's chosen people will know how to defend themselves against those threatening their existence.

The *Poema de la Reyna Ester* ends with a final prayer, in which the author's voice can be heard once more:

Ah! Del sumo Poder perfecto ejemplo,
Piedad que ampara, amor que nunca olvida,
Llegue al altar de tu divino Templo
Quien mira en ondas de temor su vida;
Que si, piedoso, su remedio ordenas,
Su gloria nace de sus mismas penas.

Gusto el dolor, regalo es el castigo
Que el justo prueba de tu santa mano,
Siendo el tormento de aquel bien testigo,
Nunca sujeto a movimiento humano:
Porque es al alma escala el sufrimiento,
Que toca el suelo y llega al firmamento.

Éste libró el Rey de aquel conflito,
Donde el blasfemo, en su poder seguro,
Cercó Sión de ejército infinito,
Negando aun ave penetrar su muro;
Desengañado cuando, en un instante,
Despojo fue de espada fulminante.

Éste al varón en sus miserias prueba,
Que humilde ve doblada recompensa;
Por éste el justo, en la encubierta cueva,
En el ungido no vengó su ofensa;
Al hombre escudo, a la ciudad es muro,
De golpe esento, de temor seguro.

Éste del mal las fuerzas deminuye
Y con sus alas siempre al bien camina
Que en la esperanza su remedio arguye,
Que firme funda en la piedad divina:
Si tu poder, si tu valor es tanto,
Al par del mundo te celebre el canto. (109–111)[25]

The lines "Porque es al alma escala el sufrimiento, / Que toca el suelo y llega al firmamento" evoke Jacob's dream of a ladder to heaven in Genesis 28:12–13 ("And he dreamed, and behold a ladder set up on the earth, and the top of it reached to heaven: and behold the angels of God ascending and descending on it"). In both the Jewish and Christian traditions, this dream has been interpreted in various ways. The Midrash B'reshith Rabba,[26] the aggadic exegesis of the book of Genesis, interprets Jacob's dream as a symbol for the migrations of the Jewish people. Israel had witnessed the rise and fall of powerful kingdoms, and Jacob's ladder symbolically stood for the ladder of history. The political dimensions of this reference are too obvious to need unfolding: the anti-Judaic Spain of the "Leaden Age" after 1492 is just one of many doomed empires that had mistreated God's people.

In the tradition of Christian exegesis, on the other hand, Jacob's ladder as a link between heaven and earth was typologically interpreted as representing Jesus. When suffering here is described as the soul's ladder guaranteeing its proximity to heaven, the lines of this stanza seem like the sum of Delgado's poeticized bible narrative. In dogmatic terms, the lines describing earthly life as futile and as a chance for the believer to prove his faith even more are "right" and familiar from both the Jewish and Christian perspectives. The fact that this text has apparently been able to pass Inquisition censorship further strengthens the argument put forth here: on the surface, everything said in Delgado's poetic bible adaptation is backed up by Christianity, since it can be reconciled with the familiar typological appropriation of the Old Testament. A closer look, however, reveals numerous, often implicit hints that it is based on a specific, nonfigural interpretation of Old Testament doctrine.

The link to the motif of Zion under threat narrows the argument in a manner that not only includes plans similar to Haman's but makes all persecution appear doubly counterproductive: threats not only strengthened Jewish faith, but there was also always the possibility that God would make one of them the instrument of their salvation. The lines "Por éste el justo, en la encubierta cueva, / En el ungido no vengó su ofensa" add another dimension to this interpretation: Delgado here alludes to the story of Saul and David's meeting in the cave of En-Gedi from 1 Samuel 24. David, who has fallen from grace with his father Saul, has the opportunity to kill the king in the cave, but for David the person of the anointed king is sacred. Even in misfortune the king is in God's realm, and David is wary of intruding into this realm, laying hands on the king, and thus taking what only God himself can grant him. In combination with 1 Chron. 16:22 ("Touch not mine anointed, and do my prophets no harm") and going beyond the story's immediate moral, this biblical passage has been conveyed as a warning to the enemies of the people of Israel, in part owing to the equation of the anointed with the entire people of Israel. In Delgado's poem, the citation of the biblical story is embedded in the logic of the relief from suffering through God. A reading of this text dedicated to Cardinal Richelieu does not end with an explicit warning but with a decided hint to consider any threat to the people of Israel, bearing in mind the history of the bond between God and his people.

In his introduction to August Wünsche's German translation of the Midrash to the book of Esther, Julius Fürst has pointed out the mutability of the Esther story and demonstrated how much the Midrashic interpretation of the Esther story is determined by historical experience:

> Each new generation brings with it its experiences, struggles, and sufferings. Before this Midrash was written down, folklore had woven all the harshness and bitterness the Jews suffered from the Romans into the Midrash; namely the Jews' sufferings under the rule of Trajan and Hadrian and the brutalities and cruelties of the Roman emperors since Constantine II have found ample expression in this Midrash.[27]

According to Fürst, the Midrash contains fragments of sermons partly in order to demonstrate how the threats of punishment issued by Moses have come true in the course of history. At the same time, it is pointed out that God has not forsaken Israel at any point in time, and that "although Israel might be enslaved, the empires were mere instruments in God's hand, none of which had acquired a right of ownership over Israel."[28] Fürst claims that the biblical figures became types in which each generation recorded its contemporary history. In the view presented here, the conclusion drawn by the Leipzig scholar regarding the Midrash to Esther more than a hundred years ago also applies to Delgado's lyrical transformation. In Delgado's adaptation, Esther appears as an example of a convert who conceals her affiliation at first but then returns to the faith of the patriarchs and comes to the aid of her threatened people. Delgado essentially inscribes two possible readings into his texts, which are structured in correspondence with the relation between the two religions of Judaism and Christianity: while the Christian reading of the Bible argues figurally, the interpretation of biblical stories presented by Delgado is an exemplary one; while the figural interpretation points to an allegorical-spiritualist level, Delgado's poetry argues literally and in a serializing manner.

Lamentaciones del Propheta Jeremías

Like the book of Esther, the book of Lamentations is one of the five Megillot of the biblical Ketuvim. The Latin title *Lamentationes* is a translation of the Hebrew קִינוֹת (*kinot*, "lamentation"), although in the Jewish tradition the book is called *Eikah* (Hebr. איכה) after its opening word. Since Jeremiah was generally assumed to be the author, both the Septuagint and Vulgate placed the book of Lamentations after the book of Jeremiah as an appendix to it, partly because of an introductory sentence describing the narrative situation: after the loss of Jerusalem, Jeremiah had written down his lament. The five lamentations are not ordered systematically and the themes overlap, yet the book's contents can be roughly summarized as follows. After an introductory, more general lament about Jerusalem, the city abandoned by its inhabitants, the second lament describes its destruction, the inhabitants' sufferings, and the adversity they are faced with. In the third lament, the narrative voice describes and reflects on its own suffering. Theological interpretations of the book of Lamentations are usually centered around this chapter and particularly on the suffering willed by God and promising hope of salvation at the same time. The fourth lamentation focuses on Jerusalem's guilt and the extent of suffering, yet it links this to a promise of forgiveness. The fifth lamentation combines the people's lament with a plea to God for forgiveness.

In formal terms, this biblical text is highly arranged: the number of stanzas in all five lamentations corresponds to the number of letters of the Hebrew alphabet (twenty-two). The first four lamentations are alphabetic acrostics.[29] In the first two poems, each letter of the alphabet introduces a stanza of three lines, and in the fourth poem a stanza of two lines. In the third poem, each of the twenty-two stanzas comprises three acrostic lines. The fifth poem is made up of twenty-two lines without an acrostic. The first two lamentations, in particular, are additionally interwoven by chiasmus. The third and fourth lamentations are linked by a symmetrical structure as well.[30]

Pinto Delgado's poem on the book of Lamentations consists of apostils of seven to twenty-five cinquains on the verses of the first two chapters of the book of Lamentations. The *mote-e-glosa* structure is a familiar structural element in Spanish poetry. In terms of form, Delgado is a Spanish poet of the sixteenth or seventeenth century in every sense. Each section is preceded by a prose translation of the respective biblical verse. Timothy Oelman has shown that the Ferrara Bible was used for this purpose[31] and has interpreted this as evidence of Delgado's clearly identifiable Jewish affiliation.[32]

The apostils are prefaced by five stanzas in which the poet dedicates his poetic texts inspired by the book of Lamentations to the Lord himself in a simultaneous gesture of dedication poem and prayer:

Senõr, mi voz imperfeta
Nacida del corazón
Que a vano error se sujeta
Hoy siga con tu Profeta
El llanto de tu Sión.

Sí del polvo a las estrellas,
Del mundo en lo más remoto,
Mostró sus vivas centellas,
El menos y el más devoto
Llore conmigo y con ellas.

Concede de alto tesoro
Tu luz a mi ciega vista,
Tu ciencia en lo que ignoro,
Porque, en ajena, mi lloro
A proprías culpas resista.

Si veo en el llanto mío
La parte de humor, que encierra
Tu fuente inmensa, confío
Que será como el rocío
Que fertiliza la tierra.

Y aunque sin alas me atrevo
A tanto vuelo, y me espante
El ver que mis labios muevo,
Inspira en mí canto nuevo,
Porque en mis lágrimas cante. (112)[33]

Delgado asks for no less than divine inspiration for his poetic composition of Jeremiah's lamentations. Two more aspects of this introductory poem are remarkable: its intended readership and the metaphor of the dewdrop. Delgado describes the reader whom he seeks to touch with his poem as "el menos y el más devoto." This may be understood as an example of an explanation of biblical poetry in emulation of Horace's concept of poetry as combining delight and instruction, "aut prodesse, aut delectare, aut etiam utrumque." In order for the Jewish-Christian sacred text to become the subject of narration or poetry, there has to be a particular instructive and annunciatory function in the literary adaptation. Delgado cites this particular merit of biblical epic poetry in his introductory poem. The status of biblical poetry, however, differs from that of the liturgical-ritual use of biblical texts. Ambiguity is introduced into a realm usually marked by a lack of ambiguity by means of poeticization. Delgado seems to understand perfectly this peculiarity of interfusing the Holy Bible and profane poetry and to purposely employ it in his composition of the sacred text. There is no reason why his version of the Lament for Zion should not be interpreted as addressed to the "menos y más devoto cristiano" (and thus as a foreseeing of the sufferings of Christ) as well as to the Jews. Beginning with its prelude, the poetic reprise of the *Lamentationes* may be understood as a work of poetry addressed to all believers who orient themselves by the sacred text, including those who have more or less departed from its Mosaic interpretation. As with the Esther poem, there are two possible readings here. From the Christian perspective, this poetic renewal of the book of Lamentations has a typological dimension referring to the sufferings of Christ; and the renewed use of the material would thus be justified as well, even from the point of view of the Inquisition, notoriously rigid with regard to authors of Jewish origin in particular. From the Jewish perspective, the poetic renewal of this material has a paradigmatic dimension: Jeremiah's lament describes the fate of the Jewish people in history, a situation of the most severe persecution from which they are nonetheless rescued time and again. Read in this manner, the text would represent an interpretation of their situation to Jews at the time, and particularly to converts—a call to master this situation not by increased self-denial but instead by a return to the faith of the patriarchs and a promise that God would come to the aid of his people if they returned to him.

This interpretation is reinforced by the fourth stanza of the dedication poem. In his request to share in the source of divine wisdom, Delgado wishes his lament might be like a dewdrop rendering the earth fertile. As has been mentioned above, in Christian symbolism the dewdrop stands for Mary and the word of Christ. In its combination with the praise of God, the symbolism in Delgado's poem points to an Old Testament meaning:

> Give ear, O ye heavens, and I will speak; and hear, O earth, the words of my mouth. My doctrine shall drop as the rain, my speech shall distil as the dew, as the small rain upon the tender herb, and as the showers upon the grass: Because I will publish the name of the Lord: ascribe ye greatness unto our God. He is the Rock, his work is perfect: for all his ways are judgment: a God of truth and without iniquity, just and right is he. (Deut. 32:1–4)

The speaking "I" of this biblical text is Moses. Given the identical structure—in both Delgado's stanza and the passage from the sacred text, language is equated to a dewdrop—it seems more likely that it is Jewish symbolism rather than the Christian interpretation that is being alluded to in Delgado's poetry. The parallels in content further support this conclusion. The sacred text continues:

> They have corrupted themselves, their spot is not the spot of his children: they are a perverse and crooked generation. Do ye thus requite the Lord, O foolish people and unwise? is not he thy father that hath bought thee? hath he not made thee, and established thee? Remember the days of old, consider the years of many generations: ask thy

> father, and he will shew thee; thy elders, and they will tell thee. When the Most High divided to the nations their inheritance, when he separated the sons of Adam, he set the bounds of the people according to the number of the children of Israel. (Deut. 32:5–8)
>
> Of the Rock that begat thee thou art unmindful, and hast forgotten God that formed thee. And when the Lord saw it, he abhorred them, because of the provoking of his sons, and of his daughters. And he said, I will hide my face from them, I will see what their end shall be: for they are a very forward generation, children in whom is no faith. They have moved me to jealousy with that which is not God; they have provoked me to anger with their vanities: and I will move them to jealousy with those which are not a people; I will provoke them to anger with a foolish nation. (Deut. 32:18–21)

The structural correspondence with Moses' warning to the people of Israel supports the aforementioned perspective that Delgado's introductory poem to his paraphrase on the *Lamentationes* opens up: the text can also be read as a warning to those who have renounced the old faith.

Following the dedication poem, the section-by-section paraphrase on the book of Lamentations begins. The following excerpt is discussed below:

> ¿Cuál desventura, o ciudad,
> Ha vuelto en tan triste estado
> Tu grandeza y majestad
> Y aquel palacio sagrado
> En estrago y soledad?
>
> . . .
>
> ¿Cuál pecado pudo tanto,
> Que no te conozco agora?
> Mas, no advirtiendo, me espanto,
> Que tú fuiste pecadora
> Y quien te ha juzgado santo.
>
> En ofenderle te empleas,
> Ya por antigua costumbre,
> Y en errores te recreas
> Y así no es mucho que veas
> Tus libres en servidumbre.
>
> . . .

La causa, porque caíste
Y porque humilde bajaste
De la gloria en que te viste,
Fue la verdad que dejaste,
La vanidad que siguiste.
. . .
Si fuiste al Señor contraria,
De los pecados el fruto,
En tu cosecha ordinaria,
Ha sido el mismo tributo
Por quien te ves tributaria.

No sólo viste perder
La honra que te adornó,
Mas tus hijos perecer,
Que el Señor los entregó
Al más tirano poder.

¿Cómo se puede alentar
Tu pueblo, entre su gemido,
Llegando a considerar
Lo que seguir ha querido,
Lo que ha querido dejar? (114–117)[34]

One peculiarity of Delgado's treatment of the book of Lamentations lies in the diversity of the speaking subjects. Lyrical speech appears in the form of an address, as the poet's first-person speech, as first-person speech by the city of Jerusalem, but also as impersonal discourse. This reflects the similarly diverse speech in the sacred text, where a personifying manner of speech referring to the daughter of Zion is linked with appeals to God and other speech situations. By transferring the biblical text into poetic form, however, lyrical subjectivity enters the liturgy's textual layers. In his *Lectures on Aesthetics*, Hegel describes wherein the principal condition of lyrical subjectivity consists, in his view, namely, to "entirely assimilate and make his own the objective subject-matter." He continues:

> For the truly lyrical poet lives in himself, treats circumstances in accordance with his own poetic individual outlook, and now, however

> variously his inner life may be fused with the world confronting him and with its situations, complexities, and fates, what he nevertheless manifests in his portrayal of this material is only the inherent and independent life of his feelings and meditations.[35]

The transformation of the book of Lamentations into the language of poetic inwardness opens the text to references not contained in the biblical source. This can be illustrated beginning with Delgado's first stanzas. While the sacred text opens with a lament in which Jerusalem is personified as "Daughter of Zion," the poem begins with stanzas inquiring about the reason for the city's punishment. These addresses also construe a "we" (stanzas 2 and 3: "Who does not lower their head in your sight"), so that the textual figure of the lyrical "you" functions as a mirror for the collective fate in the suffering of an individual figure.

Another distinctive feature of this lyrical treatment of the book of Lamentations, which has been observed for the prayerlike introductory poem as well, consists in the emphasis on guilt and the acceptance of guilt for Jerusalem's sins. The lyrical speaker stresses that God's punishment for Jerusalem's lapse was just. In the following sections, there are multiple variations of the guilt motif, all of which have the lapse from the true faith as their subject. There are recurring reflections on the joy the fall of Zion spread among the people's enemies:

> Así mientras Israel
> La Ley divina guardaba,
> Y el estatuto fiel,
> El mundo se le humillaba,
> Y sus Monarcas con él.
>
> Pero después que pecó
> Y con libertad esenta
> En sus pecados cayó,
> ¿Cuál hombre no levantó
> La mano para su afrenta? (136–137)[36]

The joy of Jerusalem's enemies over her renunciation of God is continually mirrored by verses of blame. In the following stanzas, the verdict on Jerusalem and the declaration of responsibility for her deep fall are spoken by none other than God himself as lyrical speaker:

Mi pueblo trocó su Gloria,
Formando en el culto vano,
En mi olvido, su memoria,
Y en obras de propria mano
Hizo mi ofensa notoria.

De su precioso atavío
La doncella no se olvida,
Al mar reconoce el río,
Y olvidase el pueblo mío
De mí, que soy propria vida.

Buscad y ved si se ve,
En los campos de Sión,
Donde mi viña planté,
En tantos, justo un varon,
Que yo la perdonaré. (151)[37]

This is God himself testifying that his destructive wrath was not an arbitrary act but a result of Jerusalem's previous disloyalty. At the same time, a way out of the disastrous situation is hinted at: one righteous man abiding by true faith in God would be enough for God to forgive Zion. Delgado here adopts an interpretation included in the biblical text, but he simultaneously reverses it in a specific way. In Lamentations 3:22–32, the human being in his suffering articulates his hope for God's mercy:

> It is of the Lord's mercies that we are not consumed, because his compassions fail not. They are new every morning: great is thy faithfulness. The Lord is my portion, saith my soul; therefore will I hope in him. The Lord is good unto them that wait for him, to the soul that seeketh him. It is good that a man should both hope and quietly wait for the salvation of the Lord. It is good for a man that he bear the yoke in his youth. He sitteth alone and keepeth silence, because he hath borne it upon him. He putteth his mouth in the dust; if so be there may be hope. He giveth his cheek to him that smiteth him: he

> is filled full with reproach. For the Lord will not cast off for ever: But though he cause grief, yet he will have compassion according to the multitude of his mercies.

Thus Delgado has inscribed the path he took in his own biography into the text: the return to the Jewish faith in reaction to a persecution seeming paradoxical at first, but which from the Old Testament perspective is an expectable consequence of renouncing one's faith by converting to Christianity, an idolatrous sect in the Jewish view.

With the lyrical speaker being God himself in Delgado's poem, the biblical hope for compassion turns into a promise of salvation. The latter is given a particular focus: these stanzas in which the personified city speaks as lyrical "I" appear several lines further below:

> Mis Príncipes, que me honraron,
> Mis sacerdotes perdí,
> Que, como al Señor dejaron,
> Los quiso apartar de sí,
> Y al fin de mí se apartaron.
>
> Ya su renombre perdido,
> Ya su estimado blasón,
> En infamia convertido,
> Níegan decir lo que son,
> Por no decir lo que han sido. (182)[38]

In his lyrical transformation of the material, Delgado had the full range of poetic freedom and was not fettered by the constraints of the acrostic, which had determined the choice of words in the biblical text. Thus it is by no means mere speculation to interpret the second above-cited stanza as a subtle yet very clear projection of the biblical lament of exile onto the poet's contemporary situation. In the biblical text, the believers are called upon to return repentant to faith in God, while in Delgado's poem, the call to return is nuanced as faithfulness to one's origin and affiliation: "Níegan decir lo que son / Por no decir lo que han sido." The first three lines in this cinquain support this possible interpretation, not least by the choice of the verb *convertir* in the phrase "Ya su estimado blazon, / En infamia convertido." This is a virtuosic collocation—it is an essential characteristic of the poetic text in contrast to the pragmatic text that individual words can carry a much stronger meaning as such, that is, independent of their syntactic embedding. Yet ambiguity as a characteristic feature of the literary is maintained, so that this analysis can only ever be one possible interpretation of these lines. Nevertheless, in the poetic logic of Delgado's poem, the return to the ancestral faith appears as the only path to divine forgiveness and thus to hope for liberation.

Another stanza explains the kind of light that must be sparked in dark times:

Las siete luces que ardían
Y, ardiendo, representaban
Los Astros que se movían,
Entre despojos llevaban
Los que su ser no entendían. (162)[39]

The seven lights evoke the menorah as a symbol of divine light (see Num. 8:2). This stanza is complex, for it not only connects the aspect of the eternity of divine light with the universe as a whole, it simultaneously claims its validity for those to whom the meaning of the seven lights did not reveal itself. The use of the *pretérito imperfecto* removes any temporal limitation of the described, hence this stanza bears witness to something that has repeated itself and is not finished yet. Thus the reference to the poem's contemporary situation is already inherent in its grammatical form. The divine light carries even those who are not aware of it (anymore) because they did away with the true faith ("entre despojos").

In the stanzas cited below, the image of the city of Jerusalem changes:

Cual huerto que; de mil flores
Con artificio la mano
Plantó de varias colores
Que no las secó verano,
Ni el hielo con sus rigores.
. . .

El siempre verde amaranto
Aviva allí su color;
Vese inclinado el acanto
Y la violeta que tanto
Se adorna con su palor.

El lirio blanco y celeste,
Riendo de que el rocío
Llorando se manifieste,
Al aire pide su brío
Porque sus alas le preste.

Allí; de aparencia hermosa
Y de las flores princesa,
Armada asiste la rosa
Que enseña a guardar, curiosa,
Con la virtud la belleza.

La granada abre el coral
Que por mostrarse revienta
Y en su corona real
La fe de un Rey representa
En su vasallo leal.
...
Éste, pues, donde asistía
El gusto casi inmortal,
Que por su trono escogía,
Perdiendo su monarquía,
Llora en silencio su mal.
...
Así el divino poder,
Que el huerto santo ordenó
Con soberano saber,
Las flores, que en él plantó
Eran de eterno placer. (240–243)[40]

This poetic unit of the poem, which actually comprises eighteen stanzas but has been shortened to its relevant parts for the present context, is striking in several respects. The imagery of this passage, in which the almost paradisiacal garden is compared to the as-yet-undestroyed

Jerusalem, is not contained in the biblical book of Lamentations. Delgado not only contrasts biblical metaphors (see Song of Sol. 4:13) with Baroque imagery, he emphasizes the Holy City's imperishability through the floral symbolism of his verses. Here flowers, whose beauty symbolizes the transience of all earthly things in the *vanitas* tradition of poetry, are reinterpreted as images of eternity. Neither sun nor ice can harm the holy garden of Jerusalem, and this paradisiacal garden continues to exist even in times of God's wrath. The message of these lines is that God does not punish Jerusalem permanently—in contrast to Adam, whom he banished from the Garden of Eden for all eternity. The suffering inflicted by God on his people as punishment will not last, so the hope for salvation is not in vain.

Delgado's adaptation of the book of Lamentations closes with the personified city of Jerusalem's plea to God:

Señor, pues el alma invoca
Callando, tu dulce Nombre
Que a Nuevo amor te provoca,
No sea defeto al hombre
Lo que no forma su boca.

Mira las prendas que han sido
El parto de mis entrañas,
Que, mezclando su gemido
Entre las armas estrañas,
Se escucha entre su ruido.

No soy la que tú llamabas
Tu alcázar, en que vivías,
Cuando en el Templo me honrabas:
Que, aunque antiguas mis porfías,
En ellas no me dejabas.

Acude, o Bondad eterna,
Pues nuestro error no limita
Aquella piedad paterna
Que alcanza, como infinita,
Y, como justa, gobierna.

Llegue a tus ojos el llanto
Que en este trance despide
Quien, entre mortal espanto,
Si como santo no pide,
Pide refugio al que es Santo. (313–314)[41]

The ending of Delgado's poem calls for God's renewed acceptance of Jerusalem and her deliverance from suffering through his compassion. As a path to God's mercy, the lament becomes no less than a part of the Revelation.

The decisive element marking this text regardless of its equally possible Christian reading, however, is that God's renewed embrace of his people is meant as a promise. From the Christian point of view, the embrace has already taken place through God's incarnation. Here the messianism articulated in the mode of hope is contrasted in tone as well with the triumphal messianism of the Counter-Reformation defining itself entirely in terms of the already-repaired bond with God renewed daily in the Eucharist.

Fourteen years before Delgado wrote his *Lamentaciones del Propheta Jeremias*, Francisco de Quevedo y Villegas completed his translation and commentary on the book of Lamentations' first chapter, titled *Lágrimas de Hieremías castellanas* (1613). This text was published in 1953 by Edward M. Wilson and José Manuel Blecua as a result of their cooperation in the Consejo Superior de Investigaciones Científicas[42] and to this day has received little attention in the study of Quevedo's oeuvre. The text cannot be discussed in this study to the extent it deserves, but a comparison with its treatment of the book of Lamentations will help to illustrate further the unique characteristics of Delgado's poem. In the Christian tradition, the book of Lamentations was interpreted typologically; in this interpretation, the temple stands for the body of Christ, based on John 2:19–22. Nevertheless, at the beginning of the seventeenth century, a work based on this chapter of the Bible required an explanation, as a glance at Quevedo's preface shows. Quevedo mentions a commentary on the book of Lamentations by Petrus Figueiro dating from 1596 and quotes from it: "¿Qué otra cosa es esto que confirmer a los judíos en su infidelidad y forzar a las gentes que judaícen?"[43] Quevedo considers Figueiro's interpretation at length and concludes: "Y assí no tubo razón de decir Figueiro que confirmauan a los judíos en su pertinacia estas palabras, nie que forçauan a judaizar. E referido esto para que sea cierto que mi intento no mira a otra cossa que a los dos fines dichos."[44]

First of all, this note demonstrates that using the book of Lamentations as a source was quite precarious from the point of view of a dogmatic Christian such as Quevedo. This is entirely different in Delgado's case: neither in the dedication to Cardinal Richelieu nor in the preface to the reader is there a comparable construction; on the contrary, the three biblical stories are considered particularly appropriate for the cardinal. The final section of this chapter will discuss the wording of the dedication in more detail with regard to Delgado's interpretation of history. Suffice it to note at this point that Delgado introduces the three biblical texts as particularly suitable for the truly humble:

> La historia de la Reyna Ester, las lamentaciones del Propheta Ieremias, y Rut, cuya luz siempre resplandece en el alma, aunque lo defienda el velo de la humilidad de palabras humanas, que el mundo llama adorno, tan diferente de aquella simple, y misteriosa textura, la qual dexandose entender luego, nunca se dexa totalmente penetrar, por la incapacidad de nuestra vista. (vi)[45]

Comparison with Quevedo's paraphrase and commentary on the book of Lamentations also shows how much Delgado's poems differ from the Spanish interpretive tradition of his time. The thesis outlined repeatedly in this study maintains that the poetic form produces ambiguous structures on the semantic level, which simultaneously create possible readings from a Christian perspective and entirely different ones from a Jewish perspective. At the same time, Delgado's explicit reference back to the biblical constellations is much less a matter of course than it might at first seem from today's perspective. Quevedo extracts moral aphorisms from the book of Lamentations and orders them according to the letters of the Hebrew alphabet. Both the meaning of the alphabetical acrostic in the Bible passage and the thematic references in the city of Jerusalem's lament are thus altered significantly, which the following text passage exemplifies:

Aleph

> Q[u]ien cae de la grandeza adquirida, solo iace, como la viuda a quien falta amparo: que no ai desierto como la miseria, que entre la gente lo es, y no ay título exempto de mudanza. Sola se ve la ciudad, viuda la señora.

. . .

Vav

> Adonde ai pecado, aun corporal hermosura no ai, y todo falta como falte Dios. Y assí los ricos y poderosos que le ofenden, hambrientos y pobres, en nada tienen sosiego ni hartura.

. . .

Tet

> Quien no se acordare en todas las cosas vmanas del mal fin que pueden tener, le tendrá malo, pues solo temerle malo le da bueno.[46]

In Quevedo's book, the aphorisms are followed by the translation of the Hebrew biblical text of the book of Lamentations into Spanish, as well as a commentary. The short aphorisms claim to reveal the moral content of the book of Lamentations without making direct reference to the people of Israel. Thus, the radical allegoresis has exactly that effect already systematically postulated by Augustine for the Old Testament: the removal of the text's character as a history book of a particular, namely, the Jewish, people in favor of a time-transcending, no longer locally fixed, and thus universal meaning.

Quevedo's treatment of the biblical text is structured in the following manner. The rendition of a selected passage from the Hebrew text is followed by a literal translation, then a poetic adaptation and scholarly commentary in which Quevedo discusses the existing interpretive tradition. At one point, Quevedo comments on an interpretation of the above-cited Petrus Figueiro: "Así cita Figueiro doctamente al paráphrase, y en una palabra concilia a san Hierónimo con el rigor hebreo."[47] This comment is exemplary of the entire work, for Quevedo's objective is a linguistically and theologically accurate translation of the contents of the book of Lamentations into Christian tradition as well as a defense of the Latin Vulgate. He does this as both a theologian and a poet, and from both perspectives he interprets the punishment imposed on Zion as just with regard to the New Testament while simultaneously seeking to transfer the poetic force of the Old Testament text in admiration of its poetic range of effect.

In contrast, the distinctive character of Delgado's adaptation of the book of Lamentations becomes evident once more. His lyrical transformation closely follows the content of its biblical source, without a systematic interpretation leaning in a particular denominational direction. In his poems, Delgado stages the ambivalence and ambiguity inherent in the literary text in such a virtuosic way that the text not only conforms to both Christian and Jewish dogmatic standards but also allows an interpretation from the perspectives of both religions. The fact that he achieved this in remarkable Spanish verse has been commented on by Marcelino Menéndez Pelayo in his *Historia de los heterodoxos españoles*. An excerpt from this comment has been quoted in the Introduction to this book; below is a more extensive quote from his assessment of the literary significance of Pinto Delgado's paraphrase on the book of Lamentations:

> Nunca se elevó a más altura Moseh Pinto Delgado; nunca hizo tan gallarda muestra de su fluidez métrica y de la viva penetración que tenía de las cosas bellas, como en su paráfrasis de los Trenos de Jeremías, que es la mejor corona de su memoria. Apenas hay mejores quintillas en todo el siglo XVII, y de fijo ningunas tan sencillas, inspiradas y ricas de sentimiento.[48]

Historia de Rut

Like the book of Esther, the book of Ruth (Hebr. מגילת רות) is one of the five Megillot (scrolls) of the Ketuvim. Liturgically, this biblical narrative is connected with the Jewish holiday of Shavuot. In the Septuagint, the book of Ruth is placed between Judges and Samuel. Before discussing Pinto Delgado's treatment of this material, I will give a brief summary of this biblical narrative.

Because of a famine, Elimelech, his wife Naomi, and their sons leave the city of Bethlehem in the kingdom of Judah and settle in the kingdom of Moab. Elimelech and his two sons, married to the Moabite women Ruth and Orpah, die in the foreign land. Naomi decides to return to Bethlehem. Her daughters-in-law want to accompany her on her return to Judah, but she tells them to remain in their home of Moab. While Orpah obeys her, Ruth keeps her vow to share her mother-in law's fate and not only accompanies Naomi but also converts to her faith (Ruth 1:16; 2:22–23). The two women reach Bethlehem at the beginning of the barley harvest. According to Judean law, the poor are allowed to glean, and thus Ruth sets out to gather food for herself and her mother-in-law. The field from which she gathers the leftover barley belongs to Boaz, who receives her with kindness. When she tells Naomi of her meeting with him, her mother-in-law is delighted, since she knows Boaz as a loyal friend of both her husband Elimelech and Ruth's deceased husband. Naomi advises Ruth to approach Boaz, for she sees the possibility of a Levirate marriage. Boaz does not seem to be averse to the idea but wants to examine its conditions first. After all open questions, most of which concern Naomi's land ownership, have been answered, Boaz marries Ruth and fathers a son, Obed, with her. It is prophesized in Ruth 4:17 that Obed was to become grandfather to King David. This genealogy is interesting insofar as the kingship law in Deuteronomy (Deut. 17) demands an Israelite as king and the law in Deuteronomy also forbade the inclusion of Moabites into the people of Israel (Deut. 23:4). There is a line of exegesis that interprets the story of Ruth as a post-exilic text portraying David's origin as universal.[49]

The Gospel of Matthew names Ruth alongside Tamar, Rahab, and Bathsheba as one of Jesus' female ancestors. Moshe S. Weinfeld, David Sperling, and Aaron Rothkoff also point out the remarkable nature of David's genealogy in the story of Ruth, since it shows a subtle protest against the rejection of foreign women found in Ezra (Ezra 9–10) and Nehemiah (Neh. 13:23–29) and portrays Ruth as the prototype of a just female convert.[50] From the Christian point of view, this aspect of David's genealogy has always been projected onto Jesus—who in the Christian interpretation is descended from the house of David—and subsequently rendered in a distinctly positive light. The origin of the Son of God was understood as transcending Jewish history and thus as a typological reference to the new religion's universalism. As a converted heathen, barley-gleaning Ruth typifies those who in the Christian interpretation belong among God's people not by birth but by "baptism," and she emphasizes this status by her search for the "true bread," namely, the bread of the Eucharist.

João Pinto Delgado's poem is one of the first literary treatments of this material in the Spanish language—soon followed by Tirso de Molina's drama *La major espigadera* (1634) and an *auto sacramental* on the story of Ruth by Pedro Calderón de la Barca (*Las espigas de Rut*) in 1663. Right at its beginning, Delgado's treatment of the biblical story accentuates what the poet highlights as particularly remarkable:

La conversación y bondad
De la estranjera Moabita,
Mi pluma, aunque humilde, incita
Para cantar su humildad.
...
Concede, Señor, que escriba
La que, abrazando tu Ley,
Fué su su fruto un santo Rey,
Su memoria al mundo altiva. (315–316)[51]

The wordplay *conversación/conversión* in the first line of this dedication poem to God directs attention to the story of the convert. The Moabite's conversion to the Mosaic faith is directly linked to David's royal genealogy ("La que, abrazando tu Ley / Fué su fruto un santo Rey"). The emphasis of this aspect is by no means accidental. In the poetic treatment, the story of Ruth is turned into a manifesto against xenophobia: Delgado's highlighting of Ruth's part in David's origin means the phrase referring to the sainted king ("Un santo rey") also evokes Jesus' affiliation. Thus Delgado's text focuses not on ancestry, which one cannot determine oneself, but on the decision for a faith.

The story of the migration to Moab, Elimelech's death, and Naomi's decision to return is briefly summarized in twenty-five stanzas in Delgado's poem. One of the poem's first key moments describes the decision of the two daughters-in-law in great detail. This is a prelude to a fourteen-stanza first-person speech by Naomi, who tells her daughters-in-law to remain in Moab. The first three stanzas of her request are quoted below:

Y dice: "Aunque amor profundo
No olvida el dolor que siento,
Si en vosotras represento
El bien que estimé en el mundo.

O hijas, si veo en vos
El bien de mi compañía,
Tornad, dejando la mía,
A vuestra patria las dos.

Dejadme sola y dejad
Crecer en ondas mi llanto,
Conmigo llorastes tanto,
De hoy más sin mí descansad." (321)[52]

Only one stanza is dedicated to Orpah's decision to obey her mother-in-law's request, while Ruth's resolution to disobey Naomi's instructions is described in the following stanzas:

"Sigue (le dice Naomí)
La que a sus campos volvió."
Mas ella: "Si te dejó,
No habré de dejarte a ti.

De tu voluntad verás
Que un punto no me desvío;
Tuyo será mi alvedrio,
Ni puedo ofrecerte más.

Que está, con lazo tan fuerte,
Mi alma a la tuya asida
Que, si nos juntó la vida,
Nos puede apartar la muerte." (325–326)[53]

Naomi replies, referring to the new law to which her daughter-in-law would have to subject herself were she to move to Naomi's home with her:

O hija, pues no lo entiendes
Y a nueva ley te resuelves,
Mira, si al Cielo te vuelves,
Donde tu vuelta pretendes. (327)[54]

Ruth is shown to be determined to follow her mother-in-law despite this information, and this determination is interpreted as no less than divinely inspired:

"Contigo (dice) andaré
En larga o breve distancia
Y donde hicieres la estancia,
En ella, o madre, estaré.

En esta verdad advierte
Que, siendo tu pueblo el mío,
Si en el que adoras confío,
Será la tuya mi muerte."

Naomí, que mira su vuelo,
Del mundo al cielo subido,
Le encarga el pasado olvido
En la memoria del Cielo.

Y porque le restituya
Al alma el eterno bien,
Alegre vuelve a Betlén
De Juda, que es patria suya. (327–328)[55]

In the first two lines of the third stanza quoted here, Ruth's conversion to her mother-in-law's faith depicted in the first two stanzas quoted above is described as a flight of the soul, which Naomi sees as an affirmation of her own belonging. Notably, Naomi's past is described as a space of oblivion ("Le encarga el pasado olvido"), as if she had strayed from the faith of the patriarchs during her stay in a foreign land, and as if Ruth's determined conversion to her faith reminded her of the special character of the patriarchal faith.

According to the depiction of the first encounter between Boaz and Ruth, he is so overwhelmed by the special care with which she gleans the leftover sheaves and by her overall poise, grace, and virtue that he cannot help but fall for her immediately:

Le dice: En tu acción se ve
Lo que en tu virtud contemplo.

O hija, pues muestras das
Del bien que de ti confío,
No salgas del campo mío
Y con mis mozas serás.

En esta heredad que ves,
Que toda la ofrezco a ti,
Mirando mi celo en mí,
En ella pido que estés.
...
Pues es tu pueblo Israel
Y admites, con gloria tanta,
La santa Ley, como santa
Te sea el escudo en él. (333–336)[56]

The other stanzas follow the biblical source closely. Naomi advises Ruth to approach Boaz, who is amenable to a marriage owing to her extensively described virtues but consults a council of ten community elders with whom he settles matters of land ownership first. When Boaz informs the council of his intention to marry Ruth, the elders not only do not object to the marriage but in fact see it as a virtually hallowed bond:

Todos, oyendo su intento,
Dijeron: "Como Rachel
Y Lía, que en Israel
Fueron dichoso cimiento,

Te sea Rut y el Señor
Te dé tan ancho el lugar
Como a Farés que Tamar
Parió del tribo mayor.

Y del fruto deste bien,
Que en tu virtud se dilata,
Sea el ejemplo en Efrata,
Memoria eterna en Betlén." (347)[57]

Delgado's composition of the council's reply is adopted from the biblical source, and the references to Rachel and Leah and to Tamar's son

Perez (Pharez) are contained in the sacred text as well. Sisters Rachel and Leah, daughters of Laban, with their maidservants Bilhah and Zilpah evoke the matriarchs of Israel, for Jacob fathered children with all four of these Aramean women. Tamar, daughter-in-law of Judah, who had tricked the latter and seduced him in disguise, gave birth to twins. Her firstborn, Perez, is also one of David's progenitors. These references additionally support an interpretation that prioritizes affiliation by faith over affiliation by ancestry.

The last two lines ("Sea el ejemplo en Efrata / Memoria eterna en Betlén") were added by Delgado. They illustrate very clearly the manner in which Delgado's own interpretation is embedded in his emulation of the biblical text. Ephrathah is the old Hebrew name for Bethlehem, which evokes the birthplace of Christ. The phrasing in which the example of Ephrathah is urged as an eternal reminder to Bethlehem can also be read as a warning to the members of the faith worshipping the one born in Bethlehem, namely, not to forget the lessons the ancient Hebrew city stands for. Such an interpretation is further supported by the final lines of the Ruth paraphrase:

> Nace Obed, dél Ysaí,
> De quien David procedió,
> Que su corazón llamó
> El Señor igual a sí. (348)[58]

A female convert was the ancestor not only of David but thus also implicitly of Jesus. Hence Delgado's treatment of the story of Ruth closes with an interpretation subordinating ancestry and origin to an affiliation determined by law-abidance and faith.

Pinto Delgado's Interpretation of History

In closing, I will put the rejection of a figural meaning present in Delgado's poems in relation to two texts that accompany the main text. The first of these is his preface to the reader, the other one the dedication to Cardinal Richelieu. The following is an excerpt from the preface:

> Al Lector. Lector amigo, este nombre, aunque general, particularmente procuro alcansar de ti, o grangeado si me conosces, o esperado si me conocieres. . . . Considera que no sin mucho cuidado, y dificultad se puede acomodar a la poesia humana, de que el mundo se agrada, el sagrado texto, que lleno de tantos misterios, se debe recelar no solo una palabra, mas una letra demasiada; y en lo que consiente, se siguieron las metaforas proprias, y necessarias, y contraposiciones; como luz del pecho, aliento de los ojos, y en la historia de Rut copla 10. Errado el consonante de voluntad, y Moab, en mostrarse el yerro de Elimelee por salir del culto divino a las tierras de la gentilidad, no por pobreza, mas a lo contrario, como se ve; y alfin lo que más notares no à sido por descuydo, que hará mayor la culpa quando la alles. Recibe mi offrenda con la voluntad, que de ti confio, para que me sea nuevo animo en continuar semejantes impresas, y a otros motivo para empeçarlas. El cielo te guarde. (ix)[59]

This preface may be read as an appeal for a very meticulous reading of Delgado's poems; after all, he himself postulates in his preface that his poetic composition is based on a careful reading of the biblical text. At this point, Delgado aims to say explicitly what he tried to ensure implicitly by means of a strongly rhetoricized form: he obviously wants these stories—known to everyone at the time—to be read in a new, "de-automatized" way.

Such a defamiliarizing reading of the widely known can only be intended to confront the reader with layers of meaning ignored or suppressed by the established reading—of both the Vulgate text and its Christian interpretation. Consequently, it is my hypothesis that the return to an authentic Jewish reading of the sacred text free of Christian appropriation is added as a subtext to the "narrative" of a biblical story fully accepted by Christianity and that this reading is intended as a means of interpreting the contemporary situation of the Jewish people: thus the initially puzzling fact of the persecution of converted Jews although they had become Christians is no longer incomprehensible. The persecution is a consequence of assimilation, God's punishment for renouncing the true faith. This also implies the promise that God will save his chosen people as soon as they return to the faith of their patriarchs.

The second implication of this poetic reformulation, which is mainly tied to the story of Ruth, may be described thus: In the Christian view, this Moabite woman with genealogical ties to Jesus is the typological prediction of that phase in the history of salvation in which the belief in a biblical God transcends the confines of a tribal religion and becomes universal. However, Ruth as presented in Delgado's poem is first and foremost an allegory of the free and conscious decision in matters of faith. Ruth's faith is based neither on ancestry nor on the necessities of earthly existence (since the impoverished widow marries the Jew Boaz only after she has decided to convert to the Jewish faith) but on free choice. Ruth joins the ranks of the righteous by making the decision as to which people she wants to belong to herself. In this way—and in view of the secular rulers of the time—she becomes a dual memento: first, to respect the individual's decision in his or her choice of faith, and second, not to doubt the sincerity of this decision.

It is in this light that the second accompanying text, the dedication of Delgado's work to Cardinal Richelieu quoted in excerpts below, is remarkable as well:

> Dos causas, entre las muchas, me obligaron a dedicar a V. S. Ilustrissima este trabajo de mis años, y fruto de mi humildad; si por el sujeto de los mayores que el mundo generalmente respeta. La primera fue considerar que los espiritos más generosos se emplearon en amparar los peregrinos, animandoles para se ocupar en servicio de sus Reyes, unos por armas, y otros por letras; . . . La segunda es conocer que no se alla, entre los ministros de la Real magestad, y Rey nuestro señor, cuya vida el cielo guarde, quien manifieste mayores señales de ser peregrino en todas sus acciones. . . . Viendo, pues, la obligación que V.S. Ilustrissima tiene a si mismo en aventajarse en el crédito deste honroso titulo, y amparar a los que se emplean en alguna obra, quando no para detener la velocidad de los años, por lomenos para dilatar después de la muerte su memoria, me atrevi a ofrecerle estas flores de la divinas letras, la historia de la Reyna Ester, las lamentaciones del Propheta Ieremias, y Rut, cuya luz siempre resplandece en el alma, aunque lo defienda el velo de la humilidad de palabras humanas, que el mundo llama adorno, tan diferente de aquella simple, y misteriosa textura, la qual dexandose entender luego, nunca se dexa

> totalmente penetrar, por la incapacidad de nuestra vista. Alfin, señor, si es assi que el mundo no es patria al hombre, y su patria es solo aquella, donde el tiempo con variedades no se alterna, queda obligado qualquiera a creer que es peregrino en el. Esto lo muestra bien claro el Levitico 25. quando no concediendose a ninguno vender su heredad más que asta el Iubileo dize y la tierra no se venda totalmente, porque vosotros peregrinos, y moradores mios sois. Cuyo passo confrontado con el Ps. 113. y el Hebreo 115. parece encontrarse, diciendo el cielo del Señor, y la tierra dio a los hijos de los hombres. Pues si la tierra es suya, concedida con este privilegio, como se les niega en ella la ultima, y total possession? que es esto? sino mostrarse que aunque el hombre diga. Esta es mi patria, esta la heredad me mis mayores, conosca que no la debe llamar suya, porque no offenda a la propriedad de la que espera. Animado con estos motivos me amparé de tan alto protector. (v–viii)[60]

In his dedication, Delgado links his poetic interpretation of scripture to contemporary experience—in his direct address and appeal for protection to Richelieu and the combination of the dedication of his biblical paraphrase with a reference to the divine commandment that humanity does not own the world. The interpretation of the word of God Delgado ventures in his dedication to Richelieu, which is based on direct biblical exegesis, relativizes the human definition of origin and affiliation established in this life: if the true home of the human being is the afterworld unaffected by the passage of time, then all human beings are pilgrims in this world. Even if a human being is certain of his homeland and the legacy of his ancestors, the dedication text urges restraint in order not to jeopardize what awaits him or her in the afterlife: "aunque el hombre diga. Esta es mi patria, esta la heredad de mis mayores, conosca que no la debe llamar suya, porque no offenda a la propiedad de la que espera."

Hence the warning about a lapse from the true faith and the punishment God imposes on those who are guilty of this trespass can be found not only in Delgado's lyrical texts, which in that sense might also be read as admonitions against an all too willing conversion. To recognize God's commandment appears as humanity's religious obligation in the dedication to Richelieu as well, for God had furnished humans with the sacred text and given them the ability to reflect so that they might attain knowledge. Delgado transcends the differentiation of "Old" and "New" Testament in the sense of a theologically based renunciation of worldly categories of ancestry and affiliation. The aforementioned layer of meaning of a discreet yet unmistakable warning becomes evident once more in the quotation from the dedication.

At the same time, it becomes clear that the return to one's faith urged by Delgado is a return of a different kind: it is neither a faith determined by origin nor the inquisitorial determination of origin. In the sweep of Christian universalization, Jewish faith is newly defined and reinterpreted as a decision for faith and law-abidance left to the individual. As *protector*, Richelieu is supposed to guarantee this freedom of the individual.

This text may also provide an answer to the question as to why Delgado decided on the Spanish language for his biblical paraphrases. At the time Delgado's biblical paraphrases were published, Anne of Austria was queen of France. The father of the Habsburg infanta Anna Maria Mauricia was Philip III of Spain, her mother Margaret of Austria; in November 1615, she had been married to the French king Louis XIII. The queen was fond of the arts, her native language was Spanish, her relationship to Richelieu was not without tensions, and she was known to be a devout Christian. It is possible that in his choice of the Spanish language, Delgado also wanted to demonstrate to the queen how a figural interpretation of the Old Testament may be replaced by an interpretation of scripture in the sense of a paradigmatic experience in his literary bible adaptations, whose truth prevails in recurring historical situations up until the present—and beyond.

Conclusion

Marranic Experience as a Paradigm of the Modern Age

The individual chapters have discussed authors from different periods as well as entirely different genres. What these authors have in common is that all of them in a specific way expressed a consciousness of autonomous productivity in their engagement with the sacred text, the sphere of the sacred, and the cultural constellations of their time. This is a manifestation of the ability to make the individual a subject of consideration. In the literary realm, this ability not only serves to illustrate the subject's positioning in the world, it also offers the possibility of abstraction for individual prisms of experience. Hence the contemplation of origin and affiliation can persist beyond the mere speaking about the self in broader contexts as well. The final part of this study will render the conclusions of the interpretive chapters more precise with the help of the metaphor of the Marranic.

As has previously been mentioned, the term "Marranic" is used not so much in its original historical meaning in the present context but rather as a metaphor in the sense of Dan Diner's earlier application of it to another historical constellation, namely, to Hannah Arendt's writing.[1] The term "Marranic" can be used to describe the distinctiveness of the historical experience of Jews and converts at the time. On the one hand, the concept serves to demonstrate the limits of an approach that operates on the basis of the traditional mode of national uniformity in search of its respective national literature. In this sense, the term "Marranic" represents the opposite: a perspective in the study of literature that does not put forth unambiguous cultural origin and affiliation as invariables but instead understands literature as a possible place for protecting the individual from collective impositions and codifications and that distances itself from them by contrasting them with freedom and individuality.

The texts examined in this study each in a different way articulate such a search for individuality and plurality. Thus overall they represent a form of literary writing in the early modern age that renders the diversity of Jewish and other lives visible beyond officially or ethnically defined belongings.

The representation of universal conditions and the particular challenges of affiliation of their time are inscribed into these texts in very diverse ways. The generalizations derived from their literary status do not level personal historical experience but rather maintain the resistance to cultural and linguistic attempts at eliminating otherness by means of their simultaneous existence.

The supranational as a fundamental specific of Jewish self-perception and self-characterization and the diversity of voices in those in-between spaces where belonging is impossible to define clearly—these distinctive features not only correspond with the literary status, they are characteristics of the modern age in general. This means that the texts analyzed here not only outline a unique feature of sixteenth-century literary writing but possibly a very early trend in a general development.

In his discussion of the historiography of Jewish literatures, Dan Miron has pointed out that Jews—considered both individually and collectively—could lead very different lives in different times and different places, and that each individual or collective had to merge different cultures and literatures, or rather created its own new culture and literature from these—something of one's own in the other, whose authentic roots in real life and lived historical experience deserve the designation "Jewish literature."[2] Transferring this demand to early modern Romance literatures, the origin-focused discussion of "Spanish, Portuguese, Italian, and French *converso* literature" might be replaced by another perspective that neither levels the particular character of these texts nor overlooks their encapsulation in a universal historical experience as the result of a too-narrow focus on the authors' biographies.

The individually varying engagement of the five texts with questions of origin and ancestry described in this study reveals components of a Marranic historical experience beyond the authors' affiliations.

These components seem like layers of memory that, although buried, build the foundation for the overlying layers and show through them. Not only does this mean new knowledge with regard to the multiple interlacing of affiliations in the period in question, but with regard to the existing studies of these texts it also illustrates how any reenvisioning of the past is subject to its period and context.

The analysis of these texts may also serve to initiate a fresh discussion of the complicated link between author and text, as well as of the relevance of an author's origin for an insight into aesthetic characteristics. A consideration of the hidden presence of the Marranic historical experience in early modern texts will now offer a more differentiated approach to this question than an interpretation based on the origin of an author or a complete rejection of any connection between text and author was able to do. Recourse to the author certainly is not a sufficient point of reference for interpretation, as the problematic readings of the texts discussed here show. At the same time, it has been demonstrated that the context of a text's creation can indeed provide information about the aesthetic characteristics of a work.[3]

The techniques that the analyzed texts have revealed are indeed diverse. Let me conclude by summarizing them. Despite differences in genre, subject matter, and cited intertexts, *La Celestina* and *Lazarillo de Tormes* show a strategic similarity in terms of technique. The procedure employed by both texts, by means of which semantic unambiguousness dissolves into indefinable ambiguity, has here been defined as a decontextualization followed by an "oblique" recontextualization. I will forgo repeating the individual techniques and their effects at this point. It is important to distinguish them from the carnivalesque as described by Mikhail Bakhtin.[4] Semantically, the carnivalesque employs the technique of inversion. This, too, is a decontextualizing and subsequently recontextualizing technique, yet it follows the simple pattern of a reversal into the opposite, which in itself lacks the possibility of conveying a serious statement. In some of the aforementioned cases, the oblique recontextualizing apparent in the texts analyzed in this study approaches direct inversion, yet usually keeps its distance from this simple process of mirror-image reversal. Oblique recontextualization does not directly expose the original context to ridicule but preserves it, while simultaneously questioning its exclusive claim to validity. Oblique recontextualization creates surprising perspectives for the original context, and it makes other perspectives not articulated in the text conceivable. The "one" meaning of the original context expands to diverse and in part always new attributions of meaning. It is hardly necessary to point out that a direct path leads from this technique, further perfected mainly by Cervantes in *Don Quijote*, to modern literature.

Leone Ebreo's text represents an entirely different procedure designed to create semantic hybridity. In order to characterize this procedure, the methodological key term "hybridization" commonly used in literary and cultural studies was introduced. In the *Dialoghi d'amore*, new contexts are not contrasted with familiar ones, however; instead, the boundaries between different contexts are eliminated altogether. The text's representational foundation makes way for a permanent shift of meaning. From this procedural variation, a direct path leads to the literature and literary theory of European Romanticism.

In Montaigne's *Essais*, an entirely different strategy becomes evident. What lends unity to the purposely and sometimes provocatively hybrid material that this text unfolds cannot be put in conceptual terms at all; it is a—fictitious—referential cipher: the "I" of the writer is the vanishing point of the heterogeneous. The text repeatedly emphasizes that this "I" in turn has no "substance" or "essence" beyond what it says about itself in the text. The authority attributing meaning in the text, which is marked as contingent, attempts to attribute meaning to the heterogeneous. To stage "meaning" as a nonobjective category, as a purely attributed category, and thus as a constantly newly available category is what gives Montaigne's *Essais* a dimension reaching far into the modern and even the postmodern age.

The last of the analyzed texts, by João Pinto Delgado, concludes this study mainly because it is chronologically the most recent text. Among the texts considered here, it seems the least "bold" at first glance, and as such it draws attention to the fact that processes of semantic hybridization and cultural emancipation from ancestral communities do not follow a coherent historical logic. The end of the sixteenth and beginning of the seventeenth century was largely an epoch of restoration in all of Europe. Accordingly, Pinto Delgado, who came from a family of forcibly baptized Jews and later returned to Judaism, wrote biblical poetry entirely in the style of his time, similar to Lope de Vega, Calderón de la Barca, Quevedo, and Racine.

In none of the other texts under consideration are the strategies of pluralizing the referenced "original" meaning more discreet than in this case. They essentially consist in inscribing an "original" Jewish interpretation into the broadly familiar typological interpretation of the respective Old Testament stories evoked in the texts, which does not merely historicize but refers to the contemporary situation of the Jews. I have described the tension inherent in these texts as the contrast between an "augmenting," typological, Christian concept of history and a paradigmatic-serial, virtually recursive concept of history as is common in the Jewish tradition with its still-open messianism. Regardless of its relatively traditional character, Pinto Delgado's text on an abstract level thus conceives a basic figure of modernity: the figure of competing interpretations of temporality.

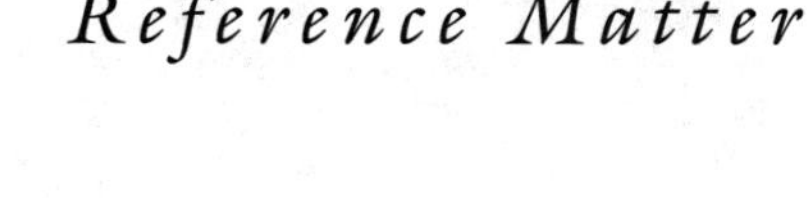
Reference Matter

Notes

Introduction

1. For the distinction between the terms "New Christian" and "Marranic," see the explanation provided at the end of this Introduction.

2. See Dan Diner, ed., *Synchrone Welten: Zeitenräume jüdischer Geschichte* (Göttingen: Vandenhoeck & Ruprecht, 2005), including suggestions for further reading.

3. "The reason was quite simple: almost all scientific and philosophical progress and the most advanced technology were the work of the Spanish Jews, the Spanish-Hebrew caste, first as Jews within the meaning of religion, and since 1492 as New Christians. . . . The cultural regression of the Spaniards since the mid-sixteenth century was not the effect of the Counter-Reformation or the anti-scientific phobia of Philip II, but simply the fear of being taken for a Jew. In the second chapter of the revised edition of my book *La realidad histórica de España* (1962) I show quite unequivocally that the notorious *limpieza de sangre* of sixteenth-century Spain, the stubborn insistence on being an 'Old Christian' and on having a genealogy without even the smallest Jewish component, was just a mere Spanish-Christian transmission of what happened among the Jews of Spain for centuries." Américo Castro, *De la edad conflictiva: Crisis de la cultura española en el siglo XVIII*, 2nd ed. (Madrid: Taurus, 1963), 54, 118–119 (author's translation; all translations henceforth are by the author unless otherwise noted). See also José Faur, *In the Shadow of History: Jews and Conversos at the Dawn of Modernity* (Albany, N.Y.: SUNY Press, 1992), 49, who also references these two passages but doesn't quote the last, rather problematic sentence about the supposed adoption of the concept of *limpieza de sangre* from Judeo-Spanish culture. In order to get a complete picture of Américo Castro's thought, however, it is necessary also to register those of his expressions that are considered outdated today.

4. Stephen Gilman, "A Generation of Conversos," *Romance Philology* 33 (1979): 87–101.

5. Claudio Sánchez-Albornoz y Menduiña (1893–1984) is one of the twentieth century's best-known Spanish medieval historians. He received honorary

doctorates from universities in Lima, Tübingen, Buenos Aires, Lisbon, Ghent, Bordeaux, Oviedo, and Valladolid. His dissertation on the monarchies of Asturia, León, and Castile from the eighth to the thirteenth century was published in 1916; he was professor of Spanish history at the universities of Barcelona, Valencia, Valladolid, and Madrid. In 1939, he was ousted from his chair at the Universidad Central because of his commitment to the republic. During its three legislative periods, Sánchez-Albornoz was a member of the republican parliament; in 1933, he became a state minister; and in 1936, he served as vice president to the parliament and ambassador to Portugal. The Spanish Civil War forced him to leave the country, going first to France. He held a chair at the University of Bordeaux until 1940 and then left Europe, first becoming a professor of medieval history at the Universidad Nacional de Cuyo in Mendoza. A year and a half later, he was appointed to the chair he was to hold until the end of his life, the chair of medieval history at the University of Buenos Aires. In the Argentine capital, he founded the Instituto de Historia de España, which started publishing the periodical *Los Cuadernos de Historia de España* in 1944. In 1983, Sánchez-Albornoz finally returned to Spain, where he died in Ávila in 1984. More than twenty monographs and far more than two hundred articles made Sánchez-Albornoz one of the leading historians in the field of Spanish medieval studies, and he never departed from his main thesis that the Spain of the *convivencia* was to be considered an inconsequential episode between Visigothic and post-Reconquista Spain.

6. "Lo judío contribuyó a la forja de lo hispano no por caminos de luz, sino por sendas tenebrosas . . . , y ningún crédito puede alegar contra nosotros, a tal punto nos legó deformaciones y desdichas y daño nuestro despliegue potencial y nuestro crédito histórico." Claudio Sánchez-Albornoz, *España: Un enigma histórico*, 4th ed. (Buenos Aires: Edhasa, 1973), 284. The reference to this quotation is taken from José Luis Abellán, "Función cultural de la presencia judía en España," in *Judios, sefarditas, conversos: La expulsión de 1492 y sus consecuencias*, ed. Ángel Alcalá Galve (Valladolid: Ámbito Ediciones, 1995), 395–407. On Claudio Sánchez-Albornoz's view of Spanish history, see Benzion Netanyahu, "Sánchez-Albornoz' View of Jewish History in Spain," in *Toward the Inquisition: Essays on Jewish and Converso History in Late Medieval Spain*, ed. Benzion Netanyahu (Ithaca, N.Y.: Cornell University Press, 1997), 126–155.

7. Essential in this context is Juan Goytisolo, *España y los españoles* (Barcelona: Lumen, 1979). Among Goytisolo's literary writings, the following deserve mention: his 1970 novel *Revindicación del Conde don Julian* (*Count Julian*), the text *Makbara* published in 1980, and the 1982 novel *Paisajes después de la batalla*. Goytisolo's occasional idealizing tendencies cannot be discussed at length at this point but need at least to be mentioned.

8. Henry Méchoulan and Gérard Nahon, eds., *Mémorial I.-S. Révah: Études sur le marranisme, l'hétérodoxie juive et Spinoza (Collection de la "Revue des Études Juives")* (Paris/Louvain: Fayard, 2001), 3–6.

9. Israël Salvator Révah, *Des marranes à Spinoza*, ed. Henry Méchoulan and Carsten Lorenz Wilke (Paris: Vrin, 1995).

10. Meyer Kayserling, *Sephardim—Romanische Poesien der Juden in Spanien: Ein Beitrag zur Literatur und Geschichte der spanisch-portugiesischen Juden* (Leipzig, 1859), viii. Following an overview of the history of the Jews in Spain up until the death of Alfonso XI, Kayserling gives an introduction to the oeuvre of Santob de Carrión as one of the most important representatives of fourteenth-century Spanish literature. He then outlines the life of a poet at the court of Juan II and in the fourth chapter gives an overview of the literature of the so-called New Christians. He subsequently describes the language and literature of the displaced Jews in both countries; the last four chapters of his book feature numerous individual studies of literary works by Spanish-Portuguese Jews.

11. Ramón Menéndez Pidal, "Catálogo del romancero judío-español," *Cultura Española* 4 (1906): 1045–1077; 5 (1907): 166–199.

12. André Stoll, "Sepharads Widerstand: Zur poetischen Produktivität der jüdischen Kultur Spaniens nach dem Vertreibungsedikt," in *Sepharden, Morisken, Indianerinnen und ihresgleichen: Die andere Seite der hispanischen Kulturen*, ed. André Stoll (Bielefeld: Aisthesis-Verlag, 1995), 15–46.

13. Manfred Tietz, "Mittelalter und Spätmittelalter," in *Spanische Literaturgeschichte*, ed. Hans-Jörg Neuschäfer (Stuttgart/Weimar: Metzler, 1997), 1–68. See also Christoph Strosetzki and Manfred Tietz, eds., *Einheit und Vielfalt der Iberoromania: Geschichte und Gegenwart*. Akten des Deutschen Hispanistentages Passau [Proceedings of the German Hispanists' meeting], February 26–March 1, 1987 (Hamburg: Buske, 1989).

14. Dietrich Briesemeister, "Mittelalterliche Fachprosa," in *Geschichte der spanischen Literatur*, ed. Christoph Strosetzki, 2nd ed. (Tübingen: De Gruyter, 1996), 27–34.

15. Alfred Gier, "12.–14. Jahrhundert: Lyrik, Epik, Roman und Drama," in Strosetzki, *Geschichte der spanischen Literatur*, 1–26.

16. Eugen Heinen, "Jüdische Spuren in der Literatur und Sprache Spaniens," in *Zur Geschichte des Iberischen Judentums, der Sepharden und Marranen*, vol. 2 of *Sephardische Spuren*, ed. Eugen Heinen (Kassel: Verlag Winfried Jenior, 2002), 169–223.

17. Norbert Rehrmann and Andreas Koechert, eds., *Spanien und die Sepharden* (Tübingen: De Gruyter, 1999). See also Rehrmann, "Der Mythos von Córdoba—Spanien, Europa und die islamische Kultur: Beispiele aus Literatur und Kulturgeschichte," *Publik: Kasseler Hochschulzeitung* 5 (1993): 5, as well as an expanded version in *Tranvía* 33 (1994): 9–16; and by the same author, *Das schwierige Erbe von Sefarad: Juden und Mauren in der spanischen Literatur—Von der Romantik bis zur Mitte des 20. Jahrhunderts* (Frankfurt a.M.: Vervuert, 2003).

18. Leo Pollmann, *Spanische Literatur zwischen Orient und Okzident* (Tübingen: Francke, 1996).

19. Iacob M. Hassán and Ricardo Izquierdo Benito, *Judíos en la literatura española: IX curso cultural hispanojudía y sefardí de la universidad de Castilla–La Mancha* (Cuenca: Ediciones Universidad de Castilla–La Mancha, 2001).

20. Felipe B. Pedraza Jiménez and Milagros Rodríguez Cáceres, "La edad media: La literatura española en su contexto: Minorías étnicas y culturales: Los judíos," in *Manual de literatura española: Edad media* (Tafalla: Cénlit, 1981, vol. 1.), 52–54. See also, by the same authors, "El mester de clerecía y otras manifestaciones poéticas del siglo XIII: Otros poemas: ¡Ay, Iherusalem!," in ibid., 318–320.

21. Ángel Sáenz-Badillos and Judit Targarona Borras, *Diccionario de autores judíos* (Córdoba: El Almendro, 1988).

22. In 1609, the *moriscos* living under the rule of the Christian kings were expelled for good. On the Islamic history of Spain, see the following essential studies: Évariste Lévi-Provençal, *Histoire de l'Espagne musulmane*, 3 vols. (facsimile reproduction of the first edition, Paris: Maisonneuve & Larose, 2000); Hans-Rudolf Singer, "Der Maghreb und die Pyrenäenhalbinsel bis zum Ausgang des Mittelalters," in *Geschichte der arabischen Welt*, ed. Ulrich Haarmann (Munich: C. H. Beck, 1987), 264–322; Ludwig Vones, *Geschichte der Iberischen Halbinsel im Mittelalter 711–1480* (Sigmaringen: Jan Thorbecke Verlag, 1993); Wilhelm Hoenerbach, *Islamische Geschichte Spaniens* (Zurich/Stuttgart: Artemis, 1970).

23. Béatrice Leroy, *Die Sephardim: Geschichte des iberischen Judentums* (Frankfurt a.M. / Berlin: Nymphenburger Verlag, 1991). See also Yitzhak Baer, *Historia de los judíos en la España cristiana* (Barcelona: Riopiedras Ediciones, 1998), as well as the first chapter of Paloma Díaz-Mas, *Sephardim: The Jews from Spain*, trans. George K. Zucker (Chicago: University of Chicago Press, 1992).

24. The Synod of Elvira issued canons regulating the relations with Jews. Canon 16, for example, prohibits marriage between Jews and Christian women. For an overview of this topic, see Heinz Schreckenberg, *Die christlichen Adversus-Judaeos-Texte und ihr literarisches und historisches Umfeld (1.–11. Jh.)*, 4th ed. (Frankfurt a.M. / Vienna: Peter Lang, 1999).

25. Norman Roth, *Conversos, Inquisition and the Expulsion of Jews from Spain* (Madison: University of Wisconsin Press, 1995).

26. See Esther Benbassa, "Questioning Historical Narratives: The Case of Balkan Sephardi Jewry," *Simon Dubnow Institute Yearbook* 2 (2003): 15–22.

27. Elias Hiam Lindo, *The History of the Jews of Spain and Portugal, from the Earliest Times to Their Final Expulsion from Those Kingdoms, and Their Subsequent Dispersion. With Complete Translations of All the Laws Made Respecting Them during Their Long Establishment in the Iberian Peninsula* (London, 1848).

28. José Amador de los Rios, *Historia social, política y religiosa de los judíos de España y Portugal*, 3 vols. (Madrid, 1875/76).

29. Yitzhak Baer, *A History of the Jews in Christian Spain*, vol. 1, *From the Age of Reconquest to the Fourteenth Century*, trans. Louis Schoffman, intro. Benjamin R. Gampel (Philadelphia/Jerusalem: Jewish Publication Society, 1992).

30. Eliyahu Ashtor, *The Jews of Moslem Spain*, trans. Aaron Klein and Jenny Machlowitz Klein, 3 vols. (Philadelphia: Jewish Publication Society of America, 1973–1984).

31. An older bibliography by Robert Singerman, *Jews in Spain and Portugal: A Bibliography* (New York: Oak Knoll Press, 1975), and his more recent bibliography with commentary, *Spanish and Portuguese Jewry: A Classified Bibliography* (Westport, Conn.: Greenwood, 1993), both provide an excellent introduction. Particularly notable among the more recent works are Yom Tov Assis, *The Jews of Spain: From Settlement to Expulsion* (Jerusalem: World Zionist Organization; Dor Hemshech: Hebrew University of Jerusalem, 1988); Haim Beinart, *The Expulsion of the Jews from Spain*, trans. Jeffrey Green (Oxford / Portland, Ore.: Littman Library of Jewish Civilization, 2002); Esther Benbassa and Aaron Rodrigue, *Sephardi Jewry: A History of the Judeo-Spanish Community, 14th–20th Centuries* (Berkeley / Los Angeles: University of California Press, 2000); Asunción Blasco, "Sefarad: Otra vision de España," in *Las Españas medievales*, ed. Julio Valderón Barique (Valladolid: Universidad de Valladolid, 1999), 113–139; Jane S. Gerber, *The Jews of Spain: A History of the Sephardic Experience* (New York: Free Press, 1992); Yosef Kaplan, *An Alternative Path to Modernity: The Western Sephardi Diaspora in the Seventeenth Century* (Leiden/Boston: Brill, 2000); Elie Kedouri, ed., *Spain and the Jews: The Sephardi Experience 1492 and After* (London: Thames & Hudson, 1992); Moshe Lazar and Stephen Haliczer, *The Jews of Spain and the Expulsion of 1492* (Lancaster, Calif.: Labyrinthos, 1997); Vivian B. Mann, Thomas F. Glick, and Jerrilynn D. Dodds, *Convivencia: Jews, Muslims, and Christians in Medieval Spain* (New York: George Braziller, 1992); Netanyahu, *Toward the Inquisition*; David Nirenberg, *Communities of Violence: Persecution of Minorities in the Middle Ages* (Princeton, N.J.: Princeton University Press, 1996); Nirenberg, "Enmity and Assimilation: Jews, Christians, and Converts in Medieval Spain," *Common Knowledge* 9 (2003): 137–155; Nirenberg, "Rasse als Begriff bei der Untersuchung spätmittelalterlicher Judenfeindschaft auf der spanischen Halbinsel," in *Jüdische Gemeinden und ihr christlicher Kontext*, ed. Christoph Cluse, Alfred Haverkamp, and Israel Yuval (Hannover: Verlag Hahnsche Buchhandlung Hannover, 2003), 49–72; Nirenberg, "Conversion, Sex, and Segregation: Jews and Christians in Medieval Spain," *American Historical Review* 107 (2002): 1065–1093; Erna Paris, *The End of Days: A Story of Tolerance, Tyranny, and the Expulsion of the Jews from Spain* (Amherst, N.Y.: Prometheus Books, 1995); Norman Roth, *Conversos, Inquisition, and the Expulsion of the Jews from Spain*; Gretchen D. Starr-LeBeau, *In the Shadow of the Virgin: Inquisitors, Friars, and* Conversos *in Guadalupe, Spain* (Princeton, N.J.: Princeton University Press, 2003); Yosef Hayim Yerushalmi, *From Spanish Court to Italian Ghetto: Isaac Cardoso—A Study in Seventeenth-Century Marranism and Jewish Apologetics* (Seattle: University of Washington Press, 1981) (an excellent selection of Yerushalmi's essential shorter studies was published in 1998: *Sefardica: Essais sur l'histoire des juifs, des marranes et des nouveaux-chrétiens d'origine hispano-portugaise* [Paris: Éditions Chandeigne, 1998]).

32. Henry Kamen, *The Spanish Inquisition: A Historical Revision* (London: Weidenfeld & Nicolson, 1997).

33. Cecil Roth, *The Spanish Inquisition* (New York: Norton, 1996).

34. Benzion Netanyahu, *The Origins of the Inquisition in Fifteenth-Century Spain*, 2nd ed. (New York: New York Review Books, 2001).

35. John Edwards, *The Spanish Inquisition* (Stroud, UK: Tempus, 1999).

36. Ángel Alcalá Galve, "Inquisitorial Control of Humanists and Writers," in *The Spanish Inquisition and the Inquisitorial Mind*, ed. Ángel Alcalá Galve (New York: Columbia University Press, 1987), 321–360.

37. Charles Amiel, "The Archives of the Portuguese Inquisition: A Brief Survey," in *The Inquisition in Early Modern Europe: Studies on Sources and Methods*, ed. Gustav Henningsen and John Tedeschi (DeKalb: Northern Illinois University Press, 1986), 79–99.

38. Francisco Bethencourt, "Les hérétiques et l'Inquisition portugaise: Représentation et pratiques de persecution," in *Ketzerverfolgung im 16. und frühen 17. Jahrhundert*, ed. Silvana Seidel Menchi (Wiesbaden: Harrassowitz, 1992), 103–117.

39. Fritz Heymann, *Tod oder Taufe: Die Vertreibung der Juden aus Spanien und Portugal im Zeitalter der Inquisition* (Frankfurt a.M.: Judischer Verlag bei Athenaum, 1988).

40. Jaime Contreras and Gustav Henningsen, "Forty-Four Thousand Cases of the Spanish Inquisition (1540–1700): Analysis of a Historical Data Bank," in *The Inquisition in Early Modern Europe*, ed. Henningsen and Tedeschi, 100–129.

41. Jean-Pierre Dedieu, "The Archives of the Holy Office of Toledo as a Source for Anthropology," in *The Inquisition in Early Modern Europe*, ed. Henningsen and Tedeschi, 158–189.

42. Mark D. Meyerson and Edward D. English, eds., *Christians, Muslims, and Jews in Medieval and Early Modern Spain: Interaction and Cultural Change* (Notre Dame, Ind.: University of Notre Dame Press, 2000).

43. Luce López Barralt, "The Legacy of Islam in Spanish Literature," in *The Legacy of Muslim Spain*, ed. Salma Khadra Jayyusi (Leiden: Brill, 1992), 1:505–552.

44. Eugenio Asensio, "La peculiaridad literaria de los conversos," *Anuario de Estudios Medievales* 4 (1967): 327–351.

45. Ángel Alcalá Galve, "From Dislike to Disguise: Jews and Conversos in Spanish Literature at the Time of the Expulsion (1474–1516)," in *Jews and Conversos at the Time of the Expulsion*, ed. Yom Tov Assis (Jerusalem: Merkaz Zalman Shazar le-Toldot YiÐraël, 1999), 109–141. See also Alcalá Galve, "Ecos antijudíos en literature aragonesa de la época de Fernando el Católico," *Trébede* 62 (2002): 27–33.

46. Eliyahu Ashtor, "Documentos españoles de la Genizah," *Sefarad* 24 (1984): 41–80.

47. Richard David Barnett, ed., *The Jews in Spain and Portugal before and after the Expulsion of 1492*, vol. 1 of *The Sephardi Heritage: Essays on the History and Cultural Contribution of the Jews of Spain and Portugal* (New York: KTAV, 1971).

48. Josep María Solá-Solé, *Sobre árabes, judíos y marranos y su impacto en la lengua y literatura españolas* (Barcelona: Puvill, 1983).

49. Ron Barkai, "Les trois cultures ibériques entre dialogue et polémique," in *Chrétiens, musulmans et juifs dans l'Éspagne médiévale*, ed. Ron Barkai (Paris: Éditions du Cerf, 1994), 227–251.

50. Ross Brann, *The Compunctious Poet: Cultural Ambiguity and Hebrew Poetry in Muslim Spain* (Baltimore: Johns Hopkins University Press, 1991).

51. Miguel Ángel de Bunes Ibarra, "Concepto y formación del patrimonio hispanojudío," in *El legado material Hispanojudío*, ed. Ana María López Alvarez and Ricardo Izquierdo Benito (Cuenca: Ediciones Universidad de Castilla–La Mancha, 1998), 79–91.

52. Enrique Cantera Montenegro, "Negación de la 'Imagen del Judío' en la intelectualidad hispano-hebrea medieval: El ejemplo del Shebet Yehudah," *Aragón en la Edad Media* 14–15 (1999): 263–274.

53. Bernard Dov Cooperman, ed., *In Iberia and Beyond: Hispanic Jews between Cultures (Proceedings of a Symposium to Mark the 500th Anniversary of the Expulsion of Spanish Jewry)* (Newark, Del. / London: University of Delaware Press, 1998).

54. Alan D. Deyermond, "Evidence for Lost Literature by Jews and Conversos in Medieval Castile and Aragon," *Donaire* 6 (1996): 19–30.

55. Eleazar Gutwirth, ed., *Ten Centuries of Hispano-Jewish Culture* (Cambridge: Cambridge University Library, 1992).

56. Miriam Bodian, "'Men of the Nation': The Shaping of Converso Identity in Early Modern Europe," *Past and Present* 143 (1994): 49–76.

57. Thomas F. Glick, "On Converso and Marrano Identity," in *Crisis and Creativity in the Sephardic World, 1391–1648*, ed. Benjamin R. Gampel (New York: Columbia University Press, 1997), 59–76.

58. Yosef Kaplan, "The Self-Definition of the Sephardic Jews of Western Europe and Their Relation to the Alien and to the Stranger," in *Crisis and Creativity in the Sephardic World, 1391–1648*, ed. Benjamin R. Gampel (New York: Columbia University Press, 1997), 121–145. See also, by the same author, "Wayward New Christians and Stubborn New Jews: The Shaping of a Jewish Identity," *Jewish History* 8, nos. 1–2 (1994): 27–41. Still essential on the above-mentioned matter is Yosef Hayim Yerushalmi, "Conversos Returning to Judaism in the Seventeenth Century: Their Jewish Knowledge and Psychological Readiness," in *Proceedings of the Fifth World Congress of Jewish Studies*, ed. Pinchas Peli (Jerusalem: World Union of Jewish Studies, 1972), 2:201–209 (Hebr.).

59. Maria Rosa Menocal, Raymond P. Scheindlin, and Michael Sells, eds., *The Literature of Al-Andalus* (Cambridge: Cambridge University Press, 2000).

60. Gregory B. Kaplan, *The Evolution of* Converso *Literature: The Writings of the Converted Jews of Medieval Spain* (Gainesville: University Press of Florida, 2002).

61. The following selection illustrates the breadth of existing individual studies: Ana María Bejarano Escanilla, "Selomoh ben Reuben Bonafed, poeta y polemista,"

Anuari de Filología 14 (1991): 87–101; Ram Ben-Shalom, "Vikuah Tortosa, Vincente Ferrer u-be'ayat ha-anusim al-pieduto shel Yitsaq Natan [The disputation of Tortosa, Vincent Ferrer and the problem of the conversos according to the testimony of Isaac Nathan]," *Zion* 56 (1991): 21–45 (Hebr.); the following anthology contains important individual studies: Isaac Benabu, ed., *Circa 1492: Proceedings of the Jerusalem Colloquium "Litterae Judaerom in Terra Hispanica"* (Jerusalem: Magnes Press, 1992); Mair José Benardete, *Hispanic Culture and Character of the Sephardic Jews*, 2nd ed., edited and augmented by Marc D. Angel (New York: Sepher-Hermon Press for the Foundation for the Advancement of Sephardic Studies and Culture and Sephardic House at Congregation Shearith Israel, 1982); Asunción Blasco, "Jewish and Convert Jongleurs, Minstrels and 'Sonadores' in Saragossa (Fourteenth and Fifteenth Centuries)," *Assaph Studies in the Arts—Orbis Musicae*, no. 12 (1998): 49–72; Fernando Díaz Esteban, "La prosa hispanohebrea," in *La vida judía en Sefarad*, ed. Elena Romero (Madrid: Ministerio de Cultura, 1992), 81–114; Lola Ferré, "Los judíos, transmisores y receptores de la sabiduría medieval," *Revista Española de Filosofía Medieval* 7 (2000): 81–93; Manuel Ferrer-Chivite, "El factor judeo-converso en el proceso de consolidación del título 'don,'" *Sefarad* 45 (1985): 131–172; David Goldstein, *The Jewish Poets of Spain: 900–1250* (Harmondsworth, UK: Penguin, 1971); Sidney David Markman, *Jewish Remnants in Spain: Wanderings in a Lost World* (Mesa, Ariz.: Scribe, 2003); Maria Rosa Menocal, *The Ornament of the World: How Muslims, Jews, and Christians Created a Culture of Tolerance in Medieval Spain* (Boston: Little, Brown, 2002); Ángeles Navarro Peiro, "Tipos sociales en la narrativa hebrea de la España cristiana," in *La sociedad medieval a través de la literatura hispanojudía*, ed. Ricardo Izquierdo Benito and Angel Sáenz-Badillos (Cuenca: Ediciones Universidad de Castilla–La Mancha, 1998), 257–277; Ángeles Navarro Peiro, *Narrativa hispanohebrea (siglos XII–XV)* (Madrid: El Almendro, 1988); Moisés Orfali Levi, *Los conversos españoles en la literatura rabínica: Problemas jurídico y opiniones legales durante los siglos XV y XVI* (Salamanca: Universidad Pontificia de Salamanca, 1982); Nicholas G. Round, "La 'peculiaridad literaria' de los conversos: ¿Unicornio o 'snark'?," in Alcalá Galve, *Judíos, sefarditas, conversos*, 557–576; Caroline Schmauser and Monika Walter, eds., *¡Bon compaño, jura Di! El encuentro de moros, judíos y cristianos en la obra cervantina* (Frankfurt a.M.: Iberoamericana, 1998); Sara Sviri, "Spiritual Trends in Pre-Kabbalistic Judeo-Spanish Literature: The Cases of Bahya Ibn Paquda and Judah Halevi," *Donaire* 6 (1996): 78–84; Frank Talmage, "The Francesc de Sant Jordi-Solomon Bonafed Letters," in *Studies in Medieval Jewish History and Literature* (Cambridge, Mass.: Center for Jewish Studies, Harvard University, 1979), 1:337–364. The following studies examine the role of Spanish Jewry for and in fifteenth-century *cancioneros*: Yirmiyahu Yovel, "Converso Dualities in the First Generation: The Cancioneros," *Jewish Social Studies* 4, no. 3 (1998): 1–28; Julio Rodríguez Puértolas, "Jews and Conversos in Fifteenth-Century Castilian

Cancioneros: Texts and Contexts," in *Poetry at Court in Trastamaran Spain: From the Cancionero de Baena to the Cancionero General*, ed. Michael E. Gerli and Julian Weiss (Tempe, Ariz.: Medieval & Renaissance Texts & Studies), 187–197.

62. Norbert Rehrmann has compiled the results of his research project on Jews and Moors in Spanish literature from the Romantic period to the mid-twentieth century in an expansive publication: see Rehrmann, *Das schwierige Erbe von Sepharad* (Frankfurt a.M.: Vervuert, 2003). See also the following publications: Seymour Resnick, "The Jew as Portrayed in Early Spanish Literature," *Hispania* 37 (1951): 54–58; and Samuel M. Stern, "Spanish Literature and the Jews," *Judaisme Sephardi* 22 (1961): 974.

63. Benbassa and Rodrigue, *Sephardi Jewry*; by the same authors, *The Jews of the Balkans* (Oxford: Blackwell, 1995).

64. Kaplan, *An Alternative Path to Modernity*.

65. Jonathan I. Israel, *Diasporas within a Diaspora: Jews, Crypto Jews, and the World of Maritime Empires (1540–1740)* (Leiden/Boston: Brill, 2002); Israel, *Empires and Entrepôts: The Dutch, the Spanish Monarchy, and the Jews, 1585–1713* (London/Ronceverte: Bloomsbury Academic, 1990); Jonathan I. Israel and Reinier Salverda, eds., *Dutch Jewry: Its History and Secular Culture (1500–2000)* (Leiden/Boston: Brill, 2002); David S. Katz and Jonathan I. Israel, eds., *Sceptics, Millenarians, and Jews* (Leiden / New York: Brill, 1990).

66. Paloma Díaz-Mas, *Sephardim*. See also her book coedited with Cristina de la Puente González, *Judaísmo e islam* (Madrid: Crítica, 2007).

67. Charles Meyers and Norman Simms, eds., *Troubled Souls: Conversos, Crypto-Jews, and Other Confused Jewish Intellectuals from the Fourteenth through the Eighteenth Century* (Hamilton, New Zealand: Outrigger Publishers, 2001).

68. Joshua Stampfer, ed., *The Sephardim: A Cultural Journey from Spain to the Pacific Coast* (Portland, Ore.: Institute for Judaic Studies, 1987).

69. Howard M. Sachar, *Farewell España: The World of the Sephardim Remembered* (New York: Vintage, 1994).

70. Ross Brann and Adam Sutcliffe, eds., *Renewing the Past, Reconfiguring Jewish Culture: From Al-Andalus to the Haskalah* (Philadelphia: University of Pennsylvania Press, 2004).

71. Yedida K. Stillman and Norman A. Stillman, eds., *From Iberia to Diaspora: Studies in Sephardic History and Culture* (Leiden/Boston: Brill, 1999). See also Israel J. Katz and M. Mitchell Serels, eds., *Studies on the History of Portuguese Jews from Their Expulsion in 1497 through Their Dispersion* (New York: Sepher Hermon Press, 2000); António José Saraiva, *The Marrano Factory: The Portuguese Inquisition and Its New Christians, 1536–1765* (Leiden/Boston: Brill, 2001); Alisa Meyuhas Ginio, ed., *Jews, Christians, and Muslims in the Mediterranean World after 1492* (London / Portland, Ore.: Frank Cass, 1992); Benjamin Arbel, *Trading Nations: Jews and Venetians in the Early Modern Eastern Mediterranean* (New York: Brill, 1995).

72. Avigdor Levy, *The Sephardim in the Ottoman Empire* (Princeton, N.J.: Darwin Press, 1994); Aron Rodrigue, ed., *Ottoman and Turkish Jewry: Community and Leadership* (Bloomington: Indiana University Turkish Studies Series, 1992); Minna Rozen, *A History of the Jewish Community of Istanbul: The Formative Years, 1453–1566* (Leiden/Boston: Brill, 2002); Paul R. Trebilco, *Jewish Communities in Asia Minor* (Cambridge / New York: Cambridge University Press, 1991); Aryeh Shmuelevitz, *The Jews of the Ottoman Empire in the Late Fifteenth and the Sixteenth Centuries: Administrative, Economic, Legal and Social Relations as Reflected in the Responsa* (Leiden: Brill, 1984); Benjamin Braude and Bernard Lewis, eds., *Christians and Jews in the Ottoman Empire: The Functioning of a Plural Society* (New York: Holmes & Meier, 1982); Mark Alan Epstein, *The Ottoman Jewish Communities and Their Role in the Fifteenth and Sixteenth Centuries* (Freiburg: Klaus Schwarz Verlag, 1980); Avigdor Levy, ed., *The Jews of the Ottoman Empire* (Princeton, N.J.: Darwin Press, 1994); Levy, ed., *Jews, Turks, Ottomans: A Shared History, Fifteenth through the Twentieth Century* (Syracuse, N.Y.: Syracuse University Press, 2002).

73. Miriam Bodian, *Hebrews of the Portuguese Nation: Conversos and Community in Early Modern Amsterdam* (Bloomington: Indiana University Press, 1997); Chaya Brasz and Yosef Kaplan, eds., *Dutch Jews as Perceived by Themselves and by Others*, Proceedings of the Eighth International Symposium on the History of the Jews in the Netherlands (Leiden/Boston: Brill, 2001); Luc Dequeker and Werner Verbeke, eds., *The Expulsion of the Jews and Their Emigration to the Southern Low Countries (15th–16th c.)* (Leuven: Leuven University Press, 1998); Piet Huisman, *Sephardim: The Spirit That Has Withstood the Times* (Son, The Netherlands: Huisman Editions, 1986); Daniel M. Swetschinski, *Reluctant Cosmopolitans: The Portuguese Jews of Seventeenth-Century Amsterdam* (London / Portland, Ore.: Littman Library of Jewish Civilization, 2000); Aron di Leone Leoni, *The Hebrew Portuguese Nations in Antwerp and London at the Time of Charles V and Henry VIII: New Documents and Interpretations* (Jersey City, N.J.: KTAV, 2005).

74. David Nirenberg, *Wie jüdisch war das Spanien des Mittelalters? Die Perspektive der Literatur* (Treves: Kliomedia, 2005).

75. Yirmiyahu Yovel, *The Other Within: Split Identity and Emerging Modernity* (Princeton, N.J.: Princeton University Press, 2009).

76. Ernst Robert Curtius, *Europäische Literatur und lateinisches Mittelalter* (Bern/Munich: Francke Verlag, 1948), esp. chap. 1, "Europäische Literatur," 13–26; chap. 2, §5, "Romania," 40–45.

77. This mainly includes the line of tradition from St. Augustine to Petrarch and possibly continuing with Luther. See Karlheinz Stierle, *Petrarca—Fragmente eines Selbstentwurfs: Essay* (Darmstadt: Carl Hanser, 1998); Andreas Kablitz, "Petrarcas Augustinismus und die écriture der *Ventoux*-Epistel," *Poetica* 26 (1994): 31–69; Joachim Küpper, *Petrarca: Das Schweigen der Veritas und die Worte des Dichters* (Berlin / New York: De Gruyter, 2002).

78. See especially Dan Diner, "Von 'Gesellschaft' zu 'Gedächtnis': Über historische Paradigmenwechsel," in *Gedächtniszeiten: Über jüdische und andere Geschichten*, ed. Dan Diner (Munich: C. H. Beck, 2003), 7–15; and Diner, "Neutralisierung und Tolerierung von Differenz: Über institutionelle Internalisierungen von Religion und Ethnos," in *Der demokratische Nationalstaat in den Zeiten der Globalisierung: Politische Leitideen für das 21. Jahrhundert*, ed. Herfried Münkler (Berlin: Akademie Verlag, 2002), 41–55.

79. Dan Diner, "Geschichte der Juden: Paradigma einer europäischen Historie," in *Annäherungen an eine europäische Geschichtsschreibung*, ed. Gerald Stourzh (Vienna: Verlag der Österreichischen Akademie der Wissenschaften, 2002), 85–102.

80. Hartmut Stenzel, *Einführung in die spanische Literaturwissenschaft* (Stuttgart/Weimar: Metzler, 2001), 123.

81. Quoted in Elizabeth Mendes da Costa, "Montaigne and the Jewish Religion," in *Troubled Souls*, ed. Meyers and Simms, 129f.

82. Carola Hilfrich, "Autobiography as a Spectropoetics of the Mother: On Hélène Cixous's Recent Works," in *Zeitgenössische jüdische Autobiographie*, ed. Christoph Miething (Tübingen: De Gruyter, 2003), 129–146; Mendes da Costa, "Montaigne and the Jewish Religion."

83. The first detailed study of Montaigne's family history appeared in a nineteenth-century monograph by Théophile Malvezin, *Michel de Montaigne, son origine, sa famille* (Bordeaux, 1875), 99–128. In contemporary scholarship, Elizabeth Mendes da Costa's aforementioned study *Montaigne and the Jewish Religion* deserves mention, as well as her essay on his travel journal: "The Jews and Montaigne's Journal de Voyage," *French Studies Bulletin* 69 (1998): 10–13.

84. "Apenas hay mejores quintillas en todo el siglo XVII, y de fijo ningunas tan sencillas, inspiradas y ricas de sentimiento." Marcelino Menéndez Pelayo, "Historia de los Heterodoxos Españoles (Madrid 1880–1882)," in Menéndez Pelayo, *Obras Completas* (Santander: Consejo Superior de Investigaciones Científicas, 1947), 38:309–310.

85. Arturo Farinelli, *Marrano: Storia di un vituperio* (Geneva: Léo S. Olschki, 1925).

86. Yakov Malkiel, *Etymology* (Cambridge: Cambridge University Press, 1993), 78–79.

87. Elaine Marks, *Marrano as Metaphor: The Jewish Presence in French Writing* (New York: Columbia University Press, 1996).

88. Yovel, *The Other Within*.

89. Dan Diner, "Marranische Einschreibungen: Erwägungen zu verborgenen Traditionen bei Hannah Arendt," *Babylon: Beiträge zur jüdischen Gegenwart* 22 (2007): 64. "In analogy with the phenomenon of Iberian late medieval–early modern Jewish convertism, the term 'Marranic' is suggested here for the encoded and concealed Jewish traces in the text. Such an impact can take different forms

and shapes. They can attend to the discursive emblems and figures in the history of Jewish emancipation in the face of its European failure; they can make use of the narrative modes of a constant alternation between the nineteenth and twentieth centuries in order to employ both a teleological and a counter-teleological strategy in the temporal overwriting of one period by another; and they can openly introduce biographical components."

Chapter 1. Skepticism and Irony

1. The archival discovery was first mentioned in an article by Manuel Serrano y Sanz, "Noticias biográficas de Fernando de Rojas, autor de *La Celestina*, y del impresor Juan de Lucena," *Revista de Archivos, Bibliotecas y Museos* 6 (1902): 245–299.

2. On the question of authorship, see the summary of research on the topic by Nicasio Salvador Miguel, "La identidad de Fernando de Rojas," in *La Celestina*, ed. Gonzalo Santonja (Madrid: Sociedad Estatal España Nuevo Milenio, 2001), 71–103.

3. Louis G. Zelson, "*The Celestina* and Its Jewish Authorship," *Jewish Forum* 8 (1930): 459–466. Zelson refers to the article by Manuel Serrano y Sanz, "Noticias biográficas de Fernando de Rojas," 459: "The failure of the Jews, for a time, to assert their rightful claim on Rojas may be explained, though only in part, by the fact that the revelation was made in a learned publication of a rather limited circulation. But as the information has since been restated in a number of studies of the *Celestina* and repeated or referred to in the recent histories of Spanish Literature, it is surprising that the interesting fact has persistently escaped the attention of writers on Jewish subjects."

4. Julio Cejador, "El bachiller Hernando de Rojas verdadero autor de *La Celestina*," *Revista Crítica Hispano-Americana* 2 (1916): 85–86.

5. Thus Fritz Vogelsang in the epilogue to his German translation of *La Celestina*.

6. Stephen Gilman, *La España de Fernando de Rojas: Panorama intelectual y social de "La Celestina"* (Madrid: Taurus, 1978). See also Gilman, "A Generation of Conversos," *Romance Philology* 33 (1979): 87–101.

7. Estrella Cardiel Sanz, "La cuestión judía en *La Celestina*," in *Actas de las jornadas de estudios sefardíes*, ed. Antonio Viudas Camarasa (Cáceres: Universidad de Extremadura, 1981), 151–159; Dwayne E. Carpenter, "A Converso Best-Seller: Celestina and Her Foreign Offspring," in *Crisis and Creativity in the Sephardic World, 1391–1648*, ed. Benjamin R. Gampel (New York: Columbia University Press, 1997), 267–281; Carpenter, "The Sacred in the Profane: Jewish Scriptures and the First Comedy in Hebrew," in *Fernando de Rojas and "Celestina": Approaching the Fifth Centenary*, ed. Ivy A. Corfis and Joseph T. Snow (Madison, Wis.: Hispanic Seminary of Medieval Studies, 1993), 229–236; Alberto M. Forcadas, "'Mira a

Bernardo' y el 'Judaísmo' de *La Celestina*," *Boletín de Filología Española* 46–49 (1973): 27–45; Jean Lemartinel, "Sobre el supuesto judaísmo de 'La Celestina,'" in *Hommage des hispanistes français a Noël Salomon* (Barcelona: Laia, 1979), 509–516; Francisco Márquez Villanueva, "*La Celestina* as Hispano-Semitic Anthropology," *Revue de Littérature Comparée* 61 (1987): 425–456; Régula Rohland de Langbehn, "Calisto, el juez y la cuestión de los conversos," in *Studia Hispanica Medievalia*, ed. L. Teresa Valdivieso and Jorge H. Valdivieso (Buenos Aires: Editorial Ergon, 1988), 2:89–98; Alfonso Vermeylen, "*La Celestina*, objeto de una enconada sospecha de judaísmo," in *Studia Hispanica Medievalia*, ed. Rosa E. Penna and María A. Rosarossa (Buenos Aires: Editorial Ergon, 1995), 3:215–222.

8. Manfred Tietz, "Mittelalter und Spätmittelalter," in *Spanische Literaturgeschichte*, ed. Hans-Jörg Neuschäfer (Stuttgart/Weimar: Metzler, 1997), 65.

9. Marcelino Menéndez Pelayo, *Orígenes de la novella* (Madrid: Bailly-Balliere e Hijos, 1915), 3:295.

10. "Pero quedo uno satisfecho al saber que el autor era judío converso. A un cristiano rancio de la Antigua España dudo que ni siquiera se le hubiera occurido tal fin." Fernando de Rojas, *La Celestina*, ed. Julio Cejador (Madrid: Espasa-Calpe, 1958), 199 n.2.

11. "El autor es un judío converso, que ha derramado en su obra los sentimientos que le indujeron a abandonar la fe de sus mayores, sin adoptar tampoco la patria nativa." Ramiro de Maeztu, *Don Quijote, Don Juan y la Celestina* (Madrid: Visor Libros, 1963), 173.

12. "[Eso recoge] la realidad espiritual de la España de entonces . . . , el ambiente de diferencias, odios e incompatibilidades de esa compleja sociedad de conversos y cristianos viejos." Emilio Orozco Díaz, "*La Celestina*: Hipótesis para una interpretación," *Ínsula* 124 (1957): 10.

13. Julio Rodríguez Puértolas, "El linaje de Calisto," *Hispanófila* 33 (1968): 1–6.

14. See Orozco Díaz, *La Celestina*, 1, 10; see also Fernando Garrido Pallardo, *Los problemas de Calixto y Melibea y el conflict de su autor* (Figueres: Canigó, 1957); and Segundo Serrano Poncela, *El secreto de Melibea y otros ensayos* (Madrid: Taurus, 1959), 7–36.

15. Gregory B. Kaplan, *The Evolution of Converso Literature: The Writings of the Converted Jews of Medieval Spain* (Gainesville: University Press of Florida, 2002), esp. 115–129.

16. Ibid., 115: "The doubt that surrounds the identities of Calisto and Melibea is the essence of Rojas' *converso* allegory. When the two become victims of 'fortune's mutations' (Gilman), the reason for their adversity is as nebulous as their socioreligious conditions. Why are Calisto and Melibea destined to live and die (without making confessions) outside the bounds of contemporary society? It may be because Rojas is condemning the type of illicit affair in which they engage, or it may be because one or both characters represent a figure that has

been relegated to a marginal existence. The fact that the reader is unsure about Calisto and Melibea does not necessarily make them *conversos*. But it does make them suspect individuals, and this, if nothing else, reflects the contemporary mistrust among individuals that could result in persecution by the Inquisition, perhaps through an accusation brought by a friend or by one family member against another. In being a *converso* lament, *Celestina*, like Cárcel and 'Diálogo,' reveals how *conversos* could be treated during the last decades of the fifteenth century."

17. Marcel Bataillon, *La Célestine selon Fernando de Rojas* (Paris: M. Didier, 1961), 168.

18. These and all subsequent quotations from the text are taken from the edition by Dorothy S. Severin, *La Celestina* (Madrid: Cátedra, 2007); subsequent references to this edition will be cited parenthetically in the text. All English translations are taken from Peter Bush's 2009 Penguin edition: "Some tut-tut, that there is no wit, that the story is too much of a muchness, that the detail is wasted, that lots more stories could have been spun. Others wax fulsome about the jokes and common adages, praising them effusively, but ignore what makes them relevant and useful. Those who find everything amusing discount the heart of the story and tell it their way, select what they think is important, laugh at what is funny, and memorise the sayings and dicta of philosophers in order to repeat them at an opportune moment. So when ten people get together to listen to this comedy being read, and all have such differing views, as is usually the case, who will deny there won't be arguments over something that can be interpreted so differently? For even the printers have added their points, have put explanations or summaries at the beginning of each act, briefly stating what happens: something quite unnecessary if one considers how the ancient writers got by without them" (213–214).

19. See José Faur, *In the Shadow of History: Jews and Conversos at the Dawn of Modernity* (Albany, N.Y.: SUNY Press, 1992), 72: "A group of ten people has no special significance in Spanish; accordingly, it will pass unnoticed. For Jews, however, a group of ten people constitutes a *minyan*, or a minimum forum required for religious service and the reading of the Tora. For a converso 'a group of ten people' evokes the Jewish *minyan*. Indeed, Rojas seems to be alluding to a ritual reading."

20. "You, who love, follow this example, / this fine armour to defend yourselves, / turn your reins, don't ruin yourselves. / Praise God by visiting his temple, / watch your step, don't court disrepute, / don't be accused by the living or dead. / You live in sin and in life lie buried, / I feel great sadness you cannot dispute" (Bush, 205–206).

21. "[CALISTO:] 'The difference between the fire in your song and the one burning me is as great as the gap between appearance and reality, life and artifice, a shadow and its source. What's more, if the fire of purgatory is anything like this, I'd prefer my spirit to follow those of brute animals than choose *that* path on my way to glory with the saints.'

[SEMPRONIO:] 'It was half right. He is mad and a heretic into the bargain,' mumbled Sempronio.

[CALISTO:] 'Didn't I tell you to speak up when you've got something on your mind?'

[SEMPRONIO:] 'I said God would never wish such a thing on you, and that what you just said is a kind of heresy.'

[CALISTO:] 'Why?'

[SEMPRONIO:] 'Because what you say goes against the Christian religion.'

[CALISTO:] 'And so what?'

[SEMPRONIO:] 'Aren't you a Christian?'

[CALISTO:] 'Me? No, I'm a Melibean. I worship Melibea, I believe in Melibea and I adore Melibea'" (Bush, 4).

22. Otis H. Green, "Fernando de Rojas, Converso and Hidalgo," *Hispanic Review* 15 (1947): 384–387.

23. "When asking what the performative contradiction at the end of *Phaidros* may actually mean beyond what was explicitly said, thus when reading it ironically, and such a reading is justified by the obvious non-sense of a non-ironic one, then a criticism of literality in a literary staging of a verbal conversation may aim at making the staging transparent by the staging itself, or put differently: at having the reader recognize that the performative character of a verbal conversation cannot be captured in writing, meaning between author and reader. On the other hand, the transmission of performance is only possible in writing, however." Klaus W. Hempfer, "Lektüren von Dialogen," in *Möglichkeiten des Dialogs: Struktur und Funktion einer literarischen Gattung zwischen Mittelalter und Renaissance in Italien*, ed. Klaus W. Hempfer (Stuttgart: Steiner, 2002), 8.

24. "[Sempronio:] 'Oh, almighty God, how impenetrable your mysteries! What power you gave love to put a lover in such a spin. You shun half measures and he's like a lover spurned. They all go too far and break free; like fighting bulls spiked in the neck and hurling nimbly over every barrier. You are a god to drive a man to forsake his mother and father for a woman and, like Calisto, not just them, but Him and His law. So, what's the big surprise: haven't sages, saints and prophets all abandoned You for the sake of love?'

[CALISTO: 'Sempronio!'

[SEMPRONIO:] 'Master.'

[CALISTO:] 'Don't leave me.'

[SEMPRONIO:] 'Ah, he's changed his tune'" (Bush, 5).

25. The biblical quotations are based on the New King James Version.

26. "Ironisch zu sein, hei ßt also, Einstellungen oder Gefühle auszudrücken, die man nicht hat, und gleichzeitig zu verstehen zu geben, daß man sie nicht hat." Ernst Lapp, *Linguistik der Ironie*, 2nd ed. (Tübingen: Narr, 1997), 141.

27. See especially Joachim Küpper, "Mittelalterlich kosmische Ordnung und rinascimentales Bewußtsein von Kontingenz: Fernando de Rojas' *Celestina* als

Inszenierung sinnfremder Faktizität (mit Bemerkungen zu Boccaccio, Petrarca, Machiavelli und Montaigne)," in *Kontingenz*, ed. Gerhart von Graevenitz and Odo Marquard (Munich: Wilhelm Fink Verlag, 1998), 173–223.

28. "[CALISTO:] 'What are you slandering me for now?'

[SEMPRONIO:] 'For making man's dignity depend on the imperfections of a weak woman.'

[CALISTO:] 'A woman? Don't insult her. She's God, God, I tell you!'

[SEMPRONIO:] 'You really think so? You must be joking?'

[CALISTO:] 'Joking? I believe she is God and I proclaim that she *is* God, and I don't believe another sovereign exists in heaven despite the fact she dwells among us.'

[SEMPRONIO:] 'Did you ever hear such blasphemy or see such blindness?' Sempronio tittered.

[CALISTO:] 'What are you laughing at now?'

[SEMPRONIO:] 'I laughed because I don't think a worse sin was ever invented in Sodom.'

[CALISTO:] 'What do you mean?'

[SEMPRONIO:] 'They were fond of abominable acts with strange angels, but you've got someone you call "God" in mind.'

[CALISTO:] 'Blast you. You've made me laugh, and that wasn't what *I* had in mind'" (Bush, 5–6).

29. "[SEMPRONIO:] 'Listen to Solomon when he says women and wine make men renege. Take advice from Seneca and read what a low opinion he has of them. Listen to Aristotle; think Bernardo. Gentiles, Jews, Christians and Moors all agree on this at least.'" (Bush, 6–7). The reference to Solomon in Sempronio's speech might be the result of a confusion of Ecclesiasticus with Ecclesiastes. The book of Sirach is also known under the title "Ecclesiasticus" in the Vulgate; the book of Kohelet / Preacher Solomon is titled "Liber Ecclesiastes."

30. "[Pármeno:] 'She . . . used these girls to make contact with women whose status confined them indoors . . . and on such holy occasions as the stations of the cross, night-time processions, dawn or midnight masses, and other special times, I saw many of these high-class ladies enter her house veiled. Hot on their heels came men barefoot and contrite, muffled up, though quick to unbutton and weep for their sins. You can't imagine the tricks she got up to! . . . She worked so hard she never missed mass or vespers or left unvisited a monastery or convent, and that's where she struck it rich and set up deals and dates'" (Bush, 15–16).

31. "[Pármeno:] 'I think cheerful poverty is the only honest policy. What's more, the poor aren't people who've got nothing but those who aspire to a lot. You can keep on that tack, but I'm not going to follow your advice. I want to live without backbiting: tough times but no fear, sleep without nasty shocks, insults I can counter, muscle that can't be sapped and hard knocks I can stand.'

[CELESTINA:] 'My son, it's not for nothing that people say wisdom comes with old age. You are very, very green'" (Bush, 25).

32. "[PÁRMENO:] 'Celestina, I really worry about following the wrong advice.'

[CELESTINA:] 'Still in the same vein? I can only repeat what Solomon said: "He who ignores good advice will trip up badly and never recover." So bye-bye, Pármeno, you've heard my last word on all this.'

And Pármeno pondered silently yet again: 'The old girl's furious with me. I have my doubts about the advice she gave me. It's wrong not to believe and wrong to believe everything. It would be only human to trust her when she's promising a future full of profit and pleasure. They say a man should believe his elders. What's she telling me to do? To make peace with Sempronio? You should never say no to peace. Blessèd [sic!] are the meek, because they shall be called the children of God. You shouldn't run away from love or do your brothers down, a few spurn their own self-interest. I'll go along with her and smile in her direction'" (Bush, 27).

33. "[CELESTINA:] 'Shut up, you fool, Elicia, let him be. We've got other important matters on our plate. Is the house empty at last? Did that lass go who was waiting for the minister?'

[ELICIA:] 'And another came and went.'

[CELESTINA:] 'And not in vain, I hope.'

[Elicia:] 'No, God forbid, she came late, but "the iron was still hot," as they say'" (Bush, 41).

34. "[MELIBEA:] 'Dear Celestina, I'm delighted to see you and chat with you again. You talk so funnily. Here's your money. God go with you because you look as if you've not eaten today.'

[CELESTINA:] 'Oh my angel face, precious pearl, dulcet tongue! I too am overjoyed to hear you speak, and you know what God said against the tempter from hell, that we can't live on bread alone? It's so true, eating alone can't sustain us'" (Bush, 50–51).

35. "[MELIBEA:] 'My good woman, I can understand nothing if you won't speak plainly. You both anger me and move me to pity. I can't give a suitable response based on the little you've revealed. Am I blessed because some soul needs a word from me to save his soul? Doing good is to be like God and does even more good when the person concerned deserves help. He who can cure the sick, and doesn't, ushers in death, so don't be afraid or embarrassed and make your request.'

[CELESTINA:] 'Lady, any fear I had vanished when I gazed on your beauty because I cannot believe God painted to no avail features that are more perfect than any other woman's, more gracious and beautiful, a fount of virtue, charity and compassion, furnishing all manner of gifts and bounties the way you do'" (Bush, 52).

36. "[CELESTINA:] 'Devil that I invoked, you granted me all I asked for! I am in your debt. Your power softened that cruel female and gave me all the time in the world to say what I wanted to, in her mother's absence. Dear old Celly! Aren't you happy? You know the battle is half won when you get off to a good start. Snake oil! White thread! How well you both worked for me! If you hadn't, I'd have broken all my ties—present and future—with the nether world and stopped believing in magic herbs, stones and spells! Rejoice, old girl, you'll make more from this job than from mending a dozen maidenheads'" (Bush, 60).

37. "[CELESTINA:] 'Who was a balm and boon to me, if it wasn't your mother, who was like a sister and a second shadow? She was so funny and easy-going, so straight and courageous! She was never scared or worried when wandering from cemetery to cemetery at midnight looking for materials for our trade, as if it were broad daylight. She'd visit the graves of Christians, Moors and Jews alike. She'd inspect by day and finish the job by night. In that way she enjoyed the dark of night as you enjoy the light of day. She said night was a sinner's cloak. . . . Well, your mother was the best in our line, if there ever was, and was known and loved as such by all and sundry: gentlemen or priests, married couples, the old, young or very young" (Bush, 80–81).

38. "[CELESTINA:] 'My son, that wasn't the only time. They seized your mother four times when your mother lived by herself. The first time they accused her of being a witch, because they'd caught her at night collecting earth by a crossroads by candlelight, and they put her in the stocks to be pilloried in the town square for half a day, with a painted cone on her head. She didn't mind. She knew we must suffer in this life to sustain our livelihood and reputation. . . . Her kind that knows what they're doing is more prone to get caught out. I suppose you've heard about that clever Virgil. They put him in a basket and hung him from a tower with all Rome watching. It didn't mean he was no longer respected or that the good name of Virgil was soiled. . . . The priest knew this better than anyone when he came to console her and said that the Holy Scriptures say: "Blessed are those persecuted by the law for they shall possess the kingdom of heaven." You must suffer a lot in this world to enjoy the glories in the next, and she suffered even more, so everyone said, because they used lying witnesses and terrible tortures, and made her confess to being what she wasn't. It was all quite unwarranted. But she reacted energetically, and as her heart was used to making the best of a bad situation, she never flinched. I heard her say a thousand times: "If I broke my foot, it was only for my own good, because now I'm better known than I was before." So your mother experienced all this down here, and, if it's true what the good priest said, then God must be rewarding her well up there. And this is my consolation. And now you be a real friend to me as she was and try to be good, because you've got someone to live up to'" (Bush, 82–83).

39. See Domenico Comparetti, *Virgilio nel Medio Evo* (Florence, 1872), and the reprint of the English translation by E. F. M. Benecke titled *Vergil in the Middle*

Ages (1895), published with an introduction by Jan M. Ziolkowski by Princeton University Press in 1997.

40. "[CALISTO:] 'I believe him now. They're ringing for mass. Get me my clothes. I'll go to Mary Magdalene and pray for God to guide Celestina and remind Melibea to remedy my heart or I'll soon be putting an end to my days'" (Bush, 98).

41. "[SEMPRONIO:] 'Master, you're in such a state and giving everybody so much cause for concern. For God's sake, try to stop the tongues wagging: spending time in church is the quickest way to get a reputation as a hypocrite. People will say you're pandering to the saints. If you've a problem, deal with it at home'" (Bush, 123).

42. "[CALISTO:] 'Cruel judge, how poorly you repaid the bread you ate from my father's table! . . . Who'd have thought you'd destroy me! Nobody is more dangerous than the surprise enemy. . . . You're the public criminal and killed men whose crimes were private. You should know private crime is less evil than public crime, and less dangerous, according to the laws of Athens, that weren't written in blood. They show in fact that it's lesser failing to sentence bandits than to punish the innocent. It's dangerous to pursue a just cause with an unjust judge! . . . Who am I talking to? Am I in my right mind? . . . Can't you see the culprit's not here? Who are you speaking to? Come to your senses. That absent fellow may be in the right. Hear both sides before you deliver your judgment. Don't you know that when carrying justice out you must forget friendship, family or servants? Don't you know the law should be the same for everyone? Look at Romulus, founder of Rome, who killed his own brother because he ignored what the law said'" (Bush, 154–155).

43. "[AREUSA:] 'You take as you find, and it's what you do that gives you pedigree. We're all children of Adam and Eve, after all. We should try to be good in ourselves and not base our virtue on the nobility of our forbears'" (Bush, 105).

44. "[PLEBERIO:] 'Life is so full of anguish, so beset by misery! World, oh world! So many have said so much about you, have questioned your great qualities, and compared you to a variety of things on mere hearsay. After the sad blow I have just been dealt, I will tell it all, as it is, as someone who bought and sold in your fairground, but never prospered. I am someone who has kept silent till now about your fraudulence so as not to inflame your ire and earn your hatred, so you didn't wither before time the flower that today you plucked with all your might. Now I am fearless, a man with nothing to lose, a man who finds your company irksome, like a poor wayfarer who walks and sings at the top of his voice, unafraid of cruel brigands. When I was young and tender, I thought you and your acts were ruled by some kind of order. Now I have seen the pros and the cons of your fair-trading, I think you are a web of deceit, a wilderness, a home to ferocious beasts, a game played by cheats and tricksters, a treacherous marsh, a realm of thorns, a craggy peak, stony ground, a meadow full of serpents,

a flowering orchard without fruit, a fount of tribulation, a river of tears, a sea of misery, toil without profit, sweet poison, vain hopes, fake cheer and true sorrow'" (Bush, 194–195).

45. "[PLEBERIO:] 'The wood that fuels your flames are [*sic*] the souls and lives of human beings, and they are many, I hardly know where to start. Christians, Gentils and Jews, all receive the same payment for serving you well. What can you tell me about Macías in our day, the way his love ended, and the way you led him to his sad demise? What did Paris do for you? Or Helen? Or Clytemnestra? Or Aegisthus? The whole world knows what happened to them. And how did you repay Sappho, Ariadne, or Leander? You couldn't even leave David and Solomon well alone. Because he was a friend of yours, Samson paid the price he deserved to pay because he trusted the person you told him to trust. I will keep my silence on the many others because my own sorrow is enough to tell' (Bush, 197–198).

46. "[PLEBERIO:] 'I reproach the world for spawning me. If it hadn't given me life, I wouldn't have fathered Melibea. If she had never been born, I wouldn't have loved her. If I hadn't loved, my last years wouldn't be sad and desolate. My good wife! My daughter broken asunder! Why didn't you let me stop you from dying? Why didn't you take pity on your dear, beloved mother? Why were you so cruel towards your dear old father? Why did you leave me when I should have left you? Why did you leave me to sorrow? Why did you leave me sad and alone in this valley of tears?'" (Bush, 198).

Chapter 2. An Aesthetics of Love

1. Benzion Netanyahu has written a book on the father's life and work, *Don Isaac Abravanel: Statesman and Philosopher* (Philadelphia: Jewish Publication Society of America, 1953).

2. Cecil Roth, introduction to *The Philosophy of Love (Dialoghi d'amore)* by Leone Ebreo, trans. F. Friedeberg-Seeley and Jean H. Barnes (London: Soncino Press, 1937), x.

3. Bernhard Zimmels, *Leo Hebreaeus, ein jüdischer Philosoph der Renaissance: Sein Leben, seine Werke und seine Lehren* (Breslau, 1886).

4. Barbara Garvin, "The Language of Leone Ebreo's *Dialoghi d'amore*," *Italia* 13–15 (2001): 181–210.

5. Shoshanna Gershenzon, "The Circle Metaphor in Leone Ebreo's *Dialoghi d'amore*," *Daat* 29 (1992): 5–17; Moshe Idel, "The Sources of the Circle Images in the *Dialoghi d'amore*," *Iyyun* 28 (1978): 156–166 (Hebr.).

6. David B. Ruderman, "Italian Renaissance and Jewish Thought," in *Renaissance Humanism: Foundations, Forms, and Legacy*, ed. Albert Rabil, Jr. (Philadelphia: University of Pennsylvania Press, 1988), 1:382–433; Paul O. Kristeller, "Jewish Contributions to Italian Renaissance Culture," *Italia* 4, no. 1 (1985): 7–20; Sergius Kodera, *Filone und Sofia in Leone Ebreos "Dialoghi d'amore": Platonische*

Liebesphilosophie der Renaissance und Judentum (Frankfurt a.M.: Peter Lang, 1995); Aaron W. Hughes, "Transforming the Maimonidean Imagination: Aesthetics in the Renaissance Thought of Judah Abravanel," *Harvard Theological Review* 97 (2004): 461–484; Giuseppe Veltri, "Leone Ebreo's Concept of Jewish Philosophy," in *Renaissance Philosophy in Jewish Garb: Foundations and Challenges in Judaism on the Eve of Modernity*, ed. Giuseppe Veltri (Leiden/Boston: Brill, 2009), 60–72.

7. Robert Bonfil, "The Historian's Perception of the Jews in the Italian Renaissance: Towards a Reappraisal," *Revue des Études Juives* 143 (1984): 59–82.

8. Heinz Pflaum [Hiram Peri], *Die Idee der Liebe: Leone Ebreo—Zwei Abhandlungen zur Geschichte der Philosophie in der Renaissance* (Tübingen: J. C. B. Mohr, 1926).

9. Ibid., 107.

10. This and all subsequent quotations in Italian are from the 2008 edition published by Editori Laterza (Rome/Bari) and edited by Delfina Giovannozzi; subsequent references to this edition will be cited parenthetically in the text. The English translations are taken from Leone Ebreo, *Dialogues of Love*, ed. Rossella Pescatori, trans. Damian Bacich and Rossella Pescatori (Toronto: University of Toronto Press, 2009): "Philo: Knowing you, Sophia, provokes in me love and desire" (Pescatori, 28).

11. Jacob Guttmann, *Die Philosophie des Salomon Ibn Gabirol* (Göttingen, 1889; repr., Hildesheim: Georg Holms Verlag, 1979), 52.

12. "Sophia: Since we have touched on this point, I would like to know how this human beatitude occurs.

Philo: There have been different opinions on the topic of happiness. Many have judged it to lie in utility and possession of the goods of fortune, and abundance thereof while life lasts. But this opinion is manifestly false. In fact, such material goods are so only in virtue of the spiritual good upon which they depend; and happiness must consist of the most excellent. All else is a means to such happiness, but itself serves no further goal, being the goal of all. Even more, such material goods rely on the power of Fortune, while happiness must only rely on the power of human beings. Some others held a different opinion; they said that beatitude consists in pleasure. . . . We said before that the end of the pleasure [*sic*] is what is honest, and happiness is not for any other goal, but is itself the final cause of all things. Therefore—without a doubt—happiness is in honest things and in the actions and faculties of the intellectual soul, which are the most excellent, and the goal of the other human faculties. Through these actions and faculties, Man is Man and more excellent than all other creatures" (Pescatori, 51–52).

13. "[H]appiness does not consist in the faculty of knowing, but in the act of knowing" (Pescatori, 56).

14. "Among the true and necessary propositions there is one which says that happiness consists in the ultimate activity of the soul as its true end. The other is that happiness consists in the actualization of the most noble and spiritual potential of the soul, and that is the intellectual one" (Pescatori, 59–60).

15. "Philo: Perfect and true love, such as I feel for you, is the father of desire and son of reason; it was generated in me by right cognitive reason. Knowing you to possess virtue, intelligence, and grace, equally admirable and wondrously attractive, my will desired your person, which reason rightly judged to be noble, excellent, and worthy of love in every thing" (Pescatori, 65–66).

16. "Philo: [L]ove fall[s] into three types: natural, sensuous, and rational-voluntary.

Sophia: Explain to me these three.

Philo: What can be found in the non-sentient bodies—such as the elements . . . (which are made of insensible compound, like metals and certain stones, and also plants, herbs, or trees) is natural knowledge, appetite, or love. All of these have a natural cognition of their aim and natural inclination to it. . . . This is called inclination, and it truly is appetite and natural love. This sensitive knowledge and appetite, or sensuous love, is what we find in irrational animals; they follow what is good for them, and they avoid what is disadvantageous. . . . Rational and voluntary knowledge and love are only in humans, because they come from and are managed by reason" (Pescatori, 80–81).

17. "Philo: The ancient poets, implied not only one, but many intentions in their poems, and these intentions are called 'senses.' First they placed the literal sense, as a kind of exterior rind, the story of some people and their noteworthy and memorable deeds. Within this same fiction they place, like an inner rind nearer to the core, the moral sense, which is useful to the active life of human beings, in approving virtuous acts and condemning vices. Beyond this, beneath those same words they signify some true knowledge of natural, celestial, astrological, or theological things, and sometimes these two or even all three scientific senses are included in the fable, like the kernels of the fruit beneath its rind. And these core senses are called 'allegorical'" (Pescatori, 106).

18. "Ganz im Geiste der Gabirol'schen Lehre ist die Ausführung über die Liebe, welche die gesammte Schöpfung, von oben nach unten, wie von unten nach oben durchdringend, alle Wesen, auch die unbelebten, dazu treibt, eine höhere Stufe des Seins zu erstreben und sich mit dem Vollkommeneren zu vereinigen. . . . So prägt auch die unendliche Schönheit Gottes nicht nach ihrem eigenen Wesen in den Geistern sich aus, sondern je nach dem Maasse der Empfänglichkeit, das diese ihr entgegenbringen. . . . Je unmittelbarer die göttliche Schönheit auf ein Wesen einwirkt, desto reiner prägt sie in demselben sich aus. . . . Um die höchste Schönheit, welche der Urquell alles Schönen ist, zu erkennen, muss der Mensch . . . sich der irdischen Leidenschaften entledigen. . . . Ist der Mensch aber mit der höchsten Schönheit erst einmal in Verbindung getreten, dann wird er von einer so mächtigen Liebe zu ihr erfasst, dass er gern allem anderen entsagt, um nur sie zu lieben, sich ganz mit ihr zu einen, und, durch die Liebe zum Schönen selber schön geworden, der höchsten Seligkeit theilhaftig zu werden." Guttmann, *Die Philosophie des Salomon Ibn Gabirol*, 54.

19. "Philo: The circle of all things is that which gradually begins from their first origin, and passing successively through each thing in turn, returns to its first origin as to its ultimate end, thus containing every degree of thing in its circular form, so that the point which is the beginning also comes to be the end. This circle has two halves, the first from the beginning to the point most distant from it, the mid-point, and the second from this mid-point to the beginning again" (Pescatori, 346–347).

20. See also Hughes, *Transforming the Maimonidean Imagination*, 465: "Although in many ways the thought of Judah Abravanel represents a continuation of medieval Jewish philosophy, a number of features mark his break with that tradition. First, the medieval philosophical tradition tended to place rhetoric among the lower forms of logic, such as those associated with Aristotle's *Rhetoric* or *Poetics*, which the medieval tradition regarded as part of Aristotle's *Organon*. Judah, however, elevates rhetoric to a position among the higher sciences, such as cosmology and epistemology. The beautiful and pleasing speech of the Torah is no longer a concession that Moses had to make for the masses; it is now part and parcel of the divine fabric. The goal of the philosopher/aesthete/artist is to imitate this to the best of his ability."

21. Klaus W. Hempfer, "Probleme traditioneller Bestimmungen des Renaissancebegriffs und die epistemologische 'Wende,'" in *Renaissance: Diskursstrukturen und epistemologische Voraussetzungen*, ed. Klaus W. Hempfer (Stuttgart: Steiner, 1993), 36.

22. Ibid., 39.

23. Klaus W. Hempfer, "Lektüren von Dialogen," in *Möglichkeiten des Dialogs: Struktur und Funktion einer literarischen Gattung zwischen Mittelalter und Renaissance in Italien,* ed. Klaus W. Hempfer (Stuttgart: Steiner, 2002), 1–38.

24. English translation by the author, following the German version by Georg Bossong, ed., *Das Wunder von al-Andalus: Die schönsten Gedichte aus dem Maurischen Spanien*, translated from Arabic and Hebrew and annotated, afterword by Edward Said (Munich: C. H. Beck Verlag, 2005), 207.

25. Ibid., 202.

26. "Because of this David says, 'By your light we see light,' and the prophet, 'Turn us unto you, O Lord, and we shall be turned,' and another says: 'Turn me, and I shall be turned; because you are the Lord my God.' For if God were to abandon us we could never return to Him of our own accord. Solomon, in his *Song of Songs*, in the name of the intellectual soul enamoured of divine Beauty, has expressed this even more plainly, saying, 'Draw me, we will run after you: the king had brought me unto his chambers: we will be glad and rejoice in you, we will remember your loves more than wine: the upright love you.' See how the intellectual soul first prays that it may be drawn in by the love of the Godhead, and then it will run swiftly in pursuit, by virtue of the love that burns within it. And the soul says that, being placed by the hand of God within His chamber, which is united by

divine grace to the very heart of the divine Beauty and majesty, it will then attain the supreme pleasure, the end of which is its love for God. Moreover, the intellectual soul will remember His love more than wine, which is the divine love that will always be present for it, remembered in the mind, unlike the love of worldly things of no greater worth than the love of wine, which intoxicates a man and leads him away from the right paths of mind. Therefore, he finishes, 'the upright love you,' which means 'You are not loved because your spirit is not pure—case of carnal love—but the upright of the soul is what loves you.' See how the intellect first speaks in the singular, saying, 'the king had brought me unto his chambers,' and again to the plural, 'we will be glad and rejoice in you, we will remember your love more than wine.' This is to show that not only the intellectual part of man, but also the created universe together with all its parts, rejoices and is made glad in union with Him. Therefore, it is said, in the plural, 'the upright love you,' because all incline to divine love through their intellectual part" (Pescatori, 354).

Chapter 3. Inquisition and Conversion

1. The printed edition of *Lazarillo*, which was published in 1554 in Medina del Campo, has been known for about fifteen years. It was found in a bricked-up den in a house in Barcarotta (Extremadura), together with nine other books and one manuscript. All ten of the volumes found in Barcarotta were on the Index. Thanks to the Biblioteca de Extremadura, they are available digitally as well: http://194.179.111.13:8080/biex/static/bb.action. On this topic, see Fernando Serrano Mangas, *El secreto de los Peñaranda: El universo judeo-converso de la Biblioteca de Barcarrota (siglos XVI y XVII)* (Huelva: Universidad de Huelva, 2004); on the Lazarillo de Barcarrota, see especially Aldo Ruffinatto, *Las dos caras del Lazarillo: Texto y mensaje* (Madrid: Editorial Castalia, 2000); see also Rosa Navarro, *Alfonso de Valdés, autor del "Lazarillo de Tormes"* (Madrid: Gredos, 2003), who interpreted the copy found in Barcarotta as evidence for her thesis on the work's authorship. An earlier version of this chapter has been published in the journal *Romanistisches Jahrbuch*: Susanne Zepp, "Ironie, Inquisition und Konversion: Parodien von Inklusionsdispositiven im *Lazarillo de Tormes*," *Romanistisches Jahrbuch* 56 (2005): 368–392.

2. Ilse Nolting-Hauff, "*La Vida de Lazarillo de Tormes* und die erasmische Satire," in *Interpretation: Das Paradigma der europäischen Renaissance-Literatur (Festschrift für Alfred Noyer-Weidner zum 60. Geburtstag)*, ed. Klaus W. Hempfer and Gerhard Regn (Wiesbaden: Steiner, 1983), 83–104.

3. "The autobiographical style is inseparable from the very attempt to bring to light a subject hitherto neglected or nonexistent. The person of the author (of Jewish descent) withdrew so much that he did not even want to reveal his name. The autobiographical dimension of the *Lazarillo* is integral to its anonymity." Américo Castro, "*El Lazarillo de Tormes*," in *Hacia Cervantes*, ed. Américo Castro (Madrid: Taurus, 1957), 137. See also Marcel Bataillon, *Erasmo y España* (Mexico

City / Buenos Aires: Fondo de Cultura Económica, 1966), who repeatedly refers to Castro's thesis in his studies of the picaresque novel, for example, in his formulation of the "posible paternidad de un converso" (the possible paternity of a *converso*; 612 n.5). Manuel Ferrer-Chivite again supported the thesis of an obvious affiliation of *Lazarillo*'s anonymous author with great vehemence in 1984: "Converso como debió ser, repito—y no soy el único, por supuesto, que le supone esa condición—, no nos debemos llamar al engaño por el diferente énfasis que adscribe a los varios rasgos de su personaje" (The author had to be a *converso*, I repeat—and of course I am not the only one who assumes this condition—, and we must not be deceived by the varying degree of emphasis with which he ascribes different sides of his personality either). "Sustratos conversos en la creación de *Lázaro de Tormes*," *Nueva Revista de Filología Hispánica* 33 (1984): 378. Additional authors who argued accordingly include Claudio Guillén, introduction to *Lazarillo de Tormes* (New York: Dell, 1966); Fernando Lázaro Carreter, *"El Lazarillo de Tormes" en la picaresca* (Barcelona: Ediciones Ariel, 1972), 185; and Francisco Rico, "Problemas del *Lazarillo*," *Boletin de la Real Academia Española* 46 (1966): 290.

4. Stephen Gilman, "The Death of Lazarillo de Tormes," *Publications of the Modern Language Association* 81 (1966): 149–166, esp. 155 n.27. In his essay "A Generation of Conversos" (*Romance Philology* 33 [1979]: 87–101), Gilman extends this perspective to all of early modern Spanish literature. See also Aron David Kossoff, "La picaresca clásica: El converso teológico y social," *La Torre: Revista de la Universidad de Puerto Rico* 1 (1987): 445–460; Victoriano Roncero López, "Lazarillo, Guzmán, and Buffoon Literature," *Modern Language Notes* 116 (2001): 235–249; Giancarlo Maiorino, *At the Margins of the Renaissance: "Lazarillo de Tormes" and the Picaresque Art of Survival* (University Park: Penn State University Press, 2003); Stanislav Zimic, *Apuntes sobre la estructura paródica y satírica del "Lazarillo de Tormes"* (Madrid / Frankfurt a.M.: Iberoamericana, 2000); Augustin Redondo, ed., *Travaux sur le "Lazarillo de Tormes"* (Paris: Éditions Hispaniques, 1993); Brian Dutton, "Unas notas sobre *Lazarillo de Tormes*," in *Busquemos otros montes y otros ríos: Estudios dedicados a Elias L. Rivers*, ed. Brian Dutton and Victoriano Roncero López (Madrid: Editorial Castalia, 1992), 113–126; and Robert Weimann, *Realismus in der Renaissance: Aneignung der Welt in der erzählenden Prosa* (Berlin/Weimar: Aufbau-Verlag, 1977), 97.

5. See the above-cited article "*La Vida de Lazarillo de Tormes* und die erasmische Satire" by Nolting-Hauff, who also points out the long tradition of this interpretation: "The assumption that *Lazarillo de Tormes* originated in the circles of Spanish Erasmism . . . was first formulated by Alfred Morel-Fatio. . . . This topic will certainly not disappear from the discussion anytime soon, since it is closely connected to other perennials in the study of *Lazarillo*, namely the question of its authorship and of the model or models with regard to its genre" (83). See also Ann Wiltrout, "The *Lazarillo de Tormes* and Erasmus' *Opulentia sordida*,"

Romanische Forschungen 81 (1969): 550–564; and Thomas Hanrahan, "*Lazarillo de Tormes*: Erasmian Satire or Protestant Reform?," *Hispania* 66 (1983): 333–339; and for the Spanish context especially, Francisco Márquez Villanueva, "La actitud spiritual del *Lazarillo de Tormes*," in *Espiritualidad y literatura en el siglo XVI*, ed. Francisco Márquez Villanueva (Madrid: Alfaguara, 1968), 67–137. Among other things, Bataillon's objections in *Erasmo y España* (esp. 609–611), in which he excludes the actual impetus of Erasmistic criticism for *Lazarillo*, refer to this essay.

6. Matthias Bauer, *Der Schelmenroman* (Stuttgart/Weimar: Metzler, 1994), 34.

7. See Antonio Rey Hazas, *La novela picaresca* (Madrid: Servicio de Publicaciones de la Universidad de Málaga, 1990), 64–65.

8. Bernhard König, "*Lazarillo de Tormes*," in *Der spanische Roman*, ed. Volker Roloff and Harald Wentzlaff-Eggebert (Stuttgart/Weimar: Cornelsen Verlag, 1995), 41. In his commendable study of the religious references in *Lazarillo*, Victor de la Concha mentions that God's name as "Dios" is mentioned sixty-six times in the novel. Additionally, there are fifteen mentions as "Señor," an allusion to "Señor Dios," and one instance of the formulation "Su Majestad." Victor de la Concha, "La intención religiosa del *Lazarillo*," *Revista de Filología Española* 55 (1972): 243–277.

9. Hans Robert Jauss, "Ursprung und Bedeutung der Ich-Form im *Lazarillo de Tormes*," *Romanistisches Jahrbuch* 8 (1957): 299.

10. All quotations are taken from Francisco Rico's edition, *La vida de Lazarillo de Tormes y de sus fortunas y adversidades* (Madrid: Cátedra, 1987); subsequent references to this edition will be cited parenthetically in the text. All English translations are from the translation by Sir Clements Markham (*The Life of Lazarillo de Tormes: His Fortunes and Adversities* [London, 1908; repr., Digireads.com, 2009]): "I had escaped from the thunder to fall under the lightning. For compared with this priest, the blind man was an Alexander the Great. I will say no more than that all the avarice in the world was combined in this man, but I know not whether it was naturally born in him or whether it was put on with the priestly habit" (Markham, 31).

11. The last supper is described in the following Gospels: Matthew 26:17–30, Mark 14:12–26, and Luke 22:7–20; see also 1 Corinthians 11:23–26. Here, Matthew 26:26–29: "Cenantibus autem eis, accepit Iesus panem et benedixit ac fregit deditque discipulis et ait: 'Accipite et comedite: hoc est corpus meum.' Et accipiens calicem gratias egit et dedit illis dicens: 'Bibite ex hoc omnes: hic est enim sanguis meus novi testamenti, qui promultis effunditur in remissionem peccatorum.' Dico autem vobis: Non bibam amodo de hoc genimine vitis usque in diem illum, cum illud bibam vobiscum novum in regno Patris mei." *Biblia sacra* iuxta vulgatam versionem, ed. Robert Weber and Bonifatius Fischer, 4th ed. (Stuttgart: Dt. Bibelges., 1994).

12. "I saw myself sinking down into the silent tomb. If God and my own intelligence had not enabled me to avail myself of ingenious tricks, there would have been no remedy for me" (Markham, 33).

13. "Look here, boy! Priests have to be very frugal in eating and drinking, and for this reason I do not feed like other people" (Markham, 33).

14. "But he lied shamefully. For at meetings and funerals where we had to say prayers and responses, and where he could get food at the expense of others, he ate like a wolf and drank more than a proposer of toasts" (Markham, 33).

15. "One day when my wretched master was out, a locksmith came to the door by chance. I thought that he was an angel sent to me by the hand of God, in the dress of a workman" (Markham, 35).

16. "I beheld the Lord's gift in the form of bread" (Markham, 35). On this topic, see Joseph V. Ricapito, "'Cara de Dios': Ensayo de rectificacion," *Bulletin of Hispanic Studies* 50 (1973): 142–146.

17. See also Anson C. Piper, "The 'Breadly Paradise' of *Lazarillo de Tormes*," *Hispania* 44 (1961): 269–271.

18. "I opened the chest as some consolation, and when I saw the bread I began to worship it, giving it a thousand kisses" (Markham, 36).

19. "What happened in the next three days I know not, for I was in the belly of the whale" (Markham, 45).

20. Robert Sitler, "The Presence of Jesus Christ in *Lazarillo de Tormes*," *Dactylus* 12 (1993): 85–97; Domingo Ynduráin, "El renacimiento de Lázaro," *Hispania* 75 (1992): 474–483.

21. Nolting-Hauff, "*La Vida de Lazarillo de Tormes* und die erasmische Satire," 85.

22. For an extensive study of this specific feature of the novel, see Manuel J. Asensio, "La intención religiosa del *Lazarillo de Tormes* y Juan de Valdés," *Hispanic Review* 27 (1959): 78–102; Stephen Gilman, "Matthew V:10 in Castilian Jest and Earnest," in *Studia Hispanica in honorem R. Lapesa*, ed. Eugenio de Bustos, Jorge Guillén, and Américo Castro (Madrid: Gredos, 1972), 257–265; and Antonio Gómez-Moriana, "The Subversion of the Ritual Discourse: An Intertextual Reading of the *Lazarillo de Tormes*," *Sociocriticism* 5 (1989): 55–81. Also of interest is the comparison with the narrative pattern of Cervantes's main work by John Incledon, "Textual Subversion in *Lazarillo de Tormes* and *Don Quixote*," *Indiana Journal of Hispanic Literatures* 5 (1994): 161–180.

23. Netanyahu, *Toward the Inquisition: Essays on Jewish and Converso History in Late Medieval Spain* (Ithaca, N.Y.: Cornell University Press, 1997); for a more extensive account of this topic, see also Netanyahu, *The Origins of the Inquisition in Fifteenth-Century Spain*, 2nd ed. (New York: New York Review Books, 2001).

24. "Over seven hundred people were burned and more than five thousand were reconciled with the church. Regularly, people were cast in prisons for four or five years that had been erected especially for that purpose. Convicts had to wear crosses and colored *Sambenitos* for a long period. The convicted were eager to take them off so that their disgrace would no longer be seen in the world." (*Sambenitos* were yellow, apronlike penitential garments, which the convicts were draped in and on which their misdeeds were pictured.) Andrés Bernáldez,

Historia de los reyes católicos don Fernando y doña Isabel (Madrid: Ediciones Atlas, 1953), 567–788.

25. See the following selection of secondary literature on the Inquisition that has been consulted for this chapter: Gerd Schwerhoff, *Die Inquisition: Ketzerverfolgung in Mittelalter und Neuzeit* (Munich: C. H. Beck, 2004); John Edwards, *Die spanische Inquisition*, trans. Harald Ehrhardt (Düsseldorf/Zurich: Artemis & Winkler, 2003) (German translation of *The Spanish Inquisition* [Stroud, UK: Tempus, 1999]); Helen Rawlings, *The Spanish Inquisition* (Oxford: Wiley, 2004); António Vieira and Sébastien Lapaque, *Sur les procédés de la Sainte Inquisition: Propositions en faveur des gens de la nation juives* (Paris: Bayard, 2004); Laurent Albaret *L'Inquisition et la répression des dissidences religieuses au Moyen Âge: Dernières recherches* (Carcassonne: Centre d'Études Cathares, 2004); León Poliakov, *Die Marranen im Schatten der Inquisition*, vol. 4 of *Geschichte des Antisemitismus* (Worms: Heintz, 1981), translated into English as *The History of Anti-Semitism: From Mohammed to the Marranos*; Marcelino Menéndez Pelayo, *Historia de los heterodoxos españoles* (Madrid: Consejo Superior de Investigaciones Científicas, 1963); Richard Kagan, *Inquisitorial Inquiries: Brief Lives of Secret Jews and Other Heretics* (Baltimore: Johns Hopkins University Press, 2004); Heymann, *Tod oder Taufe Tod oder Taufe: Die Vertreibung der Juden aus Spanien und Portugal im Zeitalter der Inquisition* (Frankfurt a.M.: Judischer Verlag bei Athenaum, 1988), 72. For a summary of the scholarly debate over whether the Inquisition was "racist" in the modern sense, as well as a decided and intelligent position on this question, see Max Sebastián Hering Torres, "'Limpieza de sangre': Rassismus in der Vormoderne?," in *Rassismus*, ed. Max Sebastián Hering Torres and Wolfgang Schmale (Innsbruck: Studien-Verlag, 2003), 20–36; on this topic, see also Yosef Yerushalmi, "Assimilierung und rassischer Antisemitismus: Die iberischen und die deutschen Modelle," in *Ein Feld in Anatot: Versuche über jüdische Geschichte*, ed. Yosef Yerushalmi (Berlin: Wagenbach, 1993), 53–80; and Jerome Friedman, "Jewish Conversion, the Spanish Pure Blood Laws and Reformation: A Revisionist View of Racial and Religious Antisemitism," *Sixteenth Century Journal* 18 (1987): 3–29.

26. "'Boy! are you seeking for a master?' I replied, 'Yes, sir!' 'Then come along with me,' he said, 'for God has shown mercy to you by letting you meet with me'" (Markham, 48).

27. "[H]e entered the principal church, and I at his heels. I saw him hear Mass and the other divine offices very devoutly" (Markham, 48).

28. For a problematization of this assumption, see Benzion Netanyahu's writings, particularly "The Racial Attack on the Conversos: Américo Castro's View of Its Origin," in *Toward the Inquisition*, 1–42.

29. "Great secrets, sir, are those which you keep and of which the world is ignorant. Who would not be deceived by that fair presence and decent cloak? And who would think that the same gentleman passed all that day without eating

anything . . . ? . . . Certainly no one would have suspected it. O Lord! How many such as him must be scattered over the world, who suffer for the jade they call honour that which they would not suffer for a friend" (Markham, 59–60).

30. "God is my witness that even now when I meet with any one dressed like this, and walking with the same pompous air, it makes me sad to think that he might be suffering what I saw my poor master suffer" (Markham, 68).

31. "I said, 'What my master has, according to what he told me, is a very good estate consisting of houses and a demolished pigeon-cote.' 'This is worth little,' they said, 'but it will do for the payment of his debts. In what part of the town is it?' 'In his own country,' I replied. 'By the Lord! This is a fine business,' they exclaimed, 'and where is his country?' 'He told me that is was in Old Castille,' I said. The officer and the scrivener laughed a good deal, and said, 'This is a good story to cover your debts!'" (Markham, 81).

32. "[M]y master was among them, saying the sweetest things that Ovid ever wrote. They had no shame in asking him to pay for their breakfasts, but he, finding that he was as cold in the purse as he was empty in the stomach, began to have that feeling which robs the face of its colour, and to make not very valid excuses. When they saw his infirmity, they went to those who were not suffering from it" (Markham, 61).

33. Hans Ulrich Gumbrecht, *Eine Geschichte der spanischen Literatur* (Frankfurt a.M.: Suhrkamp, 1990), 283–286, 302, 306–309.

34. See also the comments on *Lazarillo de Tormes* by Ruth El Saffar, "The 'I' of the Beholder: Self and Other in Some Golden Age Texts," in *Cultural Authority in Golden Age Spain*, ed. Marina S. Brownlee and Hans Ulrich Gumbrecht (Baltimore: Johns Hopkins University Press, 1995), 178–205; and Oscar Pereira Zazo, "La perspective del *Lazarillo de Tormes*," *Torre de Papel* 5 (1995): 55–79.

35. On this topic, see Rico, "Problemas del *Lazarillo*"; and Bruce W. Wardropper, "The Strange Case of Lázaro Gonzalez Pérez," *Modern Language Notes* 92, no. 2 (1977): 202–212. See also Dalai Brenes Carrillo, "¿Quién es V. M. en Lazarillo de Tormes?," *Boletin de la Biblioteca de Menéndez Pelayo* 68 (1992): 73–88; George A. Shipley, "The Critic as Witness for the Prosecution: Making the Case against Lázaro de Tormes," *Publications of the Modern Language Association* 97, no. 2 (1982): 179–194; and Peter N. Dunn, "*Lazarillo de Tormes*: The Case of the Purloined Letter," *Revista de Estudios Hispánicos* 22, no. 1 (1988): 1–14.

36. See Jauss, "Ursprung und Bedeutung der Ich-Form im *Lazarillo de Tormes*." Jauss interpreted the picaresque novel as a satire on Augustine's *Confessiones*. Margot Kruse and Peter Baumann have both raised objections to this thesis in volume 10 (1959) of the *Romanistisches Jahrbuch* (Margot Kruse, "Die parodistischen Elemente im *Lazarillo de Tormes*"; Peter Baumann, "Der *Lazarillo de Tormes*, eine Travestie der Augustinischen *Confessiones*?"). See also Judith A. Whitenack, *Confession and Conversion in Guzmán de Alfarache*, (Madison: University of Wisconsin Press, 1980), esp. 2–53.

37. "Well! your Honour must know, before anything else, that they call me Lazarillo de Tormes, and that I am the son of Thome Gonçales and Antonia Perez, natives of Tejares, a village near Salamanca. My birth was in the river Tormes, for which reason I have the river for a surname, and it was in this manner. My Father, whom God pardon, had charge of a flour mill which was on the banks of that river. He was the miller there for over fifteen years, and my mother, being one night taken with me in the mill, she gave birth to me there. So that I may say with truth that I was born in the river" (Markham, 4–5).

38. One of the most interesting among the more recent publications is by Richard Kagan (*Inquisitorial Inquiries*), who introduces six individual cases of Inquisition tribunals, transcribes excerpts from them, and contextualizes them. The description of an individual case can be found in Gillian T. W. Ahlgren, ed., *The Inquisition of Francisca: A Sixteenth-Century Visionary on Trial* (Chicago: University of Chicago Press, 2005); for individual documents, see also Louis Coronas Tejada, *Conversos and Inquisition in Jaén* (Jerusalem: Magnes Press, 1988). In 1999, a German translation of Bernardus Guidonis's *Practica officii inquisitionis* was published: *Das Buch der Inquisition: Das Originalhandbuch des Inquisitors Bernard Gui*, ed. and intro. Petra Seifert, trans. Manfred Pawlik (Augsburg: Nikol Verlagsgesellschaft, 1999). The following recent publications also provide good initial insight into the processes, formalities, and structures of the Spanish Inquisition through shorter document excerpts: Clive Griffin, *Journeymen-Printers, Heresy, and the Inquisition in Sixteenth-Century Spain* (Oxford: Oxford University Press, 2005); Robert Lemm, *Die spanische Inquisition: Geschichte und Legende* (Cologne: Anaconda, 2005); Andrew W. Keitt, *Inventing the Sacred: Imposture, Inquisition, and the Boundaries of the Supernatural in Golden Age Spain* (Leiden: Brill, 2005); and Joseph Pérez, *The Spanish Inquisition: A History*, trans. Janet Lloyd (New Haven, Conn. / London: Yale University Press, 2005). For the Roman Inquisition, following the partial opening of the Archive of the Congregation for the Doctrine of the Faith in 1998, the case records on church censorship and control of books are presently being edited (DFG-funded research project "Römische Inquisition und Indexkongregation" at Westfälische-Wilhelms-Universität Münster). See also Hubert Wolf, *Römische Inquisition und Indexkongregation: Grundlagenforschung 1814–1915* (Paderborn: Ferdinand Schöningh Verlag, 2005); and Stephan Wendehorst, ed., *The Roman Inquisition, the Index and the Jews* (Leiden: Brill, 2004).

39. The documents surviving in the Spanish National Historical Archive (Archivo Histórico Nacional, AHN) are organized according to the structure of the Inquisition—the twenty-one local tribunals in Spain, Sicily, Mexico, and Peru worked under the supervision of the central organization, the Consejo de Inquisición, or Suprema. According to the instructions by Grand Inquisitor Diego de Espinos from 1572, each local tribunal had to have a file index. The

majority of further sources on the Inquisition survive in the Archivo Diocesano de Cuenca and the Archivo General de la Nación in Mexico City. The documents in the AHN holdings are organized as follows. Since the actual case files were not bound, contrary to more general ledgers containing correspondence, criminal records, and instructions, the Inquisition files in the AHN are divided into *libros* (bound books) and *legajos* (loose files). The case files themselves are ordered by the respective offenses. In the holdings on the Inquisición de Toledo—as in most other tribunals in Spain—the header *judaizante* contains the most files, followed by witchcraft and the diverse heresies. There are many files on blasphemy as well. The *informaciones genealógicas*, which had to be submitted to the Inquisition by those wanting to hold public office or by those whose *limpieza de sangre* was doubtful, offer another large holding. On the history, structure, and organization of this archive, see the still-essential essay: Miguel Aviles, Jose Martinez Millan, and Virgilio Pinto, "El Archivo del Consejo de la Inquisición: Aportaciones para una historia de los archivos inquisitoriales," *Revista de Archivos, Bibliotecas y Museos* 81, no. 3 (1978): 459–518. The archival holdings on the Inquisition of Toledo, which are available as *legajos*, were consulted for this study. The order within the *legajos* is dictated by the individual proceedings (*expediente*). The citation of individual files gives the number of the *legajo* and the relevant *expediente*.

40. In the following transcription of the *Información genealógica*, the Inquisitor's comments in the document's header and footer are not transcribed for reasons of clarity. In order to render the document structure clear, however, the apostils are mentioned in small capitals. The top apostils are the date, confirmation of receipt, and registry entry; an official comment is recorded in the footer. Possible alternative readings are noted by subscript.

41. "Illustrious and highly esteemed Lords. This is the account of my descent, which Your Graces have demanded of me: My father is called Pedro de Ledesma, my paternal grandfather was called Andrés B$_{c}$orm$_{n}$iego de la Bibda, my grandmother was called Ionna de dios la guarde el ovejero and was the only wife of the above-mentioned Andrés B$_{c}$orm$_{n}$iego—both hailed from Pereira, land of the Ledesma. My mother is called Anna Fernandez, my maternal grandfather was called Bartholome Sanchez Ortalano and resided in an outer quarter of Santiago, my maternal grandmother was called Maria Gomez and was the only wife of the above-mentioned Bartholome Sanchez Ortalano and also lived in the suburb of the just mentioned town of Santiago. The licentiate de Ledesma."

42. See the analysis by Hugh W. Kennedy, "Lazaro y el 'coco,'" *Revista de Estudios Hispánicos* 10 (1976): 57–67.

43. "When I was a child of eight years old, they accused my father of certain misdeeds done to the sacks of those who came to have their corn ground. He was taken into custody, and confessed and denied not, suffering persecution for justice's sake. So I trust in God that he is in glory, for the Evangelist tells us that

such are blessed. . . . My widowed mother . . . and a dark-coloured man, who was one of those who had the care of the horses. They came to know each other. Sometimes he came to our house late, and went away in the morning. . . . At first I did not like him, for I was afraid of his colour and his ugly face. But when I saw that his coming was the sign of better living, I began to like him, for he always brought pieces of meat, bread, and in the winter, fuel to warm us. This intercourse went on until one day my mother gave me a pretty little brown brother, whom I played with and helped to keep warm. I remember once that when my stepfather was fondling the child, it noticed that my mother and I were white, and that he was not. It frightened the child, who ran to my mother, pointing with its finger and saying, 'Mother, he is ugly!' To this he replied laughing; but I noticed the words of my little brother, and, though so young, I said to myself, 'How many there are in the world who run from others because they do not see themselves in them'" (Markham, 5–7).

44. Heymann, *Tod oder Taufe*, 72.

45. "I hold it to be good that such remarkable things as have happened to me, perhaps never before seen or heard of, should not be buried in the tomb of oblivion. It may be that some one who reads may find something that pleases him. For those who do not go very deep into the matter there is a saying of Pliny "*that there is no book so bad that it does not contain something that is good*." Moreover, all tastes are not the same, and what one does not eat another will. Thus we see things that are thought much of by some, depreciated by others. Hence no circumstance ought to be omitted, how insignificant soever it may be, but all should be made known, especially as some fruit might be plucked from such a tree. If this were not so, very few would write at all, for it cannot be done without hard work. Authors do not wish to be recompensed with money, but by seeing that their work is known and read, and, if it contains anything that is worthy, that it is praised" (Markham, 1–2).

46. König, *Lazarillo de Tormes*; see also the following inspiring suggestions on the relation between the Inquisition and the novel's form: David M. Gitlitz, "Inquisition Confessions and *Lazarillo de Tormes*," *Hispanic Review* 68, no. 1 (2000): 53–74; Antonio Gómez-Moriana, "Autobiografía y discurso ritual: Problemática de la confesión autobiográfica destinada al tribunal inquisitorial," *Co-Textes* 8 (1984): 81–103; and Gustavo Alfaro, "Los lazarillos y la Inquisición," *Hispanófila* 26, no. 3 (1983): 11–19.

47. See Moritz Csáky, "Geschichte und Gedächtnis: Erinnerung und Erinnerungsstrategien im narrativen historischen Verfahren—Das Beispiel Zentraleuropas," in *Klio ohne Fesseln? Historiographie im östlichen Europa nach dem Zusammenbruch des Kommunismus*, ed. Alojz Ivanišević, Andreas Kappeler, Walter Lukan, and Arnold Suppan (Vienna / Frankfurt a.M.: Peter Lang, 2002), 61–80; Csáky, "Gedächtnis, Erinnerung und die Konstruktion von Identität: Das Beispiel

Zentraleuropas," in *Nation und Nationalismus in Europa: Kulturelle Konstruktion von Identitäten (Festschrift für Urs Altermatt)*, ed. Catherine Bosshart-Pfluger, Joseph Jung, and Franziska Metzger (Frauenfeld/Stuttgart/Vienna: Huber Verlag, 2002), 25–49; and especially Dan Diner, "Ereignis und Erinnerung: Über Variationen geschichtlichen Gedächtnisses," in *Shoah: Formen der Erinnerung*, ed. Nicolas Berg, Jess Jochimsen, and Bernd Stiegler (Munich: Wilhelm Fink Verlag, 1996), 13–30.

48. Horst Baader considers ambiguity an essential structural characteristic of the picaresque: "Der spanische Schelmenroman oder die Kunst der Uneindeutigkeit," in *Literatur und Spiritualität: Hans Sckommodau zum siebzigsten Geburtstag*, ed. Hans Rheinfelder, Pierre Christophorov, and Eberhard Müller-Bochat (Munich: Wilhelm Fink Verlag, 1978), 9–23.

49. "I beseech your Honour that you will accept the poor service of one who would be richer if his power was equal to his desire. Well, your Honour! This author writes what he writes, and relates his story very fully. It seemed to him that he should not begin in the middle, but quite at the beginning, so that there might be a full notice of his personality, and also that those who inherit noble estates may consider how little fortune owes them, having been so very partial to them in its gifts; and how much more those have done who, not being so favoured, have, by force and management, arrived at a good estate" (Markham, 2–3).

50. See also Reyes Coll-Tellechea and Anthony N. Zahareas, "On the Historical Function of Narrative Forms: *Lazarillo de Tormes*," *Crítica Hispánica* 19 (1997): 110–127.

51. Comparable arguments have been made by Manuel J. Asencio, "El *Lazarillo* en su circunstancia histórica," *Revista de Literatura* 54 (1992): 101–128; and James A. Parr, "Rhetoric and Referentiality: Historical Allusiveness and Artful Innuendo," *Crítica Hispánica* 19 (1997): 75–86.

Chapter 4. Marranism and Modernity

1. Denise R. Goitstein and Anne Grynberg, "French Literature," in *Encyclopedia Judaica*, ed. Michael Berenbaum and Fred Skolnik, 2nd ed. (Detroit: Macmillan Reference USA, 2007), 14:243. This is a virtually unaltered reprint of the *Encyclopedia Judaica* entry from the 1970s; only the bibliography has been updated.

2. Ibid.

3. "(1533–1592), French writer and philosopher. His mother, Antoinette de Louppes de Villanueva, came from a Spanish Jewish family. One of her ancestors, Mayer Pacagon of Catalayud, was forcibly converted to Catholicism and took the name of Lopez de Villanueva. His descendants, however, remained secretly faithful to Judaism, and several of them were persecuted by the Inquisition. One of them, Juan de Villanueva, from whom Montaigne's mother was descended, fled

to Toulouse, France[,] where he settled. She later married the Catholic Eyquem de Montaigne, her uncle's business partner. Montaigne studied at the College de Guyenne run by Portuguese New Christians and, later, at Toulouse University, a center of New Christian ferment and heterodoxy." Denise R. Goitstein, "Montaigne, Michel de," in Berenbaum and Skolnik, *Encyclopedia Judaica*, 14:453.

4. Ibid.

5. Frank-Rutger Hausmann, epilogue to *Montaigne*, by Hugo Friedrich, 3rd ed. (Tübingen/Basel: Franke, 1993), 379–393. See also Gerhard Hess, "Zu Montaignes Abstammung: Ein Bericht," *Zeitschrift für Französische Sprache und Literatur* 64 (1942): 220–227; and Walter Mönch, *Frankreichs Literatur im 16. Jahrhundert: Eine nationalpolitische Geistesgeschichte der französischen Renaissance* (Berlin: De Gruyter, 1938), 1933–1934.

6. The first reference to Montaigne's family history appears as early as the nineteenth century in a monograph by Théophile Malvezin, *Michel de Montaigne, son origine, sa famille* (Bordeaux, 1875), 99–128. Among contemporary studies, the following three very stimulating essays, which argue in different ways and focus on the question of the link between origin and oeuvre in a particular manner, deserve to be mentioned: Carola Hilfrich, "Autobiography as a Spectropoetics of the Mother: On Hélène Cixous's Recent Works," in *Zeitgenössische jüdische Autobiographie*, ed. Christoph Miething (Tübingen: De Gruyter, 2003), 129–146; Elizabeth Mendes da Costa, "Montaigne and the Jewish Religion," in Charles Meyers and Norman Simms, *Troubled Souls: Conversos, Crypto-Jews, and Other Confused Jewish Intellectuals from the Fourteenth through the Eighteenth Century* (Hamilton, New Zealand: Outrigger Publishers, 2001), 129–141; and Mendes da Costa, "The Jews and Montaigne's Journal de Voyage," *French Studies Bulletin* 69 (1998): 10–13.

7. See also Christian Schärf, *Geschichte der Essays: Von Montaigne bis Adorno* (Göttingen: Vandenhoeck & Ruprecht, 1999), 44–63. These and all subsequent citations are taken from the Pléiade edition by Jean Balsamo, Michel Magnien, and Catherine Magnien-Simonin published by Gallimard in 2007; subsequent references to this edition will be cited parenthetically in the text by book, essay, and page number. All English translations are taken from the Penguin edition of M. A. Screech's translation (London: Penguin, 2004): "I have not made my book any more than it has made me—a book of one substance with its author, proper to me and a limb of my life" (Screech, 755).

8. "All the various piece of this faggot are being bundled together on the understanding that I am only to set my hand to it in my own home and when I am oppressed by too lax an idleness. So it was assembled at intervals and at different periods, since I sometimes have occasion to be away from home for months on end. Moreover I never correct my first thoughts by second ones—well, except perhaps for the odd word, but to vary it, not to remove it. I want to remove it. I want to show my humours as they develop, revealing each element as it is born. . . .

One of the valets I used for dictation stole several pages of mine which were to his liking and thought he had acquired great plunder. It consoles me that he will no more gain anything by it than I shall lose" (Screech, 858).

9. Quoted from the English edition translated by Julia Annas and Jonathan Barnes, 2nd ed. (Cambridge: Cambridge University Press, 2000), 41.

10. "To conclude: there is no permanent existence either in our being or in that of objects. We ourselves, our faculty of judgement and all mortal things are flowing and rolling ceaselessly: nothing certain can be established about one from the other, since both judged and judging are ever shifting and changing. 'We have no communication with Being; as human nature is wholly situated, for ever, between birth and death, it shows itself only as a dark shadowy appearance, an unstable weak opinion. And if you should determine to try and grasp what Man's *being* is, it would be exactly like trying to hold a fistful of water'" (Screech, 680).

11. Verena Olejniczak Lobsien, "Heterologie: Konturen frühneuzeitlichen Selbstseins jenseits von Autonomie und Heteronomie," *Zeitschrift für Literaturwissenschaft und Linguistik* 101 (1996): 6.

12. Stephen J. Greenblatt, *Renaissance Self-Fashioning: From More to Shakespeare* (Chicago: University of Chicago Press, 1980), esp. 1–5.

13. Julia Kristeva, *Étrangers à nous-mêmes* (Paris: Gallimard, 1988).

14. "I speak about myself in diverse ways: that is because I look at myself in diverse ways. Every sort of contradiction can be found in me, . . . : timid, insolent; chaste, lecherous; talkative, taciturn; tough, sickly; clever, dull; brooding, affable; lying, truthful; learned, ignorant; generous, miserly and then prodigal—I can see something of all that in myself, depending on how I gyrate; and anyone who studies himself attentively finds in himself and in his very judgement this whirring about and this discordancy" (Screech, 377).

15. *Essais* 2.18, 703–704 (Screech, 755).

16. "Everybody looks before himself: I look inside myself; I am concerned with no one but me; without ceasing I reflect on myself, I watch myself, savour myself. . . . I turn round and round in myself" (Screech, 747).

17. "Moreover I can say that for having assayed it; in the past I made use of that freedom of personal choice and private selection in order to neglect certain details in the observances of our Church because they seemed to be rather odd or rather empty; then, when I came to tell some learned men about it, I discovered that those very practices were based on massive and absolutely solid foundations, and that it is only our ignorance and animal-stupidity which make us treat them with less reverence than all the rest. Why cannot we remember all the contradictions which we feel within our own judgement, and how many things which were articles of belief for us yesterday are fables for us today? Vainglory and curiosity are the twin scourges of our souls. The former makes us stick our noses into everything: the latter forbids us to leave anything unresolved or undecided" (Screech, 204).

18. "The first charge made against the book is that Christians do themselves wrong by wishing to support their belief with human reasons: belief is grasped only by faith and by private inspiration from God's grace. A pious zeal may be seen behind this objection; so any assay at satisfying those who put it forward must be made with gentleness and respect. It is really a task for a man versed in Theology rather than for me, who know nothing about it. Nevertheless, this [is] my verdict. . . . [C]ompare our behaviour with a Moslem's or a pagan's: you always remain lower than they are. Yet, given the advantage of our own religion, our superiority ought to outshine them, far beyond any comparison. Men ought to say: 'Are they really so just, so loving, so good? Then these people must be Christians.' All other manifestations are common to all religions. . . . The distinctive mark of the Truth we hold ought to be virtue. . . . Christians excel at hating enemies. Our zeal works wonders when it strengthens our tendency towards hatred, enmity, ambition, avarice, evil-speaking . . . and rebellion. On the other hand, zeal never makes anyone go flying towards goodness, kindness or temperance, unless he is miraculously pre-disposed to them by some rare complexion. Our religion was made to root out vices: now it cloaks them, nurses them, stimulates them" (Screech, 491–495).

19. See especially Andreas Kablitz, "Montaignes 'Skeptizismus': Zur *Apologie de Raimond Sebond* (*Essais*: II, 12)," in *Poststrukturalismus: Herausforderung an die Literaturwissenschaft*, ed. Gerhard Neumann (Stuttgart: Metzler, 1997), 504–539; Patrick Moser, "Literary Identity in Montaigne's 'Apologie de Raimond Sebond,'" *French Review* 77, no. 4 (2004): 716–727; Philip Hendrick, *Montaigne et Sebond: L'art de la traduction* (Paris: H. Champion, 1996); and Fabienne Pomel, "La fonction critique de l'ironie dans l'*Apologie de Raimond Sebond*: Montaigne, *Les Essais*, Livre II, Chapitre XII," *Bulletin de la Societé des Amis de Montaigne* 35–36 (1994): 79–89. The following anthology is essential for the discussion presented in this chapter: Claude Blum, ed., *Montaigne, "Apologie de Raimond Sebond": De la* Theologia *à la* Théologie (Paris: Librairie Honoré Champion, 1990); this publication also includes an extensive bibliography (320–334) of studies of this essay compiled by Elaine Limbrick.

20. "I am not teaching, I am relating" (Screech, 909).

21. "Si l'injonction humaniste et l'injonction religieuse prônent toutes deux la 'conversation' intérieure et la *réappropriation*, ce n'est, dans la perspective du croyant, qu'un premier temps, auquel fera suite l'obéissance à l'autorité divine, et l'espoir du salut. Pour l'humaniste qui a pris ses distances avec la dévotion, cette réappropriation, une fois réussie, est en soi un but satisfaisant. La solitude qu'il prône ne saurait se confondre avec la traditionnelle *vita contemplativa* que la religion oppose à la *vita activa*, à la vie dans le monde." Jean Starobinski, *Montaigne en mouvement* (Paris: Gallimard, 1982), 25.

22. "The means of doing good or evil can be found anywhere, but if that quip of Bias is true, that 'the evil form the larger part,' or what Ecclesiasticus says, 'One good man in a thousand have I not found' . . . " (Screech, 266).

23. "It seems to me that solitude is more reasonable and right for those who, following the example of Thales, have devoted to the world their more active, vigorous years. We have lived quite enough for others: let us live at least this tail-end of life for ourselves. Let us bring our thoughts and reflections back to ourselves and to our own well-being. Preparing securely for our own withdrawal is no light matter: it gives us enough trouble without introducing other concerns. Since God grants us leave to make things ready for our departure, let us prepare for it; let us pack up our bags and take leave of our company in good time; let us disentangle ourselves from those violent traps which pledge us to other things and which distance us from ourselves. We must unknot those bonds and, from this day forth, love this or that but marry nothing but ourselves. That is to say, let the rest be ours, but not so glued and joined to us that it cannot be pulled off without tearing away a piece of ourselves, skin and all. The greatest thing in the world is to know how to live to yourself. It is time to slip our knots with society now that we can contribute nothing to it. A man with nothing to lend should refrain from borrowing. Our powers are failing: let us draw them in and keep them within ourselves. Whoever can turn round the duties of love and fellowship and pour them into himself should do so. In that decline which makes a man a useless encumbrance importunate to others, let him avoid becoming an encumbrance, importunate and useless to himself. Let him pamper himself, cherish himself, but above all control himself, so respecting his reason and so fearing his conscience that he cannot stumble in their presence without shame" (Screech, 271–272).

24. "It happens even to us who are mere abortions of men that we can occasionally enrapture our Soul far beyond her ordinary state when she is awakened by the words or examples of another man: but it is a kind of passion which impels her, disturbs her and ravishes her somewhat outside ourselves; for once that whirlwind is over, we can see that she spontaneously relaxes and comes down, not perhaps down to the lowest stage of all but at least to less than she was" (Screech, 799).

25. "The thought of those who seek solitude for devotion's sake, filling their minds with the certainty of God's promises for the life to come, is much more sane and appropriate. Their objective is God, infinite in goodness and power: the soul can find there matters to slake her desires in perfect freedom. Pains and afflictions are profitable to them, being used to acquire eternal healing and joy; death is welcome as a passing over to that perfect state. The harshness of their Rule is smoothed by habit; their carnal appetites are rejected and lulled asleep by their denial—nothing maintains them but practicing them and using them. Only this end, another life, blessedly immortal, genuinely merits our renunciation of the comforts and sweetnesses of this life of ours. Whoever can, in reality and constancy, set his soul ablaze with the fire of this lively faith and hope, builds in his solitude a life of choicest pleasures, beyond any other mode of life" (Screech, 275).

26. "It is in our soul that evil grips us: and she cannot escape from herself. . . . So we must bring her back, haul her back, into our self. That is true solitude. It can be enjoyed in towns and in kings' courts, but more conveniently apart" (Screech, 269).

27. "That difficulty increases desire" (Screech, 694).

28. "'No reason but has its contrary,' says the wisest of the Schools of Philosophy" (Screech, 694).

29. "So it is with everything: it is difficulty which makes us prize things. The people of the Marches of Ancona more readily go to Saint James of Compostela to make their vows: those of Galicia, to Our Lady of Loreto. At Liège they sing the praises of the baths at Lucca: in Tuscany, of those of Spa-by-Liège. You hardly ever see a Roman in the fencing school of Rome: it is full of Frenchmen! Great Cato tired of his wife—just like the rest of us—while she was his: when she belonged to another he yearned for her. . . . Our appetite scorns and passes over what it holds in its hand, so as to run after what it does not have" (Screech, 696).

30. "It is an act of God's Providence to allow this Holy Church to be, as we can see she now is, shaken by so many disturbances and tempests, in order by this opposition to awaken the souls of the pious and to bring them back from the idleness and torpor in which so long a period of calm had immersed them. If we weigh the loss we have suffered by the numbers of those who have been led into error against the gain which accrues to us from our having been brought back into fighting trim, with our zeal and our strength restored to new life for the battle, I am not sure whether the befit does not outweigh the loss" (Screech, 698).

31. Sophie Jama, *L'histoire juive de Montaigne* (Paris: Flammarion, 2001), 24.

32. "You have here, Reader, a book whose faith can be trusted, a book which warns you from the start that I have set myself no other end but a private family one. I have not been concerned to serve you nor my reputation: my powers are inadequate for such a design. I have dedicated this book to the private benefit of my friends and kinsmen so that, having lost me (as they must do soon) they can find here again some traits of my character and of my humours. They will thus keep their knowledge of me more full, more alive. If my design had been to seek the favour of the world I would have decked myself out better and presented myself in a studied gait. Here I want to be seen in my simple, natural, everyday fashion, without striving or artifice: for it is my own self that I am painting. Here, drawn from life, you will read of my defects and my native form so far as respect for social convention allows: for had I found myself among those peoples who are said still to live under the sweet liberty of Nature's primal laws, I can assure you that I most willingly have portrayed myself whole, and wholly naked.

And therefore, Reader, I myself am the subject of my book: it is not reasonable that you should employ your leisure on a topic so frivolous and so vain. Therefore, Farewell: From Montaigne; this first of March, One thousand, five hundred and eighty" (Screech, lxiii). The Pléiade edition by Jean Balsamo, Michel Magnien, and Catherine Magnien-Simonin gives a variation on the date: "premier de Mars mil cinq cens quatre vingts."

33. "I am expounding a lowly, lacklustre existence. You can attach the whole of moral philosophy to a commonplace private life just as well as to one of richer stuff. Every man bears the whole Form of the human condition. Authors communicate themselves to the public by some peculiar mark foreign to themselves; I—the first ever to do so—by my universal being, not as a grammarian, poet or jurisconsult but as Michel de Montaigne. If all complain that I talk too much about myself, I complain that they never even think about their own selves" (Screech, 908).

34. "Here, my book and I go harmoniously forward at the same pace. Elsewhere you can commend or condemn a work independently of its author; but not here: touch one and you touch the other" (Screech, 909).

35. "It is no light pleasure to know oneself to be saved from the contagion of a corrupt age and to be able to say of oneself: 'Anyone who could see right into my soul would even then not find me guilty of any man's ruin or affliction, nor of envy nor of vengeance, nor of any public attack on our laws, nor of novelty or disturbance, nor of breaking my word. And even though this licentious age not only allows it but teaches it to each of us, I have nevertheless not put my hand on another Frenchman's goods or purse but have lived by my own means, in war as in peace; nor have I exploited any man's labour without due reward.' Such witnesses to our conscience are pleasant; and such natural rejoicing is a great gift: it is the only satisfaction which never fails us. Basing the recompense of virtuous deeds on another's approbation is to accept too uncertain and confused a foundation—especially since in a corrupt and ignorant period like our own to be in a good esteem with the masses is an insult: whom would you trust to recognize what was worthy of praise! May God save me from being a decent man according to the self-descriptions which I daily see everyone give to honour themselves" (Screech, 910).

36. "I have my own laws and law-court to pass judgement on me and I appeal to them rather than elsewhere" (Screech, 911).

37. "Rare is the life which remains ordinate even in privacy. Anyone can take part in a farce and act the honest man on the trestles: but to be right-ruled within, in your bosom, where anything is licit, where everything is hidden—that's what matters" (Screech, 911).

38. "When the Kings of Castile banished the Jews from their lands, King John of Portugal sold them sanctuary in his territories at eight crowns a head, on condition that they would have to leave by a particular day when he would provide vessels to transport them to Africa. The day duly arrived after which they were to remain as slaves if they had not obeyed: but too few ships were provided;

those who did get aboard were treated harshly and villainously by the sailors who, apart from many other indignities, delayed them at sea, sailing this way and that until they had used up all their provisions and were forced to buy others from them at so high a price and over so long a period that they were set ashore with the shirts they stood up in. When the news of this inhuman treatment reached those who had remained behind, most resolved to accept slavery; a few pretended to change religion. When Emmanuel, John's successor, came to the throne he first set them all free; then he changed his mind, giving them time to void his kingdom and assigning three ports for their embarkation. When the good-will he had shown in granting them their freedom had failed to convert them to Christianity, he hoped (said Bishop Osorius, the best Latin historian of our times) that they would be brought to it by the hardship of having to expose themselves as their comrades had done to thievish seamen and of having to abandon a land to which they had grown accustomed and where they had acquired great wealth, in order to cast themselves into lands foreign and unknown. But finding his hopes deceived and the Jews determined to make the crossing, he withdrew two of the ports he had promised in order that the length and difficulty of the voyage would make some of them think again—or perhaps it was to pile them all together in one place so as the more easily to carry out his design, which was to tear all the children under fourteen from their parents and to transport them out of sight and out of contact, where they could be taught our religion. This deed is said to have produced a dreadful spectacle, as the natural love of parents and children together with their zeal for their ancient faith rebelled against this harsh decree: it was common to see fathers and mothers killing themselves or—an even harsher example—throwing their babes down wells out of love and compassion in order to evade that law. Meanwhile the allotted time ran out: they had no resources, so returned to slavery. Some became Christians: even today a century later few Portuguese trust in their sincerity or in that of their descendants, even though the constraints of custom and of long duration are as powerful counsellors as any other" (Screech, 55–56).

Chapter 5. Sacred Text and Poetic Form

1. Francisco Marquez de Sousa Viterbo, *Notícia acerca a vida e obras de João Pinto Delgado* (Lisbon: Typ. da Academia, 1910).

2. Israël Salvator Révah, "Autobiographie d'un marrane: Édition partielle d'un manuscrit de João Pinto Delgado," *Revue des Études Juives* 119 (1961): 41–130. About fifteen years later, an English edition was published by Herman Prins Salomon ("The 'De Pinto' Manuscript: A Seventeenth-Century Marrano Family History," *Studia Rosenthaliana* 9, no. 1 [1975]: 1–62).

3. Among these, the following essential study by Cecil Roth particularly deserves mention: "João Pinto Delgado: A Literary Disentanglement," *Modern*

Language Review 30 (1935): 19–25. For a broader yet no less pertinent study by the same author, see "Les marranes à Rouen: Un chapitre ignoré de l'histoire des juifs en France," *Revue des Études Juives* 88 (1929): 113–155.

4. Edward W. Wilson has discussed this question by means of a comparison of the Esther and Ruth poems and argued for the use of the Hebrew original as source; see his essay "The Poetry of João Pinto Delgado," *Journal of Jewish Studies* 1, no. 3 (1949): 131–142.

5. A. D. H. Fishlock, "The Rabbinic Material in the *Ester* of Pinto Delgado," *Journal of Jewish Studies* 2, no. 1 (1950): 37–50.

6. "Quevedo also wrote a poetic paraphrase on the first chapter of Lamentations, and in this, too, each section is prefaced by a supposedly literal prose translation from the Hebrew. This work was composed before 1613, but never saw print until the nineteenth century; it is not impossible that Pinto saw a manuscript version." Wilson, "The Poetry of João Pinto Delgado," 142.

7. See the summary in Albert I. Baumgarten, S. David Sperling, and Shalom Sabar, "Scroll of Esther," in Michael Berenbaum and Fred Skolnik, *Encyclopedia Judaica*, 2nd ed. (Detroit: Macmillan Reference USA, 2007), 16:215–220. The still-essential article on this topic is by Jacob Hoschander, "The Book of Esther in the Light of History," *Jewish Quarterly Review* 9 (1918): 1–41. For an introduction to the interpretive tradition, see Elias Bickerman, *Four Strange Books of the Bible* (New York: Schocken Books, 1967); and Barry Dov Walfish, *Esther in Medieval Garb: Jewish Interpretation of the Book of Esther in the Middle Ages* (Albany, N.Y.: SUNY Press, 1993).

8. "A qué grandeza mi valor se estiende, / Si el alma veo a la pasión rendida? / Vasallo soy deste dolor que ofende, / En la dura prisión, mi propia vida. / ¿Cuál libertad de mi corona heredo? / ¿Qué puedo, al fin, si mi querer no puedo?" (17; My kingdom shrinks to this one doleful thought, / and I am become a vassal to my pain. / My courtiers are ghostly presences / I barely notice, locked inside my brain / as if in a dungeon, and I do not grant / that clemency I beg of myself. I can't [Slavitt, 25]). All quotations from João Pinto Delgado's poems are taken from the edition by Israël Salvator Révah (Lisbon: Institut Français au Portugal, 1954); references to this edition will be cited parenthetically by page number. There are two English translations of the Esther chapter of Delgado's book, one by Timothy Oelman, *Marrano Poets of the Seventeenth Century: An Anthology of the Poetry of João Pinto Delgado, Antonio Enríquez Gómez, and Miguel Barrios* (London/Toronto: Fairleigh Dickinson University Press, 1982), and a complete yet more liberal translation by David R. Slavitt, *The Poem of Queen Esther* (Oxford / New York 1999). I cite to the latter.

9. "I envy simple tradesmen in the streets / and even peasants, who are, compared to me, / happy in their lives, for their desires / are subject to their wills, and they are free / as I can never be. The joys they feel / are small and simple perhaps, but they are real" (Slavitt, 25).

10. "He has an orphaned cousin he has reared, / Esther, a girl of striking beauty, grace, / and virtue. She is the solace of his life / of exile that is gentled by her face / and its serene expression. Like the sun, / she warms the world and dazzles everyone. // Her eyes, those windows of the soul, are full / of understanding, kindness and a rare / compassion. When she raises them heavenward / in a fervor of humility and prayer, / simply to be near her is a gift— / a flower from which the sweetest perfumes drift. // Her lips are like that blossom's inner petals, / delicate, soft, and of a subtle hue / roses might envy, and her smile can gleam / brighter than the pearls one compares it to. / Have you ever, in a meadow at dawn, felt bliss / at its perfection? Esther's like this" (Slavitt, 26).

11. "La dulce boca que a gustar convida / un humor entre perlas destilado / y a no envidiar aquel licor sagrado / que a Júpiter ministra a el garzón de Ida" (The sweet mouth that invites you to taste / A liquid that is distilled through pearls, / Not to envy of that sacred liquor / That the boy from Ida served to Jove). Luis de Góngora y Argote, *La dulce boca* (1584), quoted from *Obras completas*, 5th ed. (Madrid 1961), 452.

12. Renate Schumacher-Wolfgarten, "Rose," in *Lexikon der christlichen Ikonographie*, ed. Engelbert Kirschbaum, vol. 3 (Rome: Verlag Herder, 1971), cols. 563–568; Norbert H. Ott, "Rosen," in *Lexikon des Mittelalters*, ed. Robert-Henri Bautier et al. (Munich: Artemis-Verlag, 1995), 7:1031–1032; Charles Sears Baldwin, *Medieval Rhetoric and Poetic* (New York: Peter Smith, 1928).

13. See also A. D. H. Fishlock, "Lope de Vega's 'La Hermosa Ester' and Pinto Delgado's 'Poema de la Reyna Ester': A Comparative Study," *Bulletin of Hispanic Studies* 32 (1955): 81–97.

14. "The courtiers bow as low before him as / before their emperor or their god. In this / offense to heaven he takes outrageous pleasure. / That something in their behavior—or in his— / is blasphemous never crosses his mind at all / or that, given enough time, such pride must fall. // The only man who appears to have no fear / (or hopes of gain from Haman's fickle favor / that can produce the same servility) / is Mordecai, whose heart seems not to quaver / at Haman's scowls and frowns, however black. / In bland assurance, Mordecai stares back" (Oelman, 35).

15. Volker Roloff, "Der fremde Calderón: Sartre und das spanische Barock-Theater," in *Literarische Begegnungen: Romanistische Studien zur kulturellen Identität, Differenz und Alterität (Festschrift für Karl Hölz zum 60. Geburtstag)*, ed. Frank Leinen (Berlin: Erich Schmidt Verlag, 2002), 232.

16. Hans Gerd Schulte, *El desengaño: Wort und Thema in der spanischen Literatur des Goldenen Zeitalters* (Munich: Wilhelm Fink Verlag, 1969).

17. "'How does your majesty allow,' he asks, / 'an alien element here who do not observe / your laws but keep their own? How can you let / such insolence go unpunished? They do not serve / your majesty but a god they cannot see. / They defy you and they live! How can this be? . . . The good will of the people is all

very well, / but a demonstration of force will better compel / correct behavior, here in the capital city, / and out in the provinces where rumor runs / with reports of the dire punishments that follow / insult or disobedience—anyone's. / Harshness is not in your nature, but you may find / it gentler, sometimes, than being kind'" (Oelman, 39–40).

18. Fishlock, "The Rabbinic Material in the *Ester* of Pinto Delgado." On the interpretation of Mordecai, see also the following Midrashic commentary on the book of Esther: *Midrash Rabbah*, vol. 9, *Esther*, ed. Harry Freedman and Maurice Simon, trans. Maurice Simon, 3rd ed. (London: Soncino Press, 1983). See also Dagmar Börner-Klein, *Eine babylonische Auslegung der Ester-Geschichte* (Frankfurt a.M.: Peter Lang, 1991).

19. "Now separated from the sacred Wall, / from the holy Temple rite, our kings all dead, / the imperiled people as leaves upon the wind, / subject to the fief of divers foreign laws / in the depths of affliction and seized by dread, / rumor assails and points the finger at them. // Who so humble as keeps silence at our wrong? / Who does not rejoice to hear our suffering? / And what fabricating tongue does not condemn / the innocent before the world's opinion? / For in such hatred, rejoicing at our change, / in our ill-fate they find their own well-being" (Oelman, 87–88).

20. Salomo Ibn Verga, *Schevet Jehuda*, ed. and trans. Sina Rauschenbach (Berlin: Parerga Verlag, 2006), 242.

21. "How is it, Lord, that the weight of our offense / thus forces you to take pleasure in our ill? / It is a cloud across an infinite sun, / and a mountain against your sea of mercies; / unless it be, though others worse condemning, / your light engulf, your sea arrest our error. // Behold, Lord, you were a brief sanctuary / for the people that now bewails your absence, / and though their sin has become a stumbling block, / you once loved and have not now forgotten them; / in such dire straits may the sound of their lament / break through the skies and rise to reach your hearing. // Whenever you desired to unsheathe your sword / to exact vengeance for the greatest sin, / you in mercy hearkened to your servant's zeal" (Oelman, 89).

22. "'Woe!' they answer him. 'If that which the heart / imprints in sketchy outline forebodes the truth, / it is not for naught the soul in fear freezes, / though the force of your position urge it on; / for fortune in its gifts is often cruel, / harsh towards the good, but to the wicked mild. // 'If it is from Judah that your conflict springs, / just is your grief and just the fear you feel, / for when Judah falls, he humbly falls to earth / and when he rises, rises proud to heaven; / for he is like the dust, he is like the stars, / prostrate in the dust, or raised up to the stars'" (Oelman, 91).

23. *Midrash Rabbah*, vol. 9, *Esther*, 29.

24. "Si el menor instrumento el verdadero / Sujeto fué de sublimar tu gloria / El dulce efeto a mi deseo espero / Y tu grandeza, en mi humildad, notoria: / Ya

nuevo aplauso escuchan mis oídos / Y vencedores vueltos los vencidos" (80; If it could be that the smallest instrument / could be the right one to exalt your glory, / I have hope my wish will gain its sweet intent / and humbly wait on your greatness known to all: / already a new applause comes to my ears / and those once vanquished now are turned to victors" [Oelman, 95]).

25. "Oh, perfect example of the highest Power, / mercy which succors, love which never forgets, / let him who sees his life sink in waves of dread, approach the altar of your divine Temple; / for if in mercy you ordain his ransom, / out of his very pain is born his triumph. // Sorrow is pleasure, reward the punishment / that the just man endures at your holy hand, / his torment bearing witness to that blessing, / which is to human feeling never subject: / because suffering is a ladder for the soul, / which stands on earth and rises to the heavens. // He it was who released the king from that strait / where blasphemy, secure in its own power, / encircled Zion with an infinite host, / denying even birds entry to its walls, / in an instant stripped of its illusions, when / it became the victim of the flashing blade. // He it is who shows the worthy in his depths / that, humble, he receives reward in double; / for his sake the just one in the hidden cave / did not take vengeance on the Lord's anointed; / to men he is a shield, to the city a wall, / from blows protected, from fear kept secure. // He it is who weakens the strength of evil / and with his wings leads goodness ever on, / for in hope he shows us his salvation, / which on his divine mercy he firmly founds: / if your power is such, if such your valor, / may you be throughout the world extolled in song" (Oelman, 97).

26. I have consulted the following German translation: *Der Midrasch Bereschit Rabba*, trans. August Wünsche (Leipzig, 1881).

27. Julius Fürst, introduction to *Der Midrasch zum Buche Esther*, trans. August Wünsche (Leipzig, 1881), vi.

28. Ibid., vii.

29. See the entry on the book of Lamentations by Jeffrey Howard Tigay, Alan Cooper, and Bathja Bayer, "Lamentations, Book of," in Berenbaum and Skolnik, *Encyclopedia Judaica*, 12:446–451. Norman K. Gottwald has argued that the acrostics reflect the immensity of the suffering described in the book's content in a sort of A–Z spectrum (*Studies in the Book of Lamentations*, 2nd ed. [London: Wipf & Stock, 1962]).

30. See Renate Brandscheidt, *Gotteszorn und Menschenleid: Die Gerichtsklage des leidenden Gerechten nach Klgl 3* (Treves: Paulinus Verlag, 1983).

31. Oelman, *Marrano Poets of the Seventeenth Century*, 133. A paperback edition of this book was published in 2007.

32. "The use of the Ferrara Bible looks like a gesture of affirmation of the poet's Jewishness, while by contrast he shows a preference in the poem itself for the interpretations of the Vulgate—indicating perhaps the hold of his upbringing on his aesthetic taste and outlook." Ibid.

33. "Lord, my imperfect voice / sprung from the heart / subjecting itself to the vain error, / today joins your prophet / to lament your Zion. // So that from the dust of the earth to the stars / from the world to the greatest remoteness / the vivid rays may appear / and the less and the more devout / may cry with me and them. // Grant from the highest treasure / your light to my blindness / your wisdom for what I do not understand / so that in a foreign land my lament may resist / its own negligence. / If I see in my lament / the smallest drop of that / which your immeasurable source contains, / I trust that my lament will be like the dew, / that makes our earth fertile. // And even if without wings I dare / to attempt such a flight, / and am afraid to move my lips, / inspire my lament anew / so that I may sing in tears."

34. "What misfortune, O City, / has brought to such a sad estate / your greatness and your majesty / and that most holy palace / to ruin and to solitude? // What sin has power to do so much / that I no longer know you now? / But, since I do not know, I fear, / for you were indeed a sinner / and he who judged you holy. // You spend your time in his offense, / through a habit long established, / and take delight in evil ways, / and so it is of no surprise / to see your freemen all enslaved. . . . // The reason why you tumbled down / and why you descended, humbled, / from the glory wherein you were / lies in the truth that you forsook, / in the vanity you followed. . . . // If you rebelled against the Lord, / the fruits which you garnered / in your customary harvest / have been the selfsame tribute / which makes you tributary now. // Not only have you seen the loss / of the honor which adorned you, / but you have seen your children die, / for the Lord has delivered them / into the greatest tyrant's hand. // How can your people find comfort / for themselves, amid their wailing, / when they come to consider / what paths they have wished to follow, / what paths they have wished to forsake" (Oelman, 98–103).

35. G. W. F. Hegel, *Aesthetics: Lectures on Fine Art*, trans. T. M. Knox (Oxford: Oxford University Press, 1975), 2:1118.

36. "While Israel / preserved the divine law / and remained true to its order / the world bowed before them / as did its monarchs. // But after it had sinned / and in exaggerated freedom / fell to its sins, / who did not / raise his hand to shame Zion?"

37. "My people changed their destiny, / when they turned to a vain cult, and / neglected me in their memory / and thus by their own hands / made their offense against me notorious. // A noblewoman never forgets / her precious jewelry, / the river recognizes the sea, / yet my people have forgotten me, / me, who is life itself. // Go and see if you find / in the fields of Zion, / where I planted my grape, / just one single righteous man among the many, / so that I could forgive Zion."

38. "I have lost my noblemen, who once honored me, / and also my priests; / when they abandoned the Lord / he turned away from them, so that / they parted

from me in the end. // Already the glory has been lost, / just as the esteemed crest / has converted to infamy. / They refuse to say who they are, / in order not to say what they were."

39. "The seven burning lights / representing in their burning the / moving stars / even in their bare form / carried those / who did not understand their existence."

40. "She is a garden planted / with a thousand flowers of myriad / hues by the skillful hand of God / which the summer did not parch dry / nor the ice's harshness wither. . . . // The ever-verdant amaranth / enlivens there its color; / the bowed acanthus may be seen / and the violet, whose pallor / so fittingly adorns it. // The lily, celestial and white, / laughing that the morning dew / should manifest itself in tears, / begs the wind its liveliness / so that it might lend her wings. // There beautiful in appearance / and princess of all flowers, / sits the rose arrayed with arms, / teaching that we should keep beauty / pure and guarded round with virtue. / The pomegranate opens up / its coral, which bursts to show itself, / and in the royal crown it wears / it demonstrates the faith a king / may have in a loyal vassal. . . . // This garden, then, in which there dwelt / pleasure near to everlasting, / where she chose to set her throne, / now her monarchy is ended / bemoans in silence her ill fate" (Oelman, 110–115).

41. "Lord, since the soul silently / calls your sweet name / to bring back your love / let that not be to man's disadvantage / which he does not articulate. // See the victims those became / who sprang from me / whose sighs blend / with the sound of foreign weapons, / sighs still audible in the noise of battle. // I no longer am the city that you / called your castle, that you lived in / while your temple still honored me. / Although my sins are old / you did not leave me. // Come to our aid, eternal goodness, / for our mistake does not limit / the fatherly mercy / which is infinite / and governs justly. // Hear the lament / a farewell stricken with fear, / with which we ask protection from the Saints."

42. Francisco de Quevedo, "Advertencia," in *Lágrimas de Hieremías Castellanas*, ed., intro., and commentary by Edward M. Wilson and José Manuel Blecua (Madrid: Consejo Superior de Investigaciones Científicas, 1953).

43. Ibid., 7 (fol. 2 in the MS). "What else is it but an affirmation of the Jews in their infidelity and a reassurance of those who Judaize?"

44. Ibid. "Thus Figueiro was not right when he said the words [of the book of Lamentations] confirmed the Jews in their pertinacity, nor did they induce them to Judaize. I say this in order to be sure that my intention is none other than the two objectives given." Quevedo had previously explained why he had attempted a commentary on the *Lamentationes*: "Dos cosas me an de disculpar: la una auer querido dar a mi lengua esta paraphrasi; la otra, defender con razones la Vulgata. Cosas, la una importante a mi nación; la otra, necessaria para reprehender el descuydo de los que pudiéndolo hacer mexor no lo hizieron" (ibid.; Two mitiga-

ting things must be considered: first that I wanted to attempt this paraphrase in my language, and second that I want to defend the Vulgate with reason. The first is important for my nation, the second is necessary so that those do not attempt such a thing who do it carelessly and had better not begin it).

45. "The story of Queen Esther, the lamentations of the prophet Jeremiah and the book of Ruth: the light that illuminates these stories does always warm the soul, even if they are veiled by human words in a way that the world calls embellishment, so different compared to that simple and mysterious texture of the Bible that can never be fully penetrated due to the inability of our gaze."

46. Quevedo, "Advertencia," 29–35. "Alef: He who falls from acquired greatness is as powerless alone as the widow lacking protection. There is no greater emptiness than the misery that exists among people, and there is no title not subject to change. One sees the city deserted, the woman widowed. . . . Vav: Where there is sin, even if there is no physical beauty, everything is missing, as God is missing. Thus the rich and powerful revolt just as the hungry and the poor, nothing gives them peace or satisfaction. . . . Tet: He who does not see the bad ending of human deeds will end badly, for one achieves good only through fear of evil."

47. Ibid., 112. "Hence Figueiro quotes the paraphrase in a scholarly manner, thus reconciling St. Jerome with Hebrew severity."

48. Marcelino Menéndez Pelayo, *Historia de los heterodoxos españoles* (Madrid: Consejo Superior de Investigaciones Científicas, 1963), 309–310. "Never again did Moshe Pinto Delgado reach such poetic heights, never again did he give such an impressive example of his metric elegance and vital penetration of the beautiful as in his paraphrase on the book of Lamentations, which forms the crown of his oeuvre and the memory thereof. There hardly are better *quintillas* in the entire 17th century and certainly none so free of pomposity, so inspired, and so rich in sentiment."

49. See Gillian Feeley-Harnik, "Naomi and Ruth: Building Up the House of David," in *Text and Tradition: The Hebrew Bible and Folklore*, ed. Susan Niditch (Atlanta: Scholars Press, 1990), 163–191; Derek Robert George Beattie, "The Book of Ruth as Evidence for Israelite Legal Practice," *Vetus Testamentum* 24 (1974): 251–267; Beattie, *Jewish Exegesis of the Book of Ruth* (Sheffield, UK: JSOT, 1977); and Jack M. Sasson, *Ruth: A New Translation with a Philological Commentary and a Formalist-Folklorist Interpretation*, 2nd ed. (Sheffield, UK: Sheffield University Press, 1989).

50. Moshe S. Weinfeld, David Sperling, and Aaron Rothkoff, "Ruth, Book of," in Berenbaum and Skolnik, *Encyclopedia Judaica*, 17:593.

51. "Discourse and kindness / of Ruth the Moabitess, / inspire my equally humble pen / to praise her humility. // . . . // Grant me, o Lord, that I write / about the one that accepted thy law / and who gave birth to a holy king / so that the haughty world may hear her example."

52. "And she says, 'Even if deep love / doesn't let me forget my pain / I see in you all the good that I / value in the world. // Daughters, even though I see in you / the good of my family, / you two should leave my country and go back / to yours. // Leave me alone and let my / tears be like waves, / you've cried with me so much, that from / today on you shall rest without me.'"

53. "'Follow her (Naomi tells her) who has / returned to her fields.' / But she responds: 'Since she left you, / I must not leave you. // You will see that I will differ from your / will in one point only: / yours is now my free will, / I can't offer you anything more. // With such strong ties my / soul is tied to yours, / that if this life united us / even death cannot separate us.'"

54. "Oh daughter, you do not understand, / you bind yourself to a new law. / Look up to Heaven / at which your conversion is directed."

55. "'With you (she says) I will go / be it near or far, / and where you choose to stay / I will, oh mother, stay with you. // Note this to be true / that if your people are now also mine / if I trust in the one you worship / I want to die where you die.' // Naomi, who observes the flight of Ruth's soul / from the world to heaven, / remembers her own faith / that she had forgotten in the past. // And because the soul is restored to the / eternal good / she returns happy to Bethlehem / in Judea, her homeland."

56. "He says: 'In your actions one can see / what virtue looks like. // Oh daughter, you are showing such signs of / the good that I see in you. / Do not leave my field / and stay with my maids. // All this estate that you see / I offer it to you, / it is my desire that you stay with me, / I beg that you stay. // . . . // Now you belong to the people of Israel / and take part in our glory, / accept the holy law like a saint, / may it be your escutcheon and protection."

57. "When they heard of his plans / they said, 'As Rachel and Leah / were the fortuitous foundation / for Israel, // Ruth shall be yours, may the Lord / give you such a home as / he did to Phares, who was born / by Tamar from highest family. // And the fruit of that good / born from your virtue, / shall be the example in Ephrathah, / eternal memory in Bethlehem.'"

58. "Obed was born, and from him Jesse, / from whom David descended, / whose heart the Lord / called equal."

59. "To the reader: Reader, dear friend, I am trying to gain your friendship, although this term is so general—this is exactly what I'm trying to do: to gain your friendship if you know me and to hope for it if you are only getting to know me. . . . Bear in mind that it requires great care and effort to meld the sacred text and human poetry in a manner that meets worldly tastes. The sacred text contains so many mysteries that one cannot trust one additional word, or even an additional letter. The changes one allows must preserve the metaphors and similes proper and necessary to the sacred text, as for example 'Light of my heart, breath of my eyes' and in the book of Ruth verse 10. And Moab, the wrong word is chosen to explain why Elimelech left [this place of] religious worship

for the land of the Gentiles, not because of poverty but on the contrary, as you know. Ultimately the most notable [errors] are not the result of carelessness, which would make them worse. Accept my offering with the benevolence I trust to find in you, for this may give me the courage to continue similar enterprises and begin new ones. May Heaven protect you."

60. "Two reasons among many have influenced me, your most famous Grace, to dedicate to you this labor of my recent years and fruit of my humility; just as the subject is among the greatest the world generally respects. The first reason was the consideration that the most generous spirits advocate protecting foreigners and encouraging them to put themselves at the service of their kings, some with arms and others with literature. . . . The second reason is the knowledge that among the servants of the royal Highness our Lord the King whose life Heaven may protect, no one else proves to be in all of his actions such a true pilgrim as your Grace. . . . Thus I recognized the obligation Your most famous Grace accepts by dint of the faith placed in you as expressed in Your most honorable title to protect those who make the effort to compose an artwork that, while it cannot halt the speed of years passing, at least may delay the death of remembrance. Hence I dared lay these flowers of divine literature at your feet: The Story of Queen Esther, the Lamentations of the Prophet Jeremiah, and the Book of Ruth. The light that illuminates these stories does always warm the soul, even if they are veiled by human words in a way that the world calls embellishment, so different compared to that simple and mysterious texture of the Bible that can never be fully penetrated owing to the inability of our gaze. Finally, Lord, if it is true that this world is not man's home, but the world where time does not change, then everybody is obliged to believe themselves a pilgrim in it. This is shown very clearly in Leviticus 25, when no one is permitted to sell his land until the Year of Jubilee, and where it is said that land must not be sold as a whole, for you are pilgrims and my inhabitants. If we compare this passage with Psalm 113 and Hebrews 115, there seems to be a contradiction, for it says that Heaven belongs to the Lord, and he gave the earth to the children of men. Well, if the earth belongs to humankind and we are equipped with that privilege, how can you deny them the possession of land in the latter? What does this mean? It means that even if a man says 'This is my country, this is the inheritance of my ancestors,' he must always know not to call it his own, so he does not sin against the property of God and jeopardize what awaits him. It is for these reasons that I ask the protection of such a high protector."

Conclusion

1. Dan Diner, "Marranische: Erwägungen zu verborgenen Traditionen bei Hannah Arendt," *Babylon: Beiträge zur jüdischen Gegenwart* 22 (2007): 68–71. It is important to note in this context that this is a notional constellation that is of

interest to both cultural and Jewish studies in multiple ways. An important example is the research by Andreas Kilcher at ETH Zürich, with whom I discussed on several occasions a discursive actualization of the concept of Marranism. Kilcher understands the term "Marranism" as a means of explaining Jewish history in the context of the opposing interests of universalism and particularism, either by direct reference or by means of analogy.

2. Dan Miron, *Verschränkungen: Über jüdische Literaturen* (Göttingen: Vandenhoeck & Ruprecht, 2007), 168.

3. See Fotis Jannidis, Gerhard Lauer, Matías Martínez, and Simone Winko, eds., *Die Rückkehr des Autors: Zur Erneuerung eines umstrittenen Begriffs* (Tübingen: De Gruyter, 1999), especially the essay by Matías Martínez, "Autorschaft und Intertextualität" (465–479, esp. 474: "If I support the thesis in this essay that the author is a necessary point of reference for any interpretation of his work, this only applies to the author in the sense of the work's conceptual creator"), and the introduction, "Rede über den Autor an die Gebildeten unter seinen Verächtern," esp. 15–18.

4. See Bakhtin's studies on Dostoyevsky and Rabelais: Mikhail M. Bakhtin, *Problems of Dostoevsky's Poetics*, ed. and trans. Caryl Emerson (Minneapolis: University of Minnesota Press, 1984); and *Rabelais and His World*, trans. Hélène Iswolsky (Bloomington: Indiana University Press, 1993).

Bibliography

Primary Sources

Biblia sacra iuxta vulgatam versionem. Edited by Robert Weber and Bonifatius Fischer. 4th ed. Stuttgart: Dt. Bibelges., 1994.

Delgado, João Pinto. *Poema de la Reyna Ester, Lamentaciones del Propheta Jeremias y Historia de Rut y varias poesías*. Introduction by Israël Salvator Révah. Lisbon: Institut Français au Portugal, 1954.

——. *The Poem of Queen Esther*. Translated by David R. Slavitt. Oxford / New York: Oxford University Press, 1999.

Ebreo, Leone. *Dialoghi d'amore*. Edited by Delfina Giovannozzi. Introduction by Eugenio Canone. Rome/Bari: Editori Laterza, 2008.

——. *Dialoghi d'amore: Hebräische Gedichte*. Mit einer Darstellung des Lebens und Werkes Leones. Bibliographie, Register zu den Dialoghi, Übertragung der hebräischen Texte, Regesten, Urkunden und Anmerkungen. Edited by Carl Gebhard. Heidelberg, 1929.

——. *Dialogues of Love*. Edited by Rossella Pescatori. Translated by Damian Bacich and Rossella Pescatori. Toronto: University of Toronto Press, 2009.

——. *The Philosophy of Love (Dialoghi d'amore)*. Translated by F. Friedeberg-Seeley and Jean H. Barnes. Introduction by Cecil Roth. London: Soncino Press, 1937.

——. [Hébreu, Léon]. *Dialogues d'amour*. Translation by Pontus de Tyard (1551). Text established by Tristan Dagron and Saverio Ansaldi. Introduction and notes by Tristan Dagron. Paris: Librairie Philosophique J. Vrin, 2006.

The Holy Bible: King James Version. New York: American Bible Society, 1999.

Ibn Verga, Salomo. *Schevet Jehuda: Ein Buch über das Leiden des jüdischen Volkes im Exil*. Edited and translated by Sina Rauschenbach. Berlin: Parerga Verlag, 2006.

The Life of Lazarillo de Tormes: His Fortunes and Adversities. Translated by Sir Clements Markham. London, 1908. Reprint, Digireads.com, 2009.

Der Midrasch Bereschit Rabba. Translated by August Wünsche. Leipzig, 1881.

Midrash Rabbah. Vol. 9, *Esther*. Edited by Harry Freedman and Maurice Simon. Translated by Maurice Simon. 3rd ed. London: Soncino Press, 1983.

Der Midrasch zum Buche Esther. Translated by August Wünsche. Eingeleitet und mit Noten versehen von Rabb. Dr. Julius Fürst. Leipzig, 1881.

Montaigne, Michel de. *Les Essais*. Edited by Jean Balsamo, Catherine Magnien-Simonin, and Michel Magnien. Paris: Gallimard, 2007.

———. *Essais*. Hg. und mit einem Nachwort versehen von Ralph-Rainer Wuthenow. Revidierte Fassung der von Johann Joachim Bode übertragenen Auswahl. Frankfurt a.M.: Insel Verlag, 2001.

———. *Essais*. Erste moderne Gesamtübersetzung von Hans Stilett. Frankfurt a.M.: Eichborn, 1998.

———. *Essais* [Versuche], nebst des Verfassers Leben. Nach der Ausgabe von Pierre Coste ins Deutsche übersetzt von Johann Daniel Tietz. Leipzig 1753, satzfaksimilierter Nachdruck Zürich: Diogenes, 1991–1992.

———. *Les Essais*. Text established and edited by Albert Thibaudet. Paris: Gallimard, 1950.

———. *The Complete Essays*. Translated by M. A. Screech. London: Penguin, 2004.

Rojas, Fernando de. *La Celestina*. Translated and edited by Dorothy S. Severin. Introduction by Stephen Gilman. Madrid: Cátedra, 2007.

———. *Celestina*. Translated by Peter Bush. London: Penguin, 2009.

———. *La Celestina oder Tragikomödie von Calisto und Melibea*. Translation and epilogue by Fritz Vogelsang. Frankfurt a.M.: Insel Verlag, 1990.

———. *La Celestina*. Edited by Julio Cejador. Madrid: Espasa-Calpe, 1958.

Vega, Garcilaso de la (El Inca). *Traducción de los Diálogos de Amor de León Hebreo*. 1590. Edited and with prologue by Andrés Soria Olmedo. Madrid: Biblioteca Castro, 1995.

La vida de Lazarillo de Tormes y de sus fortunas y adversidades. Edited by Francisco Rico. Madrid: Cátedra, 1987.

Secondary Sources

Abellán, José Luis. "Función cultural de la presencia judía en España." In Alcalá Galve, *Judíos, sefarditas, conversos*, 395–407.

Adler, Robert L. "Modernization of Spain and the Converso in the Work of Mariano José de Larra." *Hispania: A Journal Devoted to the Teaching of Spanish and Portuguese* 72 (1989): 483–490.

Agüera, Victorio G. "Salvación del cristiano nuevo en el 'Guzmán de Alfarache.'" *Hispania: A Journal Devoted to the Teaching of Spanish and Portuguese* 57 (1974): 23–30.

Ahlgren, Gillian T. W., ed. *The Inquisition of Francisca: A Sixteenth-Century Visionary on Trial*. Chicago: University of Chicago Press, 2005.

Albaret, Laurent. *L'Inquisition et la répression des dissidences religieuses au Moyen Âge: Dernières recherches*. Carcassonne: Centre d'Études Cathares, 2004.

Alcalá Galve, Ángel. "Ecos antijudíos en literatura aragonesa de la época de Fernando el Católico." *Trébede* 62 (2002): 27–33.

——. "From Dislike to Disguise: Jews and Conversos in Spanish Literature at the Time of the Expulsion (1474–1516)." In *Jews and Conversos at the Time of the Expulsion*, edited by Yom Tov Assis and Joseph Kaplan, 109–141. Jerusalem: Merkaz Zalman Shazar le-Toldot YiĐraël, 1999.

——. "Inquisitorial Control of Humanists and Writers." In *The Spanish Inquisition and the Inquisitorial Mind*, edited by Ángel Alcalá Galve, 321–360. New York: Columbia University Press, 1987.

——, ed. *Judíos, sefarditas, conversos: La expulsion de 1492 y sus consecuencias*. Valladolid: Ámbito Ediciones, 1995.

——. "El mundo converso en la literatura y la mística del Siglo de Oro." *Manuscrits* 10 (1992): 91–118.

——, ed. *The Spanish Inquisition and the Inquisitorial Mind*. New York: Columbia University Press, 1987.

Alegre, Atanasio. "Los criptojudíos españoles, una comunidad amurallada." *Revista Universidad de Antioquia* 273 (2003): 103–111.

Alfaro, Gustavo. "Los lazarillos y la Inquisición." *Hispanófila* 26, no. 3 (1983): 11–19.

Altmann, Alexander. "Ars Rhetorica as Reflected in Some Jewish Figures of the Italian Renaissance." In Cooperman, *Jewish Thought in the Sixteenth Century*, 1–22.

Amador de los Rios, José. *Historia social, política y religiosa de los judíos de España y Portugal*. 3 vols. Madrid, 1875/76.

Amiel, Charles. "The Archives of the Portuguese Inquisition: A Brief Survey." In Henningsen and Tedeschi, *The Inquisition in Early Modern Europe*, 79–99.

——. "La 'pureté de sang' en Espagne." *Études Inter-Ethniques* 6 (1983): 28–45.

Arbel, Benjamin. *Trading Nations: Jews and Venetians in the Early Modern Eastern Mediterranean*. New York: Brill, 1995.

Armbruster, Claudius. "Iberien und/oder Europa: Iberische Identitätskonstruktionen in den Literaturen Spaniens und Portugals." In *Dulce et decorum est philologiam colere (Festschrift für Dietrich Briesemeister zu seinem 65. Geburtstag)*, edited by Sybille Grosse and Axel Schönberger, 1485–1514. Berlin: Domus Editoria Europea, 1999.

——. "Iberische Wurzeln und Rhizome: Postkoloniale und periphere Identitätsbegründungen auf der Iberischen Halbinsel." In *Minorisierte Literaturen und Identitätskonzepte in Spanien und Portugal: Sprache, Narrative Entwürfe, Texte*, edited by Javier Gómez-Montero, 223–245. Darmstadt: Wissenschaftliche Buchgesellschaft, 2001.

——. "Inszenierungen von Religion und Politik: Tradition und Moderne des Mysterienspiels in den iberischen und iberoamerikanischen Kulturen und Literaturen." In *Pasajes–Passages–Passagen: Homenaje a / Mélanges offerts à / Festschrift für Christian Wentzlaff-Eggebert*, edited by Susanne Grunwald, Claudia Hammerschmidt, Valérie Heinen and Gunnar Nilsson, 713–728. Seville: Secretariado de Publicaciones de la Universidad de Sevilla, 2004.

Aronson-Friedman, Amy. "Identifying the Converso Voice in Fernando de Rojas' *La Celestina*." *Mediterranean Studies* 13 (2004): 77–105.

Artigas, María del Carmen. "Un breve comentario sobre el converso en *El licenciado Vidriera*." *Romance Notes* 43 (2002): 37–41.

Asensio, Eugenio. "La peculiaridad literaria de los conversos." *Anuario de Estudios Medievales* 4 (1967): 327–351.

Asencio, Manuel J. "La intención religiosa del *Lazarillo de Tormes* y Juan de Valdés." *Hispanic Review* 27 (1959): 78–102.

——. "El *Lazarillo* en su circunstancia histórica." *Revista de Literatura* 54 (1992): 101–128.

Ashtor, Eliyahu. "Documentos españoles de la Genizah." *Sefarad* 24 (1984): 41–80.

——. *The Jews of Moslem Spain*. Translated from the Hebrew by Aaron Klein and Jenny Machlowitz Klein. 3 vols. Philadelphia: Jewish Publication Society of America, 1973–1984.

Assis, Yom Tov. *The Golden Age of Aragonese Jewry: Community and Society in the Crown of Aragon, 1213–1327*. London / Portland, Ore.: Littman Library of Jewish Civilization, 1997.

——. *The Jews of Spain: From Settlement to Expulsion*. Jerusalem: World Zionist Organization; Dor Hemshech: Hebrew University of Jerusalem, 1988.

Aviles, Miguel, Jose Martinez Millan, and Virgilio Pinto. "El Archivo del Consejo de la Inquisición: Aportaciones para una historia de los archivos inquisitoriales." *Revista de Archivos, Bibliotecas y Museos* 81, no. 3 (1978): 459–518.

Ayala, Jorge M. "La tensión razón-fe en la filosofía judeo-musulmana de Al-Andalus." *Revista Española de Filosofía Medieval* 3 (1993): 21–29.

Azevedo, João Lúcio de. *História dos Cristãos-Novos Portugueses*. Lisbon: Clássica Editora, 1922.

Baader, Horst. "Der spanische Schelmenroman oder die Kunst der Uneindeutigkeit." In *Literatur und Spiritualität: Hans Sckommodau zum siebzigsten Geburtstag*, edited by Hans Rheinfelder, Pierre Christophorov, and Eberhard Müller-Bochat, 9–23. Munich: Wilhelm Fink Verlag, 1978.

Baer, Yitzhak. *Historia de los judíos en la España cristiana*. Barcelona: Riopiedras Ediciones, 1998.

——. *A History of the Jews in Christian Spain*. Vol. 1, *From the Age of Reconquest to the Fourteenth Century*. Translated from the Hebrew by Louis Schoffman.

Introduction by Benjamin R. Gampel. Philadelphia/Jerusalem: Jewish Publication Society, 1992.

Bakhtin, Mikhail M. [Bachtin, Michail M.] *Literatur und Karneval: Zur Romantheorie und Lachkultur*. Translated by Alexander Kaempfe. Frankfurt a.M.: Fischer Taschenbuch, 1990.

——. *Problems of Dostoevsky's Poetics*. Edited and translated by Caryl Emerson. Minneapolis: University of Minnesota Press, 1984.

——. *Rabelais and His World*. Translated by Hélène Iswolsky. Bloomington: Indiana University Press, 1993.

Baldwin, Charles Sears. *Medieval Rhetoric and Poetic*. New York: Peter Smith, 1928.

Barbera, Raymond E. "Fernando de Rojas, Converso." *Hispania: A Journal Devoted to the Teaching of Spanish and Portuguese* 51 (1968): 140–144.

Barkai, Ron. "Les trois cultures ibériques entre dialogue et polémique." In *Chrétiens, musulmans et juifs dans l'Espagne médiévale: De la convergence à l'expulsion*, edited by Ron Barkai, 227–251. Paris: Éditions du Cerf, 1994.

Barnett, Richard David, ed. *The Jews in Spain and Portugal before and after the Expulsion of 1492*. Vol. 1 of *The Sephardi Heritage: Essays on the History and Cultural Contribution of the Jews of Spain and Portugal*. New York: KTAV, 1971.

Barros, Carlos, ed. *Xudeus e conversos na historia*. Vol. 1, *Mentalidades e cultura*. Santiago de Compostela: Carlos Barros, 1994.

Bataillon, Marcel. *La Celestine selon Fernando de Rojas*. Paris: M. Didier, 1961.

——. *Erasmo y España*. Mexico City / Buenos Aires: Fondo de Cultura Económica, 1966.

——. "Melancolía renacentista o melancolía judía?" In *Estudios hispánicos: Homenaje a Archer M. Huntington*, 39–50. Wellesley, Mass.: Spanish Department, Wellesley College, 1952.

——. "Les nouveaux chrétiens de Segovie en 1510." *Bulletin Hispanique* 58, no. 2 (1956): 207–231.

——. "Pérégrinations espagnoles du juif errant." *Bulletin Hispanique* 43, no. 2 (1941): 81–122.

——. *Le roman picaresque*. Paris: La Renaissance du Livre, 1931.

Battesti-Pelegrin, Jeanne, and Monique de Lope. "Problèmes de la caractérisation du juif-converso dans la poésie des chansonniers du XVe siècle: Signes et marques du convers (Espagne, XVe–XVIe siècles)." *Études Hispaniques* 20 (1993): 31–61.

Bauer, Matthias. *Der Schelmenroman*. Stuttgart/Weimar: Metzler, 1994.

Baumann, Peter. "Der *Lazarillo de Tormes*, eine Travestie der Augustinischen Confessiones?" *Romanistisches Jahrbuch* 63 (2012): 285–291.

Baumgarten, Albert I., S. David Sperling, and Shalom Sabar. "Scroll of Esther." In Berenbaum and Skolnik, *Encyclopedia Judaica*, 16:215–220.

Beattie, Derek Robert George. "The Book of Ruth as Evidence for Israelite Legal Practice." *Vetus Testamentum* 24 (1974): 251–267.

——. *Jewish Exegesis of the Book of Ruth*. Sheffield, UK: JSOT, 1977.

Bautier, Robert-Henri, et al., eds. *Lexikon des Mittelalters*. Vol. 7. Munich: Artemis-Verlag, 1995.

Beinart, Haim. "The Converso Community in 15th Century Spain." In Barnett, *The Jews in Spain and Portugal*, 425–456.

——. "The Converso Community in 16th and 17th Century Spain." In Barnett, *The Jews in Spain and Portugal*, 457–478.

——. *Los conversos ante el tribunal de la Inquisición*. Barcelona: Riopiedras Ediciones, 1983.

——. *The Expulsion of the Jews from Spain*. Translated by Jeffrey Green. Oxford / Portland, Ore.: Littman Library of Jewish Civilization, 2002.

Bejarano Escanilla, Ana María. "Selomoh ben Reuben Bonafed, poeta y polemista." *Anuari de Filología* 14 (1991): 87–101.

Bellón, Juan Alfredo. "Judíos y conversos 'en el Cancionero de obras de burlas provocantes a risa' (Valencia, 1519)." *Miscelanea de Estudios Árabes y Hebraicos II: Filología Hebrea, Biblia y Judaismo* 32 (1982): 133–149.

Benabu, Isaac, ed. *Circa 1492: Proceedings of the Jerusalem Colloquium "Litterae Judaeorum in Terra Hispanica."* Jerusalem: Magnes Press, 1992.

Benardete, Mair José. *Hispanic Culture and Character of the Sephardic Jews*. 1952. 2nd ed. Edited and augmented by Marc D. Angel. New York: Sepher-Hermon Press for the Foundation for the Advancement of Sephardic Studies and Culture and Sephardic House at Congregation Shearith Israel, 1982.

Benbassa, Esther. "Questioning Historical Narratives: The Case of Balkan Sephardi Jewry." *Simon Dubnow Institute Yearbook* 2 (2003): 15–22.

Benbassa, Esther, and Aron Rodrigue. *The Jews of the Balkans*. Oxford: Blackwell, 1995.

——. *Sephardi Jewry: A History of the Judeo-Spanish Community, 14th–20th Centuries*. Berkeley / Los Angeles: University of California Press, 2000.

Benito Ruano, Eloy. "El memorial contra los conversos del bachiller Marcos García de Mora (Marquillos de Mazarambroz)." *Sefarad* 17 (1957): 314–351.

——. *Los orígenes del problema converso*. Barcelona: Ediciones El Albir, 1976.

Ben-Shalom, Ram. "Vikuah Tortosa, Vincente Ferrer u-be'ayat ha-anusim al-pi eduto shel Yitshaq Natan [The disputation of Tortosa, Vincent Ferrer, and the problem of the conversos according to the testimony of Isaac Nathan]." *Zion* 56 (1991): 21–45 (Hebr.).

Berenbaum, Michael, and Fred Skolnik. *Encyclopedia Judaica*. 2nd ed. Detroit: Macmillan Reference USA, 2007.

Bernáldez, Andrés. *Historia de los reyes católicos don Fernando y doña Isabel*. Madrid: Ediciones Atlas, 1953.

Bethencourt, Francisco. "Les hérétiques et l'Inquisition portugaise: Représentation et pratiques de persécution." In *Ketzerverfolgung im 16. und frühen 17. Jahrhundert*, edited by Silvana Seidel Menchi, 103–117. Wiesbaden: Harrassowitz, 1992.

Beusterien, John. "Blotted Genealogies: A Survey of the *Libros Verdes*." *Bulletin of Hispanic Studies* 78 (2001): 183–197.

Bickerman, Elias. *Four Strange Books of the Bible*. New York: Schocken Books, 1967.

Bjornson, Richard. "Guzman de Alfarache: Apologia for a 'Converso.'" *Romanische Forschungen* 85 (1973): 314–329.

Blasco, Asunción. "Jewish and Convert Jongleurs, Minstrels and 'Sonadores' in Saragossa (Fourteenth and Fifteenth Centuries)." *Assaph Studies in the Arts--Orbis Musicae*, no. 12 (1998): 49–72.

———. "Sefarad: Otra visión de España." In *Las Españas medievales*, edited by Julio Valderón Barique, 113–139. Valladolid: Universidad de Valladolid, 1999.

Blum, Claude, ed. *Montaigne, "Apologie de Raimond Sebond": De la* Theologia *à la* Théologie. Paris: Librairie Honoré Champion, 1990.

Bodian, Miriam. *Hebrews of the Portuguese Nation: Conversos and Community in Early Modern Amsterdam*. Bloomington: Indiana University Press, 1997.

———. "'Men of the Nation': The Shaping of Converso Identity in Early Modern Europe." *Past and Present* 143 (1994): 48–76.

Bonfil, Robert. "The Historian's Perception of the Jews in the Italian Renaissance: Towards a Reappraisal." *Revue des Études Juives* 143 (1984): 59–82.

Börner-Klein, Dagmar. *Eine babylonische Auslegung der Ester-Geschichte*. Frankfurt a.M.: Peter Lang, 1991.

Bossong, Georg, ed. *Das Wunder von al-Andalus: Die schönsten Gedichte aus dem Maurischen Spanien*. Translated from Arabic and Hebrew and annotated. Afterword by Edward Said. Munich: C. H. Beck Verlag, 2005.

Brandscheidt, Renate. *Gotteszorn und Menschenleid: Die Gerichtsklage des leidenden Gerechten nach Klgl 3*. Treves: Paulinus-Verlag, 1983.

Brann, Ross. *The Compunctious Poet: Cultural Ambiguity and Hebrew Poetry in Muslim Spain*. Baltimore: Johns Hopkins University Press, 1991.

Brann, Ross, and Adam Sutcliffe, eds. *Renewing the Past, Reconfiguring Jewish Culture: From Al-Andalus to the Haskalah*. Philadelphia: University of Pennsylvania Press, 2004.

Brasz, Chaya, and Yosef Kaplan, eds. *Dutch Jews as Perceived by Themselves and by Others: Proceedings of the Eighth International Symposium on the History of the Jews in the Netherlands*. Leiden/Boston: Brill, 2001.

Braude, Benjamin, and Bernard Lewis, eds. *Christians and Jews in the Ottoman Empire: The Functioning of a Plural Society*. New York: Holmes & Meier, 1982.

Brenes Carrillo, Dalai. "¿Quién es V. M. en *Lazarillo de Tormes*?" *Boletin de la Biblioteca de Menéndez Pelayo* 68 (1992): 73–88.

Brenner, Frédéric, dir. *Les derniers Marranes* (documentary film). Paris: Les Film d'Ici, 1990.

Brenner, Michael. "Das Judentum in Europa: Geschichte und Gegengeschichte." *Concilium: Internationale Zeitschrift für Theologie* 40 (2004): 162–167.

Briesemeister, Dietrich. "Mittelalterliche Fachprosa." In *Geschichte der spanischen Literatur*, edited by Christoph Strosetzki, 2nd ed., 27–34. Tübingen: De Gruyter, 1996.

Brownlee, Marina S., and Hans Ulrich Gumbrecht, eds. *Cultural Authority in Golden Age Spain*. Baltimore: Johns Hopkins University Press, 1995.

Das Buch der Inquisition: Das Originalhandbuch des Inquisitors Bernard Gui. Edited by and with an introduction by Petra Seifert. Translated by Manfred Pawlik. Augsburg: Nikol Verlagsgesellschaft, 1999.

Bunes Ibarra, Miguel Ángel de. "Concepto y formación del patrimonio hispanojudío." In *El legado material hispanojudío*, edited by Ana María López Alvarez and Ricardo Izquierdo Benito, 79–91. Cuenca: Ediciones Universidad de Castilla–La Mancha, 1998.

Bürger, Peter. *Das Verschwinden des Subjekts: Eine Geschichte der Subjektivität von Montaigne bis Barthes*. Frankfurt a.M.: Suhrkamp Verlag, 1998.

Burke, Peter. *Montaigne zur Einführung*. 3rd ed. Hamburg: Junius, 2004.

Busse, Winfried. "Die Sprache(n) der Sepharden: Ladino." In Rehrmann and Koechert, *Spanien und die Sepharden*, 133–143.

Cabezudo Astrain, José. "Los conversos aragoneses según los procesos de la Inquisición." *Sefarad* 18 (1958): 272–282.

Campose, Edmund Valentine. "Jews, Spaniards, and Portingales: Ambiguous Identities of Portuguese Marranos in Elizabethan England." *English Literary History* 69 (2002): 599–616.

Canelo, David Augusto. *O resgate dos marranos portugueses*. Belmonte, Portugal: D. A. Canelo, 1996.

Cantera Burgos, Francisco. "*El Cancionero de Baena*: Judíos y conversos en él." *Sefarad* 27 (1967): 71–111.

Cantera Montenegro, Enrique. "Negación de la 'Imagen del Judío' en la intelectualidad hispano-hebrea medieval: El ejemplo del Shebet Yehudah." *Aragón en la Edad Media*, nos. 14–15 (1999): 263–274.

Cardiel Sanz, Estrella. "La cuestión judía en *La Celestina*." In *Actas de las jornadas de estudios sefardíes*, edited by Antonio Viudas Camarasa, 151–159. Cáceres: Universidad de Extremadura, 1981.

Carpenter, Dwayne E. "A Converso Best-Seller: *Celestina* and Her Foreign Offspring." In *Crisis and Creativity in the Sephardic World, 1391–1648*, edited by Benjamin R. Gampel, 267–281. New York: Columbia University Press, 1997.

——. "The Sacred in the Profane: Jewish Scriptures and the First Comedy in Hebrew." In *Fernando de Rojas and "Celestina": Approaching the Fifth Centenary*, edited by Ivy A. Corfis and Joseph T. Snow, 229–236. Madison, Wis.: Hispanic Seminary of Medieval Studies, 1993.

Carrasco, Rafael. "El veritables senyals d'identitat dels jueus conversos espanyols." *L'Avenç* 210 (1997): 40–45.

Carrete Parrondo, Carlos, Marcelo Dascal, Francisco Márquez Villanueva, and Ángel Sáenz Badillos, eds. *Encuentros and Desencuentros: Spanish Jewish Cultural Interaction throughout History*. Tel Aviv: University Publishing Projects, 2000.

Castro, Américo. *Aspectos del vivir hispánico*. Madrid: Alianza, 1970.

——. *Aspectos del vivir hispánico: Espiritualismo, mesianismo, actitud personal en los siglos XIV al XVI*. Santiago de Chile: Cruz del Sur, 1949.

——. *"La Celestina" como contienda literaria: Castas y casticismos*. Madrid: Revista de Occidente, 1965.

——. *De la edad conflictiva: Crisis de la cultura española en el siglo XVII*. 2nd ed. Madrid: Taurus, 1963.

——. *España en su historia: Cristianos, moros y judíos*. Barcelona: Crítica, 2001.

——, ed. *Hacia Cervantes*. Madrid: Taurus, 1957.

——. "El *Lazarillo de Tormes*." In Castro, *Hacia Cervantes*, 135–141.

——. "Juan de Mal Lara y su 'Filosofía vulgar'" In Castro, *Hacia Cervantes*, 142–182.

——. *La realidad histórica de España*. Mexico City: Porrúa, 1954.

——. *Spanien: Vision und Wirklichkeit* [*La realidad histórica de España*]. Translated by Suzanne Heintz. Cologne: Kiepenheuer & Witsch, 1957.

Cejador, Julio. "El bachiller Hernando de Rojas verdadero autor de *La Celestina*." *Revista Crítica Hispano-Americana* 2 (1916): 85–86.

Chamorro Martínez, Jose Maria. "Vida y costumbres de los judeo-conversos, según los procesos inquisitoriales." *Revista de Dialectología y Tradiciones Populares* 48 (1993): 57–84.

Coll-Tellechea, Reyes, and Anthony N. Zahareas. "On the Historical Function of Narrative Forms: *Lazarillo de Tormes*." *Crítica Hispánica* 19 (1997): 110–127.

Comparetti, Domenico. *Vergil in the Middle Ages*. Translated by E. F. M. Benecke, with an introduction by Jan M. Ziolkowski. Princeton, N.J.: Princeton University Press, 1997.

——. *Virgilio nel medio evo*. Florence, 1872.

Concha, Victor de la. "La intención religiosa del *Lazarillo*." *Revista de Filología Española* 55 (1972): 243–277.

Contreras, Jaime. "Aldermen and Judaizers: Cryptojudaism, Counter-Reformation, and Local Power." In *Culture and Control in Counter-Reformation Spain*, edited by Anne J. Cruz and Mary Elizabeth Perry, 93–123. Minneapolis: University of Minnesota Press, 1992.

——. "Conversos y judaizantes después de 1492: Una relación desigual." In *Los judíos de España: Historia de una diáspora, 1492–1992*, edited by Henry Méchoulan, 60–70. Madrid: Agapea, 1993.

——. "Domínguez Ortiz y la historiografía sobre judeo-conversos." *Manuscrits* 14 (1996): 59–79.

——. "Limpieza de sangre, cambio social y manipulación de la memoria." In Asociación de Amigos del Museo Sefardí, *Inquisición y conversos*, 81–101. Toledo: Asociación de Amigos del Museo Sefardí–Caja de Castilla–La Mancha, 1994.

Contreras, Jaime, and Gustav Henningsen. "Forty-Four Thousand Cases of the Spanish Inquisition (1540–1700): Analysis of a Historical Data Bank." In Henningsen and Tedeschi, *The Inquisition in Early Modern Europe*, 100–129.

Cooperman, Bernard Dov, ed. *In Iberia and Beyond: Hispanic Jews between Cultures (Proceedings of a Symposium to Mark the 500th Anniversary of the Expulsion of Spanish Jewry)*. Newark, Del. / London: University of Delaware Press, 1998.

——, ed. *Jewish Thought in the Sixteenth Century*. Cambridge, Mass.: Center for Jewish Studies, Harvard University, 1983.

Cordero Cuevas, Idalia. "El 'vivir desviviéndose' de un judeoconverso español." *Revista de Estudios Hispanicos* 21 (1994): 57–67.

Coronas Tejada, Luis. *Conversos and Inquisition in Jaén*. Jerusalem: Magnes Press, 1988.

Csáky, Moritz. "Gedächtnis, Erinnerung und die Konstruktion von Identität: Das Beispiel Zentraleuropas." In *Nation und Nationalismus in Europa: Kulturelle Konstruktion von Identitäten (Festschrift für Urs Altermatt)*, edited by Catherine Bosshart-Pfluger, Joseph Jung, and Franziska Metzger, 25–49. Frauenfeld/Stuttgart/Vienna: Huber Verlag, 2002.

——. "Geschichte und Gedächtnis: Erinnerung und Erinnerungsstrategien im narrativen historischen Verfahren–Das Beispiel Zentraleuropas." In *Klio ohne Fesseln? Historiographie im östlichen Europa nach dem Zusammenbruch des Kommunismus*, edited by Alojz Ivanišević, Andreas Kappeler, Walter Lukan, and Arnold Suppan, 61–80. Vienna / Frankfurt a.M.: Peter Lang, 2002.

Curtius, Ernst Robert. *Europäische Literatur und lateinisches Mittelalter*. Bern/Munich: Francke Verlag, 1948.

Davidson, Herbert. "Medieval Jewish Philosophy in the Sixteenth Century." In Cooperman, *Jewish Thought in the Sixteenth Century*, 106–144.

Dedieu, Jean-Pierre. "The Archives of the Holy Office of Toledo as a Source for Historical Anthropology." In Henningsen and Tedeschi, *The Inquisition in Early Modern Europe*, 158–189.

——. "Pecado original o pecado social? Reflexiones en torno a la constitución y la definición del grupo judeo-converso en Castilla." *Manuscrits* 10 (1992): 61–76.

Dequeker, Luc, and Werner Verbeke, eds. *The Expulsion of the Jews and Their Emigration to the Southern Low Countries (15th–16th c.)*. Leuven: Leuven University Press, 1998.

Deyermond, Alan D. "Evidence for Lost Literature by Jews and Conversos in Medieval Castile and Aragon." *Donaire* 6 (1996): 19–30.

Díaz Esteban, Fernando. "La prosa hispanohebrea." In *La vida judía en Sefarad*, edited by Elena Romero, 81–114. Madrid: Ministerio de Cultura, 1992.

Díaz Esteban, Máximo. "La expulsión y la justificación de la conversión simulada." *Sefarad* 56 (1996): 251–263.

Díaz-Mas, Paloma. *Los sefardíes: Historia, lengua y cultura*. Barcelona: Riopiedras Ediciones, 1986.

———. *Sephardim: The Jews from Spain*. Translated by George K. Zucker. Chicago: University of Chicago Press, 1992.

Díaz-Mas, Paloma, and Cristina de la Puente González, eds. *Judaísmo e islam*. Madrid: Crítica, 2007.

DiFranco, Ralph. "Hispanic Biographical Criticism: The Converso Question." *Michigan Academician: Papers of the Michigan Academy of Science, Arts, and Letters* 12 (1979): 85–96.

Dille, Glen. "Antonio Enríquez Gómez: The *Converso* and the Picaresque Novel." *Pe'amim: Studies in the Cultural Heritage of Oriental Jewry* 46 (1991): 222–234 (Hebr.).

Diner, Dan. "Ereignis und Erinnerung: Über Variationen historischen Gedächtnisses." In *Shoah: Formen der Erinnerung*, edited by Nicolas Berg, Jess Jochimsen, and Bernd Stiegler, 13–30. Munich: Wilhelm Fink Verlag, 1996.

———. "From Society to Memory: Reflections on a Paradigm Shift." In *On Memory: An Interdisciplinary Approach*, edited by Doron Mendels, 149–164. Oxford: Peter Lang International Academic Publishers, 2007.

———. "Geschichte der Juden: Paradigma einer europäischen Historie." In *Annäherungen an eine europäische Geschichtsschreibung*, edited by Gerald Stourzh, 85–102. Vienna: Verlag der Österreichischen Akademie der Wissenschaften, 2002.

———. "Jüdische Minderheitenerfahrung: Von der Korporation zur Nationalität." In *Mut zur Freiheit: Ein Leben voller Projekte (Festschrift zum 80. Geburtstag von Wolfgang Marcus)*, edited by Mike Schmeitzner and Heinrich Wiedemann, 425–432. Berlin: LIT, 2007.

———. "Marranische Einschreibungen: Erwägungen zu verborgenen Traditionen bei Hannah Arendt." *Babylon: Beiträge zur jüdischen Gegenwart* 22 (2007): 62–71.

———. "Neutralisierung und Tolerierung von Differenz: Über institutionelle Internalisierungen von Religion und Ethnos." In *Der demokratische Nationalstaat in den Zeiten der Globalisierung: Politische Leitideen für das 21. Jahrhundert*, edited by Herfried Münkler, 41–55. Berlin: Akademie Verlag, 2002.

——, ed. *Synchrone Welten: Zeitenräume jüdischer Geschichte*. Göttingen: Vandenhoeck & Ruprecht, 2005.

——. "Von 'Gesellschaft' zu 'Gedächtnis': Über historische Paradigmenwechsel." In *Gedächtniszeiten: Über jüdische und andere Geschichten*, edited by Dan Diner, 7–15. Munich: C. H. Beck, 2003.

Domínguez Ortiz, Antonio. *Los judeoconversos en España y América*. Madrid: Istmo, 1971.

——. *Los judeoconversos en la España moderna*. Madrid: MAPFRE, 1992.

——. "Los judeoconversos en la vida española del Renacimiento." In *Actas de las Jornadas de Estudios Sefardíes*, edited by Antonio Viudas Camarasa, 189–200. Cáceres: Universidad de Extremadura, 1981.

DuBois, Gene W., and Colbert I. Nepaulsingh. "Letters on 'Monocultural Criticism.'" *La Corónica* 29 (2000): 231–237.

Duke, Alastair C. "A Footnote to 'Marrano Calvinism' and the Troubles of 1566–1567 in the Netherlands." *Bibliothèque d'Humanisme et Renaissance* 30 (1968): 147–148.

Dunn, Peter N. "*Lazarillo de Tormes*: The Case of the Purloined Letter." *Revista de Estudios Hispánicos* 22, no. 1 (1988): 1–14.

Dutton, Brian. "Unas notas sobre *Lazarillo de Tormes*." In *Busquemos otros montes y otros ríos: Estudios dedicados a Elias L. Rivers*, edited by Brian Dutton and Victoriano Roncero López, 113–126. Madrid: Editorial Castalia, 1992.

Edwards, John. "The Beginnings of a Scientific Theory of Race? Spain, 1450–1600." In Stillman and Stillman, *From Iberia to Diaspora*, 179–196.

——. "The Conversos: A Theological Approach." *Bulletin of Hispanic Studies* 62 (1985): 39–49.

——. "Jewish Testimony to the Spanish Inquisition: Teruel, 1484–87." *Revue des Études Juives* 143 (1984): 333–350.

——. "'Raza' y religión en la España de los siglos XVI y XVII: Una revisión de los estatutos de 'limpieza de sangre.'" *Anales de la Universidad de Alicante: Historia Medieval* 7 (1988): 243–261.

——. *Religion and Society in Spain, c. 1492*. Aldershot: Ashgate Variorum, 1996.

——. *The Spanish Inquisition*. Stroud, UK: Tempus, 1999. Translated into German as *Die spanische Inquisition* by Harald Ehrhardt. Düsseldorf/Zurich: Artemis & Winkler, 2003.

——. "Was the Spanish Inquisition Truthful? Review Essay." *Jewish Quarterly Review* 87 (1997): 351–366.

Edwards, John, David Gitlitz, Martha Krow-Lucal, Francisco Márquez Villanueva, Mark Meyerson, David Nirenberg, Angel Sáenz-Badillos, Judit Targarona, and John Zemke. "Inflecting the *Converso* Voice." *La Corónica* 25, no. 2 (1997): 159–194.

Empiricus, Sextus. *Grundriß der pyrrhonischen Skepsis*. Edited, translated, and introduction by Malte Hossenfelder. 2nd ed. Frankfurt a.M.: Suhrkamp, 1993.

Epstein, Mark Alan. *The Ottoman Jewish Communities and Their Role in the Fifteenth and Sixteenth Centuries*. Freiburg: Klaus Schwarz Verlag, 1980.

Escudero, José Antonio. "Netanyahu y los orígenes de la Inquisición española." *Revista de la Inquisición* 7 (1998): 9–46.

Ettinghausen, Henry. "Quevedo's *Converso pícaro*." *Modern Language Notes* 102 (1987): 241–254.

Farinelli, Arturo. *Marrano: Storia di un vituperio*. Geneva: Léo S. Olschki, 1925.

Faur, José. *In the Shadow of History: Jews and Conversos at the Dawn of Modernity*. Albany, N.Y.: SUNY Press, 1992.

Feeley-Harnik, Gillian. "Naomi and Ruth: Building Up the House of David." In *Text and Tradition: The Hebrew Bible and Folklore*, edited by Susan Niditch, 163–191. Atlanta: Scholars Press, 1990.

Feingold, Ben-Ami. "Historical Dramas on the Inquisition and Expulsion." *Journal of Theatre and Drama* 1 (1995): 9–30.

Feldman, Seymour. *Philosophy in a Time of Crisis: Don Isaac Abravanel, Defender of the Faith*. London: Psychology Press, 2003.

———. "Platonic Cosmologies in the *Dialoghi d'amore* of Leone Ebreo (Judah Abravanel)." *Viator* 36 (2005): 557–582.

Ferré, Lola. "Los judíos, transmisores y receptores de la sabiduría medieval." *Revista Española de Filosofía Medieval* 7 (2000): 81–93.

Ferrer-Chivite, Manuel. "Las *Coplas del Provincial*: Sus conversos y algunos que no lo son." *La Corónica* 10, no. 2 (1982): 156–178.

———. "El factor judeo-converso en el proceso de consolidación del título 'don.'" *Sefarad* 45 (1985): 131–173.

———. "Sustratos conversos en la creación de *Lázaro de Tormes*." *Nueva Revista de Filología Hispánica* 33 (1984): 352–379.

Fishlock, A. D. H. "Lope de Vega's 'La Hermosa Ester' and Pinto Delgado's 'Poema de la Reyna Ester': A Comparative Study." *Bulletin of Hispanic Studies* 32 (1955): 81–97.

———. "The Rabbinic Material in the *Ester* of Pinto Delgado." *Journal of Jewish Studies* 2, no. 1 (1950): 37–50.

Fontes, Manuel da Costa. *The Art of Subversion in Inquisitorial Spain*. West Lafayette, Ind.: Purdue University Press, 2004.

———. "Four Portuguese Crypto-Jewish Prayers and Their 'Inquisitorial' Counterparts." *Mediterranean Language Review* 6–7 (1993): 67–104.

———. "The Idea of Exile in *La lozana andaluza*: An Allegorical Reading." In *Jewish Culture and the Hispanic World: Essays in Memory of Joseph H. Silverman*, edited by Samuel G. Armistead, Mishael M. Caspi, and Murray Baumgarten, 145–160. Newark, N.J.: Juan de la Cuesta, 2001.

Forcadas, Alberto M. "'Mira a Bernardo' y el 'Judaísmo' de *La Celestina*." *Boletín de Filología Española* 46–49 (1973): 27–45.

Freund, Scarlett, and Teofilo F. Ruiz. "Jews, Conversos, and the Inquisition in Spain, 1391–1492: The Ambiguities of History." In *Jewish-Christian Encounters over the Centuries: Symbiosis, Prejudice, Holocaust, Dialogue*, edited by Marvin Perry and Frederick M. Schweitzer, 169–195. New York: Peter Lang, 1994.

Friedman, Jerome. "Jewish Conversion, the Spanish Pure Blood Laws and Reformation: A Revisionist View of Racial and Religious Antisemitism." *Sixteenth Century Journal* 18 (1987): 3–29.

Friedrich, Hugo. *Montaigne*. 3rd ed. Tübingen/Basel: Franke, 1993.

Garrido Pallardo, Fernando. *Los problemas de Calixto y Melibea y el conflicto de su autor*. Figueres: Canigó, 1957.

Garvin, Barbara. "The Language of Leone Ebreo's *Dialoghi d'amore*." *Italia* 13–15 (2001): 181–210.

Gerber, Jane S. *The Jews of Spain: A History of the Sephardic Experience*. New York: Free Press, 1992.

Gerli, E. Michael. "The Ambivalent Converso Condition." Review of *The Evolution of Converso Literature: The Writings of the Converted Jews of Medieval Spain*, by Gregory B. Kaplan. *Calíope: Journal of the Society for Renaissance & Baroque Hispanic Poetry* 9 (2003): 93–102.

———. "Performing Nobility: Mosén Diego de Valera and the Poetics of Converso Identity." *La Corónica* 25, no. 1 (1996): 19–36.

Gershenzon, Shoshanna. "The Circle Metaphor in Leone Ebreo's *Dialoghi d'amore*." *Daat* 29 (1992): 5–17.

Gessmann, Martin. *Montaigne und die Moderne: Zu den philosophischen Grundlagen einer Epochenwende*. Hamburg: Meiner, 1997.

Gier, Alfred. "12.–14. Jahrhundert: Lyrik, Epik, Roman und Drama." In *Geschichte der spanischen Literatur*, edited by Christoph Strosetzki, 2nd ed., 1–26. Tübingen: Max Niemeyer Verlag, 1996.

Gil, Juán. *Los conversos y la Inquisición sevillana: Ensayo de prosopografía*. Seville: Universidad de Sevilla, 2001.

Gilman, Stephen. "The Case of Diego Alonso: Hypocrisy and the Spanish Inquisition." *Daedalus* (June 1979): 135–144.

———. "The 'Conversos' and the Fall of Fortune." In Hornik, *Collected Studies in Honour of Américo Castro's Eightieth Year*, 127–136.

———. "The Death of Lazarillo de Tormes." *Publications of the Modern Language Association* 81 (1966): 149–166.

———. *La España de Fernando de Rojas: Panorama intelectual y social de "La Celestina."* Madrid: Taurus, 1978.

———. "A Generation of Conversos." *Romance Philology* 33 (1979): 87–101.

———. "Matthew V:10 in Castilian Jest and Earnest." In *Studia Hispanica in honorem R. Lapesa*, edited by Eugenio de Bustos, Jorge Guillén, and Américo Castro, 257–265. Madrid: Gredos, 1972.

——. *The Spain of Fernando de Rojas: The Intellectual and Social Landscape of "La Celestina."* Princeton, N.J.: Princeton University Press, 1972.

Giovanni, Norman Thomas di, and Susan Ashe. "A Marrano on Trial: Before the Holy Office of the Inquisition." *Hopscotch* 1 (1999): 102–115.

Gitlitz, David M. "Divided Families in 'Converso' Spain." *Shofar* 11 (1993): 1–19.

——. "Hybrid Conversos in the 'Libro llamado el Alboraique.'" *Hispanic Review* 60 (1992): 1–17.

——. "Inquisition Confessions and *Lazarillo de Tormes*." *Hispanic Review* 68, no. 1 (2000): 53–74.

——. *Secrecy and Deceit: The Religion of the Crypto-Jews*. Philadelphia: Jewish Publication Society, 1996.

Glick, Thomas F. "On Converso and Marrano Identity." In *Crisis and Creativity in the Sephardic World, 1391–1648*, edited by Benjamin R. Gampel, 59–76. New York: Columbia University Press, 1997.

Goitstein, Denise R., and Anne Grynberg. "French Literature." In Berenbaum and Skolnik, *Encyclopedia Judaica*, 14:238–252.

Goldstein, David. *The Jewish Poets of Spain: 900–1250*. Harmondsworth, UK: Penguin, 1971.

Gómez-Moriana, Antonio. "Autobiografía y discurso ritual: Problemática de la confesión autobiográfica destinada al tribunal inquisitorial." *Co-Textes* 8 (1984): 81–103.

——. "The Subversion of the Ritual Discourse: An Intertextual Reading of the *Lazarillo de Tormes*." *Sociocriticism* 5 (1989): 55–81.

Góngora y Argote, Luis de. *Obras Completas*. 5th ed. Madrid: Aguilar, 1961.

González Cañal, Rafael. "Judíos y conversos en la poesía satírica del barroco." In *Judeoconversos y moriscos en la literatura del Siglo de Oro*, edited by Irene Andrés-Suárez, 101–128. Neuchâtel: Presses Universitaires de Franche-Comté, 1995.

Gonzalo Maeso, David. "Sobre la etimología de la voz 'marrano' (criptojudío)." *Sefarad* 25 (1955): 373–385.

Goodman, Lenn E. *Neoplatonism and Jewish Thought*. Albany, N.Y.: SUNY Press, 1992.

Gottwald, Norman K. *Studies in the Book of Lamentations*. 2nd ed. London: Wipf & Stock, 1962.

Goytisolo, Juan. *España y los españoles*. Barcelona: Lumen, 1979.

Graetz, Heinrich. *Geschichte der Juden: Von den ältesten Zeiten bis auf die Gegenwart*. Leipzig, 1896.

Graizbord, David L. *Souls in Dispute: Converso Identities in Iberia and the Jewish Diaspora, 1580–1700*. Philadelphia: University of Pennsylvania Press, 2004.

Green, Otis H. "Fernando de Rojas, Converso and Hidalgo." *Hispanic Review* 15 (1947): 384–387.

Greenblatt, Stephen J. *Renaissance Self-Fashioning: From More to Shakespeare*. Chicago: University of Chicago Press, 1980.

Griffin, Clive. *Journeymen-Printers, Heresy, and the Inquisition in Sixteenth-Century Spain*. Oxford: Oxford University Press, 2005.

Guillén, Claudio. Introduction to *Lazarillo de Tormes*, edited by Claudio Guillén. New York: Dell, 1966.

Gumbrecht, Hans Ulrich. *Eine Geschichte der spanischen Literatur*. Frankfurt a.M.: Suhrkamp, 1990.

——. "Konsequenzen der Rezeptionsästhetik oder Literaturwissenschaft als Kommunikationssoziologie." *Poetica* 7 (1975): 388–413.

——. "Literarische Gegenwelten, Karnevalskultur und die Epochenschwelle vom Spätmittelalter zur Renaissance." In *Literatur in der Gesellschaft des Spätmittelalters*, edited by Hans Ulrich Gumbrecht, 95–149. Heidelberg: Winter Verlag, 1980.

——. "Zur Pragmatik der Frage nach persönlicher Identität." In *Identität: Poetik und Hermeneutik*, vol. 8, edited by Odo Marquard and Karlheinz Stierle, 674–684. Munich: Wilhelm Fink Verlag, 1979.

Guttmann, Jacob. *Die Philosophie des Salomon Ibn Gabirol*. Göttingen, 1889. Reprint, Hildesheim: Georg Holms Verlag, 1979.

Gutwirth, Eleazar. "From Jewish to Converso Humour in Fifteenth-Century Spain." *Bulletin of Hispanic Studies* 67 (1990): 253–264.

——. "Lineage in XVth Century Hispano-Jewish Thought." *Miscelánea de Estudios Árabes y Hebraicos* 34 (1985): 85–91.

——, ed. *Ten Centuries of Hispano-Jewish Culture*. Cambridge: Cambridge University Library, 1992.

Hanrahan, Thomas. "*Lazarillo de Tormes*: Erasmian Satire or Protestant Reform?" *Hispania* 66 (1983): 333–339.

Hassán, Iacob M., and Ricardo Izquierdo Benito. *Judíos en la literatura española: IX curso cultural hispanojudía y sefardí de la universidad de Castilla–La Mancha*. Cuenca: Ediciones Universidad de Castilla–La Mancha, 2001.

Hausmann, Frank-Rutger. "Nachwort zur dritten Auflage." In Friedrich, *Montaigne*, 379–393.

Hegel, Georg Wilhelm Friedrich. *Ästhetik*. Berlin: Aufbau Verlag, 1955.

——. *Hegel's Aesthetics: Lectures on Fine Art*. Translated by T. M. Knox. Oxford: Oxford University Press, 1975.

Heinen, Eugen. "Jüdische Spuren in der Literatur und Sprache Spaniens." In *Zur Geschichte des Iberischen Judentums, der Sepharden und Marranen*, vol. 2 of *Sephardische Spuren*, edited by Eugen Heinen, 169–223. Kassel: Verlag Winfried Jenior, 2002.

Hempfer, Klaus W. "Lektüren von Dialogen." In *Möglichkeiten des Dialogs: Struktur und Funktion einer literarischen Gattung zwischen Mittelalter und Renaissance in Italien*, edited by Klaus W. Hempfer, 1–38. Stuttgart: Steiner, 2002.

——. "Probleme traditioneller Bestimmungen des Renaissancebegriffs und die epistemologische 'Wende.'" In *Renaissance: Diskursstrukturen und epistemologische Voraussetzungen: Literatur, Philosophie, Bildende Kunst*, edited by Klaus W. Hempfer, 9–45. Stuttgart: Steiner, 1993.

Hendrick, Philip. *Montaigne et Sebond: L'art de la traduction*. Paris: H. Champion, 1996.

Henningsen, Gustav, and John Tedeschi. *The Inquisition in Early Modern Europe: Studies on Sources and Methods*. DeKalb: Northern Illinois University Press, 1986.

Hering Torres, Max Sebastián. "'Limpieza de sangre': Rassismus in der Vormoderne?" In *Rassismus*, edited by Max Sebastián Hering Torres and Wolfgang Schmale, 20–36. Innsbruck: Studien-Verlag, 2003.

Herskovits, Andrew. "Towards a Positive Image of the Jew in the *Comedia*." *Bulletin of the Comediantes* 57 (2005): 251–282.

Hess, Gerhard. "Zu Montaignes Abstammung: Ein Bericht." *Zeitschrift für Französische Sprache und Literatur* 64 (1942): 220–227.

Heymann, Fritz. *Tod oder Taufe: Die Vertreibung der Juden aus Spanien und Portugal im Zeitalter der Inquisition*. Frankfurt a.M.: Judischer Verlag bei Athenaum, 1988.

Hilfrich, Carola. "Autobiography as a Spectropoetics of the Mother: On Hélène Cixous's Recent Works." In *Zeitgenössische jüdische Autobiographie*, edited by Christoph Miething, 129–146. Tübingen: De Gruyter, 2003.

Hoenerbach, Wilhelm. *Islamische Geschichte Spaniens*. Zurich/Stuttgart: Artemis, 1970.

Hornik, Marcel P., ed. *Collected Studies in Honour of Américo Castro's Eightieth Year*. Oxford: Lincombe Lodge Research Library, 1965.

——. "Introduction: Profiles of Conversos." In Hornik, *Collected Studies in Honour of Américo Castro's Eightieth Year*, 7–20.

Hoschander, Jacob. "The Book of Esther in the Light of History." *Jewish Quarterly Review* 9 (1918): 1–41.

Hughes, Aaron W. "Transforming the Maimonidean Imagination: Aesthetics in the Renaissance Thought of Judah Abravanel." *Harvard Theological Review* 97 (2004): 461–484.

Huisman, Piet. *Sephardim: The Spirit That Has Withstood the Times*. Son, The Netherlands: Huisman Editions, 1986.

Hutcheson, Gregory S. "Cracks in the Labyrinth: Juan de Mena, Converso Experience, and the Rise of the Spanish Nation." *La Corónica* 25 (1996): 37–52.

——. "Inflecting the Converso Voice." *La Corónica* 25 (1996): 3–5.

Idel, Moshe. "The Sources of the Circle Images in the *Dialoghi d'amore*." *Iyyun* 28 (1978): 156–166 (Hebr.).

Incledon, John. "Textual Subversion in *Lazarillo de Tormes* and *Don Quixote*." *Indiana Journal of Hispanic Literatures* 5 (1994): 161–180.

Israel, Jonathan I. *Diasporas within a Diaspora: Jews, Crypto-Jews, and the World of Maritime Empires (1540–1740)*. Leiden/Boston: Brill, 2002.

——. *Empires and Entrepôts: The Dutch, the Spanish Monarchy, and the Jews, 1585–1713*. London/Ronceverte: Bloomsbury Academic, 1990.

Israel, Jonathan I., and Reinier Salverda, eds. *Dutch Jewry: Its History and Secular Culture (1500–2000)*. Leiden/Boston: Brill, 2002.

Ivry, Alfred. "Remnants of Jewish Averroism in the Renaissance." In Cooperman, *Jewish Thought in the Sixteenth Century*, 243–265.

Izquierdo Benito, Ricardo, and Angel Sáenz-Badillos, eds. *La sociedad medieval a través de la literatura hispanojudía*. Cuenca: Ediciones Universidad de Castilla–La Mancha, 1998.

Jama, Sophie. *L'histoire juive de Montaigne*. Paris: Flammarion, 2001.

Jannidis, Fotis, Gerhard Lauer, Matías Martínez, and Simone Winko, eds. *Die Rückkehr des Autors: Zur Erneuerung eines umstrittenen Begriffs*. Tübingen: De Gruyter, 1999.

Jauss, Hans Robert. "Ursprung und Bedeutung der Ich-Form im *Lazarillo de Tormes*." *Romanistisches Jahrbuch* 8 (1957): 290–311.

Kablitz, Andreas. "Montaignes 'Skeptizismus': Zur *Apologie de Raimond Sebond* (*Essais*: II, 12)." In *Poststrukturalismus: Herausforderung an die Literaturwissenschaft*, edited by Gerhard Neumann, 504–539. Stuttgart: Metzler, 1997.

——. "Petrarcas Augustinismus und die écriture der *Ventoux*-Epistel." *Poetica* 26 (1994): 31–69.

Kagan, Richard. *Inquisitorial Inquiries: Brief Lives of Secret Jews and Other Heretics*. Baltimore: Johns Hopkins University Press, 2004.

Kamen, Henry. *Crisis and Change in Early Modern Spain*. London: Variorum, 1993.

——. "Limpieza and the Ghost of Américo Castro: Racism as a Tool of Literary Analysis." *Hispanic Review* 64, no. 1 (1996): 19–29.

——. *The Spanish Inquisition: A Historical Revision*. London: Weidenfeld & Nicolson, 1997.

——. "Una crisis de conciencia en la Edad de Oro en España: La Inquisición contra 'limpieza de sangre.'" *Bulletin Hispanique* 88, nos. 3–4 (1996): 321–356.

Kaplan, Gregory B. *The Evolution of* Converso *Literature: The Writings of the Converted Jews of Medieval Spain*. Gainesville: University Press of Florida, 2002.

——. "In Search of Salvation: The Deification of Isabel la Católica in Converso Poetry." *Hispanic Review* 66 (1998): 289–308.

——. "Jews and Judaism in the Political and Social Thought of Spain in the Sixteenth and Seventeenth Centuries." In *Anti-Semitism through the Ages*, edited by Shmuel Almog, 153–160. Oxford: Pergamon Press, 1988.

——. "Toward the Establishment of a Christian Identity: The Conversos and Early Castilian Humanism." *La Corónica* 25 (1996): 53–68.

Kaplan, Yosef. *An Alternative Path to Modernity: The Western Sephardi Diaspora in the Seventeenth Century*. Leiden/Boston: Brill, 2000.

——. "The Self-Definition of the Sephardic Jews of Western Europe and Their Relation to the Alien and to the Stranger." In *Crisis and Creativity in the Sephardic World, 1391–1648*, edited by Benjamin R. Gampel, 121–145. New York: Columbia University Press, 1997.

——. "Wayward New Christians and Stubborn New Jews: The Shaping of a Jewish Identity." *Jewish History* 8, nos. 1–2 (1994): 27–41.

Katz, David S., and Jonathan I. Israel, eds. *Sceptics, Millenarians, and Jews*. Leiden / New York: Brill, 1990.

Katz, Israel J., and M. Mitchell Serels, eds. *Studies on the History of Portuguese Jews from Their Expulsion in 1497 through Their Dispersion*. New York: Sepher Hermon Press, 2000.

Kayserling, Meyer. *Geschichte der Juden in Spanien und Portugal*. 2 vols. 1861. Reprint, Hildesheim: Gerstenberg, 1978.

——. *Sephardim–Romanische Poesien der Juden in Spanien: Ein Beitrag zur Literatur und Geschichte der spanisch-portugiesischen Juden*. Leipzig, 1859.

Kedourie, Elie, ed. *Spain and the Jews: The Sephardi Experience 1492 and After*. London: Thames & Hudson, 1992.

Keitt, Andrew W. *Inventing the Sacred: Imposture, Inquisition, and the Boundaries of the Supernatural in Golden Age Spain*. Leiden: Brill, 2005.

Kennedy, Hugh W. "Lazaro y el 'coco.'" *Revista de Estudios Hispanicos* 10 (1976): 57–67.

King, Edmund L. "A Note on *El licenciado Vidriera*." *Modern Language Notes* 69 (1954): 99–102.

Kirschbaum, Engelbert, ed. *Lexikon der christlichen Ikonographie*. Vol. 3. Rome: Herder Verlag, 1971.

Kodera, Sergius. *Filone und Sofia in Leone Ebreos "Dialoghi d'amore": Platonische Liebesphilosophie der Renaissance und Judentum*. Frankfurt a.M.: Peter Lang, 1995.

König, Bernhard. "*Lazarillo de Tormes*." In *Der spanische Roman*, edited by Volker Roloff and Harald Wentzlaff-Eggebert, 30–45. Stuttgart/Weimar: Cornelsen Verlag, 1995.

Kossoff, Aron David. "La picaresca clásica: El converso teológico y social." *La Torre: Revista de la Universidad de Puerto Rico* 1 (1987): 445–460.

Kramer-Hellinx, Nechama. "Antonio Enríquez Gómez (1600–1662): Desafío de la Inquisición." In Barros, *Xudeus e conversos na historia*, vol. 1, *Mentalidades e cultura*, 289–307.

——. "The Edicts of the Inquisition as Reflected in the Literary Work of the Spanish Converso Antonio Enríquez Gómez (1600–1663)." *Queens College Journal of Jewish Studies* 7 (2005): 19–33.

——. "Polemical Disputation and Jewish Theology in the Poetry of the Spanish Converso Ferrant Sánchez de Talavera." *Queens College Journal of Jewish Studies* 6 (2004): 21–36.

Krewitt, Ulrich. *Metapher und tropische Rede in der Auffassung des Mittelalters*. Ratingen/Kastellaun/Wuppertal: Aloys Henn, 1971.

Kriegel, Maurice. "Entre 'question' des 'nouveaux-chrétiens' et expulsion des juifs: La double mentalité des procés d'exclusion dans l'Espagne du XVe siècle." In Barros, *Xudeus e conversos na historia*, vol. 1, *Mentalidades e cultura*, 171–194.

——. "La liquidation du pluralisme réligieux dans l'Espagne des rois catholiques: Limites et eficacité de l'approche 'internaliste.'" *Temas Medievales* 4 (1994): 35–46.

——. "Le marranisme: Histoire intelligible et mémoire vivante." *Annales: Histoire, Sciences Sociales* 57 (2002): 323–334.

Kristeller, Paul O. "Jewish Contributions to Italian Renaissance Culture." *Italia* 4, no. 1 (1985): 7–20.

——. *Renaissance Philosophy and the Medieval Traditions*. Latrobe, Pa.: Archabbey Press, 1966.

Kristeva, Julia. *Étrangers à nous-mêmes*. Paris: Gallimard, 1988.

Krobb, Florian. *Kollektivautobiographien, Wunschautobiographien: Marranenschicksal im deutsch-jüdischen historischen Roman*. Würzburg: Konigshausen & Neumann, 2002.

Kruse, Margot. "Die parodistischen Elemente im *Lazarillo de Tormes*." *Romanistisches Jahrbuch* 10 (1959): 292–304.

Küpper, Joachim. *Diskurs-Renovatio bei Lope de Vega und Calderón: Untersuchungen zum spanischen Barockdrama*. Tübingen: Narr, 1990.

——. "Mittelalterlich kosmische Ordnung und rinascimentales Bewußtsein von Kontingenz: Fernando de Rojas' *Celestina* als Inszenierung sinnfremder Faktizität (mit Bemerkungen zu Boccaccio, Petrarca, Machiavelli und Montaigne)." In *Kontingenz*, edited by Gerhart von Graevenitz and Odo Marquard, 173–223. Munich: Wilhelm Fink Verlag, 1998.

——. *Petrarca: Das Schweigen der Veritas und die Worte des Dichters*. Berlin / New York: De Gruyter, 2002.

——. "Philology and Theology in Petrarch." *Modern Language Notes* 122, no. 1 (2007): 133–147.

——. "Was ist Literatur?" *Zeitschrift für Ästhetik und Allgemeine Kunstwissenschaft* 45, no. 2 (2001): 187–215.

Lacouture, Jean. *Michel de Montaigne: Ein Leben zwischen Politik und Philosophie*. Frankfurt a.M. / New York: Campus Verlag, 1998.

Lapp, Ernst. *Linguistik der Ironie*. 2nd ed. Tübingen: Narr, 1997.

Lawee, Eric. *Isaac Abrabanel's Stance toward Tradition: Defense, Dissent, and Dialogue*. Albany, N.Y.: SUNY Press, 2001.

Lazar, Moshe, and Stephen Haliczer. *The Jews of Spain and the Expulsion of 1492*. Lancaster, Calif.: Labyrinthos, 1997.

Lázaro Carreter, Fernando. *El "Lazarillo de Tormes" en la picaresca*. Barcelona: Ediciones Ariel, 1972.

Lemartinel, Jean. "Sobre el supuesto judaísmo de 'La Celestina.'" In *Hommage des hispanistes français à Noel Salomon*, 509–516. Barcelona: Laia, 1979.

Lemm, Robert. *Die spanische Inquisition: Geschichte und Legende*. Cologne: Anaconda, 2005.

Leone Leoni, Aron di. *The Hebrew Portuguese Nations in Antwerp and London at the Time of Charles V and Henry VIII: New Documents and Interpretations*. Jersey City, N.J.: KTAV, 2005.

Leroy, Béatrice. *Die Sephardim: Geschichte des iberischen Judentums*. Frankfurt a.M. / Berlin: Nymphenburger Verlag, 1991.

Lesley, Arthur M. "The Place of the *Dialoghi d'amore* in Contemporaneous Jewish Thought." In *Essential Papers on Jewish Culture in Renaissance and Baroque Italy*, edited by David B. Ruderman, 170–188. New York: NYU Press, 1992.

———. "Proverbs, Figures and Riddles: The Dialogues of Love as a Hebrew Humanist Composition." In *Midrashic Imagination: Jewish Exegesis, Thought, and History*, edited by Michael Fishbane, 204–225. Albany, N.Y.: SUNY Press, 1993.

Lévi-Provençal, Évariste. *Histoire de l'Espagne musulmane*. 3 vols. Faksimile reproduction of the first edition, Paris: Maisonneuve & Larose, 2000.

Levy, Avigdor, ed. *The Jews of the Ottoman Empire*. Princeton, N.J.: Darwin Press, 1994.

———, ed. *Jews, Turks, Ottomans: A Shared History, Fifteenth through the Twentieth Century*. Syracuse, N.Y.: Syracuse University Press, 2002.

———. *The Sephardim in the Ottoman Empire*. Princeton, N.J.: Darwin Press, 1992.

Levy, Ze'ev. "On the Concept of Beauty in the Philosophy of Yehudah Abrabanel." In *New Horizons in Sephardic Studies*, edited by Yehida K. Stillman and George K. Zuker, 37–44. Albany, N.Y.: SUNY Press, 1993.

Limbrick, Elaine. "Bibliographie de l'*Apologie de Raimond Sebond*." In Blum, *Montaigne, "Apologie de Raimond Sebond,"* 320–334.

Lindo, Elias Hiam. *The History of the Jews of Spain and Portugal, from the Earliest Times to Their Final Expulsion from Those Kingdoms, and Their Subsequent Dispersion. With Complete Translations of All the Laws Made Respecting Them during Their Long Establishment in the Iberian Peninsula*. London, 1848.

Lobsien, Verena Olejniczak. "Heterologie: Konturen frühneuzeitlichen Selbstseins jenseits von Autonomie und Heteronomie." *Zeitschrift für Literaturwissenschaft und Linguistik* 101 (1996): 6–36.

Lokos, Ellen. "The Politics of Identity and the Enigma of Cervantine Genealogy." In *Cervantes and His Postmodern Constituencies*, edited by Anne J. Cruz and Carroll B. Johnson, 116–133. New York: Psychology Press, 1999.

Lope, Monique de. *Le grotesque dans la représentation du converso: Signification d'une carnavalisation littéraire sui generis*. Aix-en-Provence: PUP, 1993.

López, Victoriano Roncero. "Lazarillo, Guzmán, and Buffoon Literature." *Modern Language Notes* 116 (2001): 235–249.

López Baralt, Luce. "The Legacy of Islam in Spanish Literature." In *The Legacy of Muslim Spain*, edited by Salma Khadra Jayyusi, 1:505–552. Leiden: Brill, 1992.

Lozoya, Marqués de. "Andrés Laguna y el problema de los conversos segovianos." In Hornik, *Collected Studies in Honour of Américo Castro's Eightieth Year*, 311–316.

MacKay, Angus. "The Hispanic-Converso Predicament." *Transactions of the Royal Historical Society* 35 (1985): 159–179.

———. "El problema converso en la literatura del Renacimiento." *Manuscrits* 11 (1993): 127–141.

Maeztu, Ramiro de. *Don Quijote, Don Juan y la Celestina*. Madrid: Visor Libros, 1963.

Maiorino, Giancarlo. *At the Margins of the Renaissance: Lazarillo de Tormes and the Picaresque Art of Survival*. University Park: Penn State University Press, 2003.

Malkiel, Yakov. *Etymology*. Cambridge: Cambridge University Press, 1993.

Malvezin, Théophile. *Michel de Montaigne, son origine, sa famille*. Bordeaux, 1875.

Mann, Vivian B., Thomas F. Glick, and Jerrilynn D. Dodds, eds. *Convivencia: Jews, Muslims, and Christians in Medieval Spain*. New York: George Braziller, 1992.

Markman, Sidney David. *Jewish Remnants in Spain: Wanderings in a Lost World*. Mesa, Ariz.: Scribe, 2003.

Marks, Elaine. *Marrano as Metaphor: The Jewish Presence in French Writing*. New York: Columbia University Press, 1996.

Márquez Villanueva, Francisco. "*La Celestina* as Hispano-Semitic Anthropology." *Revue de Littérature Comparée* 61 (1987): 425–256.

———. "The Converso Problem: An Assessment." In Hornik, *Collected Studies in Honour of Américo Castro's Eightieth Year*, 317–333.

———. "La criptohistoria morisca: Los otros conversos." *Cuadernos Hispanoamericanos* 390 (1982): 517–534.

———. *Espiritualidad y literatura en el siglo XVI*. Madrid: Alfaguara, 1968.

———. "Nacer y morir como bestias (criptojudaísmo y criptoaverroísmo)." In *Inquisição: Ensaios sobre mentalidade, heresias e arte*, edited by Anita Novinsky and Maria Luiza Tucci Carneiro, 11–34. Rio de Janeiro / São Paulo: Universidade de São Paulo, 1992.

———. *Orígenes y sociología del tema celestinesco*. Barcelona: Anthropos Editorial, 1993.

———. "Presencia judía en la literatura española: Releyendo a Américo Castro." In Izquierdo Benito and Sáenz-Badillos, 11–28.

Martínez, Matías. "Das lyrische Ich: Verteidigung eines umstrittenen Begriffs." In *Autorschaft: Positionen und Revisionen*, edited by Heinrich Detering, 376–389. Stuttgart/Weimar: Metzler, 2002.

———. "Narrative Motivation: Erzähltheoretische Einführung." In *Doppelte Welten: Struktur und Sinn zweideutigen Erzählens*, edited by Matías Martínez, 13–36. Göttingen: Vandenhoeck & Ruprecht, 1996.

Martínez Miller, Orlando. *La ética judía y "La Celestina" como alegoría*. Miami: Ediciones Universal, 1978.

Martz, Linda. "Converso Families in Fifteenth- and Sixteenth-Century Toledo: The Significance of Lineage." *Sefarad* 48 (1988): 1–79.

———. "Implementation of Pure-Blood Statutes in Sixteenth-Century Toledo." In Cooperman, *In Iberia and Beyond*, 245–271.

———. "Pure Blood Statutes in Sixteenth-Century Toledo: Implementation as Opposed to Adoption." *Sefarad* 54 (1994): 83–107.

Méchoulan, Henry. *Le sang de l'autre ou l'honneur de Dieu: Indiens, juifs, mauresques au Siècle d'or*. Paris: Fayard, 1979.

Méchoulan, Henry, and Gérard Nahon. *Mémorial I.-S. Révah: Études sur le marranisme, l'hétérodoxie juive et Spinoza*. Paris/Louvain: Fayard, 2001.

Melammed, Renée Levine. *Heretics or Daughters of Israel? The Crypto-Jewish Women of Castile*. Oxford: Oxford University Press, 1999.

———. "Judaizers and Prayer in Sixteenth Century Alcázar." In Cooperman, *In Iberia and Beyond*, 173–195.

Mendes da Costa, Elizabeth. "The Jews and Montaigne's Journal de Voyage." *French Studies Bulletin* 69 (1998): 10–13.

———. "Montaigne and the Jewish Religion." In Meyers and Simms, *Troubled Souls*, 129–141.

Menéndez Pelayo, Marcelino. *Historia de los heterodoxos españoles*. Madrid: Consejo Superior de Investigaciones Científicas, 1963.

———. "Historia de los heterodoxos españoles (Madrid 1880–1882)." In Marcelino Menéndez Pelayo, *Obras completas*, vol. 38. Santander: Consejo Superior de Investigaciones Científicas, 1947.

———. *Orígenes de la novela*. Vol. 3. Madrid: Bailly-Balliere e Hijos, 1915.

Menéndez Pidal, Ramón. "Catálogo del romancero judío-español." *Cultura Española* 4 (1906): 1045–1077; 5 (1907): 166–199.

Menocal, Maria Rosa. *The Ornament of the World: How Muslims, Jews, and Christians Created a Culture of Tolerance in Medieval Spain*. Foreword by Harold Bloom. Boston: Little, Brown, 2002.

Menocal, Maria Rosa, Raymond P. Scheindlin, and Michael Sells, eds. *The Literature of Al-Andalus*. Cambridge: Cambridge University Press, 2000.

Meyer-Minnemann, Klaus. "El género de la picaresca." In Meyer-Minnemann and Schlickers, *La novela picaresca*, 13–40.

Meyer-Minnemann, Klaus, and Sabine Schlickers, eds. *La novela picaresca: Concepto genérico y evolución del género (siglos XVI y XVII)*. Madrid: Iberoamericana/Vervuet, 2008.

Meyers, Charles, and Norman Simms. *Troubled Souls: Conversos, Crypto-Jews, and Other Confused Jewish Intellectuals from the Fourteenth through the Eighteenth Century*. Hamilton, New Zealand: Outrigger Publishers, 2001.

Meyerson, Mark D., and Edward D. English, eds. *Christians, Muslims, and Jews in Medieval and Early Modern Spain: Interaction and Cultural Change*. Notre Dame, Ind.: University of Notre Dame Press, 2000.

Meyuhas Ginio, Alisa, ed. *Jews, Christians, and Muslims in the Mediterranean World after 1492*. London / Portland, Ore.: Frank Cass, 1992.

——. "Self-Perception and Images of the Judeoconversos in Fifteenth-Century Spain and Portugal." *Tel Aviver Jahrbuch für Deutsche Geschichte* 22 (1993): 127–152.

Milburn, Alan Ray. "Leone Ebreo and the Renissance." In *Isaac Abravanel: Six Lectures*, edited by J. B. Trend and Herbert Loewe, 131–156. Cambridge: Cambridge University Press, 1937.

Miron, Dan. *Verschränkungen: Über jüdische Literaturen*. Göttingen: Vandenhoeck & Ruprecht, 2007.

Mönch, Walter. *Frankreichs Literatur im 16. Jahrhundert: Eine nationalpolitische Geistesgeschichte der französischen Renaissance*. Berlin: De Gruyter, 1938.

Moser, Patrick. "Literary Identity in Montaigne's 'Apologie de Raimond Sebond.'" *French Review* 77, no. 4 (2004): 716–727.

Navarro, Rosa. *Alfonso de Valdés, autor del "Lazarillo de Tormes."* Madrid: Gredos, 2003.

Navarro Peiro, Ángeles. *Narrativa hispanohebrea (siglos XII–XV)*. Madrid: El Almendro, 1988.

——. "Tipos sociales en la narrativa hebrea de la España cristiana." In Izquierdo Benito and Sáenz-Badillos, *La sociedad medieval a través de la literatura hispanojudía*, 257–277.

Nepaulsingh, Colbert I. *Apples of Gold in Filigrees of Silver: Jewish Writing in the Eye of the Inquisition*. New York: Holmes & Meier, 1995.

Netanyahu, Benzion. *Don Isaac Abravanel: Statesman and Philosopher*. Philadelphia: Jewish Publication Society of America, 1953.

——. *The Marranos of Spain: From the Late 14th to the Early 16th Century, According to Contemporary Hebrew Sources*. Ithaca, N.Y.: Cornell University Press, 1999.

——. "On the Historical Meaning of the Hebrew Sources Related to the Marranos: A Reply to Critics." *Hispania Judaica* 1 (1980): 79–102.

——. *The Origins of the Inquisition in Fifteenth-Century Spain*. 2nd ed. New York: New York Review Books, 2001.

——. "The Racial Attack on the Conversos: Américo Castro's View of Its Origin." In Netanyahu, *Toward the Inquisition*, 1–42.

——. "Sánchez-Albornoz' View of Jewish History in Spain." In Netanyahu, *Toward the Inquisition*, 126–155.

——. *Toward the Inquisition: Essays on Jewish and Converso History in Late Medieval Spain*. Ithaca, N.Y.: Cornell University Press, 1997.

Neuschäfer, Hans-Jörg. "Selbstbestimmung und Identität im *Don Quijote*: Das Zusammenspiel von Haupthandlung und Eingeschobenen Geschichten." In *Welterfahrung–Selbsterfahrung: Konstitution und Verhandlung von Subjektivität in der spanischen Literatur der frühen Neuzeit*, edited by Wolfgang Matzat und Bernhard Teuber, 293–303. Tübingen: Stauffenburg, 2000.

——, ed. *Spanische Literaturgeschichte*. 3rd ed. Stuttgart: Metzler, 2006.

Neves, Amaro. *Judeus e cristãos-novos de Aveiro e a Inquisição*. Aveiro: Fedrave, 1997.

Niemeyer, Katharina. "' . . . el ser de un pícaro el sujeto deste libro': La primera parte de Guzmán de Alfarache (Madrid 1599)." In Meyer-Minnemann and Schlickers, *La novela picaresca*, 77–116.

——. "'¿Quién creerá que no he de decir más mentiras que letras?' El *Libro de entretenimiento de la pícara Justina*, de Francisco López de Úbeda (Medina del Campo, 1605)." In Meyer-Minnemann and Schlickers, *La novela picaresca*, 193–222.

Nieto, José C. *El Renacimiento y la otra España: Visión cultural socioespiritual*. Geneva: Librairie Droz, 1997.

Nirenberg, David. "The Birth of the Pariah: Jews, Christian Dualism, and Social Science." *Social Research* 70, no. 1 (2003): 201–236.

——. *Communities of Violence: Persecution of Minorities in the Middle Ages*. Princeton, N.J.: Princeton University Press, 1996.

——. "El concepto de la raza en la España medieval." *Edad Media* 3 (2000): 39–60.

——. "Conversion, Sex, and Segregation: Jews and Christians in Medieval Spain." *American Historical Review* 107 (2002): 1065–1093.

——. "Enmity and Assimilation: Jews, Christians, and Converts in Medieval Spain." *Common Knowledge* 9 (2003): 137–155.

——. "Mass Conversion and Genealogical Mentalities: Jews and Christians in Fifteenth-Century Spain." *Past and Present* 174 (2002): 3–41.

——. "Rasse als Begriff bei der Untersuchung spätmittelalterlicher Judenfeindschaft auf der spanischen Halbinsel." In *Jüdische Gemeinden und ihr christlicher Kontext*, edited by Christoph Cluse, Alfred Haverkamp, and Israel Yuval, 49–72. Hannover: Verlag Hahnsche Buchhandlung Hannover, 2003.

——. *Wie jüdisch war das Spanien des Mittelalters? Die Perspektive der Literatur*. Treves: Kliomedia, 2005.

Nitsch, Wolfram. "Barocke Dezentrierung: Spiel und Ernst in Lope de Vegas Dorotea." In *Diskurse des Barock: Dezentrierte oder rezentrierte Welt?*, edited by Joachim Küpper and Friedrich Wolfzettel, 219–244. Munich: Wilhelm Fink Verlag, 2000.

——. *Barocktheater als Spielraum: Studien zu Lope de Vega und Tirso de Molina*. Tübingen: Narr, 2000.

Nitsch, Wolfram, and Bernhard Teuber, eds. *Zwischen dem Heiligen und dem Profanen: Religion, Mythologie, Weltlichkeit in der spanischen Literatur und Kultur der frühen Neuzeit*. Munich: Wilhelm Fink Verlag, 2008.

Nolting-Hauff, Ilse. "*La Vida de Lazarillo de Tormes* und die erasmische Satire." In *Interpretation: Das Paradigma der europäischen Renaissance-Literatur (Festschrift für Alfred Noyer-Weidner zum 60. Geburtstag)*, edited by Klaus W. Hempfer and Gerhard Regn, 83–104. Wiesbaden: Steiner, 1983.

Oelman, Timothy, ed. *Marrano Poets of the Seventeenth Century: An Anthology of the Poetry of João Pinto Delgado, Antonio Enríquez Gómez, and Miguel Barrios*. Oxford: Littman, 2007.

——. "The Religious Views of Antonio Enríquez Gómez: Profile of a Marrano." *Bulletin of Hispanic Studies* 60 (1983): 201–209.

——. "Tres poetas marranos." *Nueva Revista de Filología Hispánica* 30 (1981): 184–206.

Orfali Levi, Moisés. *Los conversos españoles en la literatura rabínica: Problemas jurídicos y opiniones legales durante los siglos XII–XVI*. Salamanca: Universidad Pontificia de Salamanca, 1982.

Orozco Díaz, Emilio. "*La Celestina*: Hipótesis para una interpretación." *Ínsula* 124 (1954): 1–10.

Ortiz, Antonio Dominguez. "Historical Research on Spanish Conversos in the Last Fifteen Years." In Hornik, *Collected Studies in Honour of Américo Castro's Eightieth Year*, 63–82.

Ott, Norbert H. "Rosen." In Angermann, *Lexikon des Mittelalters*, 7:1031–1032.

Parello, Vincent. *Les judéo-convers: Tolède, XVe–XVIe siècles: De l'exclusion à l'intégration*. Paris: Éditions L'Harmattan, 1999.

Paris, Erna. *The End of Days: A Story of Tolerance, Tyranny, and the Expulsion of the Jews from Spain*. Amherst, N.Y.: Prometheus Books, 1995.

Parr, James A. "Rhetoric and Referentiality: Historical Allusiveness and Artful Innuendo." *Crítica Hispánica* 19 (1997): 75–86.

Pecellín Lancharro, Manuel. "B. A. Montano, íntimo de judeoconversos, familistas y procesados por la Inquisición." In *Jornadas extremeñas de estudios judaicos: Raíces hebreas en Extremadura: Del candelabro a la encina*, edited by Fernando Cortés Cortés and Lucía Castellano Barrios, 351–374. Badajoz: Excelentísima Diputación Provincial de Badajoz, 1996.

Pedraza Jiménez, Felipe B., and Milagros Rodríguez Cáceres. "La edad media: La literatura española en su contexto: Minorías étnicas y culturales: Los judíos." In *Manual de literatura española: Edad media*, 1:52–54. Tafalla: Cénlit, 1981.

———. "El mester de clerecía y otras manifestaciones poéticas del siglo XIII: Otros poemas: ¡Ay, Iherusalem!" In *Manual de literatura española: Edad media*, 1:318–320. Tafalla: Cénlit, 1981.

Pedrosa, José Manuel. "La bendición del día y Dios delante y yo detrás: Correspondencias cristianas y judías de dos oraciones hispanoportuguesas." *Romanistisches Jahrbuch* 45 (1994): 262–270.

Pereira Zazo, Oscar. "La perspectiva del Lazarillo de Tormes." *Torre de Papel* 5 (1995): 55–79.

Pérez, Joseph. *The Spanish Inquisition: A History*. Translated by Janet Lloyd. New Haven, Conn. / London: Yale University Press, 2005.

Pescatori, Rossella. "Elementi cabalistici in Giovanni Pico della Mirandola e Leone Ebreo." *Annali d'Italianistica* 26 (2008): 97–110.

Pflaum, Heinz [Peri, Hiram]. *Die Idee der Liebe: Leone Ebreo-Zwei Abhandlungen zur Geschichte der Philosophie in der Renaissance*. Tübingen: J. C. B. Mohr, 1926.

Pike, Ruth. "The Conversos in *La Lozana andaluza*." *Modern Language Notes* 84 (1969): 304–308.

———. *Linajudos and Conversos in Seville: Greed and Prejudice in Sixteenth- and Seventeenth-Century Spain*. New York: Peter Lang International Academic Publishers, 2000.

Pines, Shlomo. "Medieval Doctrines in Renaissance Garb: Some Jewish and Arabic Sources of Leone Ebreo's Doctrine." In Cooperman, *Jewish Thought in the Sixteenth Century*, 365–398.

Piper, Anson C. "The 'Breadly Paradise' of Lazarillo de Tormes." *Hispania* 44 (1961): 269–271.

Pliny the Younger. *Epistulae* 3–5. Munich: Deutscher Taschenbuch Verlag, 1984.

Poliakov, Léon. *Die Marranen im Schatten der Inquisition*. Vol. 4 of *Geschichte des Antisemitismus*. Worms: Heintz, 1981.

Pollmann, Leo. *Spanische Literatur zwischen Orient und Okzident*. Tübingen: Francke, 1996.

Pomel, Fabienne. "La fonction critique de l'ironie dans l'*Apologie de Raimond Sebond*." *Bulletin de la Societé des Amis de Montaigne* 35–36 (1994): 79–89.

Popkin, Richard H. "Jewish Christians and Christian Jews in Spain, 1492 and After." *Judaism* 41 (1992): 248–267.

Pulido Serrano, Ignacio. *Injurias a Cristo: Religión, política y antijudaísmo en el siglo XVII*. Alcalá: Instituto Internacional de Estudios Sefardíes y Andalusíes, 2002.

Quevedo, Francisco de. "Advertencia." In *Lágrimas de Hieremías Castellanas*, edited and with an introduction and commentary by Edward M. Wilson and

José Manuel Blecua. Madrid: Consejo Superior de Investigaciones Científicas, 1953.

Rawlings, Helen. *The Spanish Inquisition*. Oxford: Wiley, 2004.

Redondo, Augustin, ed. *Travaux sur le "Lazarillo de Tormes."* Paris: Éditions Hispaniques, 1993.

Regev, Shaul. "The Attitude Towards the Conversos in 15th–16th Century Jewish Thought." *Revue des Études Juives* 156 (1997): 1–2, 117–134.

Rehrmann, Norbert. "Der Mythos von Córdoba-Spanien, Europa und die islamische Kultur: Beispiele aus Literatur und Kulturgeschichte." *Publik: Kasseler Hochschulzeitung* 5 (1993): 5; expanded version: *Tranvía* 33 (1994): 9–16.

——. *Das schwierige Erbe von Sefarad: Juden und Mauren in der spanischen Literatur–Von der Romantik bis zur Mitte des 20. Jahrhunderts*. Frankfurt a.M.: Vervuert, 2003.

Rehrmann, Norbert, and Andreas Koechert, eds. *Spanien und die Sepharden*. Tübingen: De Gruyter, 1999.

Resnick, Seymour. "The Jew as Portrayed in Early Spanish Literature." *Hispania* 37 (1951): 54–58.

Révah, Israël Salvator. "Autobiographie d'un marrane: Édition parcielle d'un manuscrit de João Pinto Delgado." *Revue des Études Juives* 119 (1961): 41–130.

——. *Des marranes à Spinoza*. Edited by Henry Méchoulan and Carsten Lorenz Wilke. Paris: Vrin, 1995.

——. "Les marranes." *Revue des Études Juives* 1 (1959/60): 29–77.

——. "Le procès inquisitorial contre Rodrigo Méndez Silva, historiographe du roi Philippe IV." *Bulletin Hispanique* 67 (1965): 225–252.

——. "Une famille de 'nouveaux-chrétiens': Les Bocarro Frances." *Revue des Études Juives* 116 (1957): 73–86.

Rey Hazas, Antonio. *La novela picaresca*. Madrid: Servicio de Publicaciones de la Universidad de Málaga, 1990.

Ricapito, Joseph V. "'Cara de Dios': Ensayo de rectificación." *Bulletin of Hispanic Studies* 50 (1973): 142–146.

Rico, Francisco. "Problemas del *Lazarillo*." *Boletín de la Real Academia Española* 46 (1966): 277–296.

Rivkin, Ellis. "How Jewish Were the New Christians?" *Hispania Judaica* 1 (1980): 105–115.

Rodrigue, Aron, ed. *Ottoman and Turkish Jewry: Community and Leadership*. Bloomington: Indiana University Turkish Studies Series, 1992.

Rodríguez Moñino, Antonio. "Les judaisants à Badajoz de 1493 à 1599." *Revue des Études Juives* 115 (1956): 73–86.

Rodríguez Puértolas, Julio. "Jews and Conversos in Fifteenth-Century Castilian Cancioneros: Texts and Contexts." In *Poetry at Court in Trastamaran Spain:*

From the Cancionero de Baena *to the* Cancionero General, edited by E. Michael Gerli and Julian Weiss, 187–197. Tempe, Ariz.: Medieval & Renaissance Texts & Studies, 1998.

——. "El linaje de Calisto." *Hispanófila* 33 (1968): 1–6.

Rohland de Langbehn, Regula. "Calisto, el juez y la cuestión de los conversos." In *Studia Hispanica Medievalia*, edited by L. Teresa Valdivieso and Jorge H. Valdivieso, 89–98. Buenos Aires: Editorial Ergon, 1988.

Roloff, Volker. "Der fremde Calderón: Sartre und das spanische Barock-Theater." In *Literarische Begegnungen: Romanistische Studien zur kulturellen Identität, Differenz und Alterität (Festschrift für Karl Hölz zum 60. Geburtstag)*, edited by Frank Leinen, 231–245. Berlin: Erich Schmidt Verlag, 2002.

Romano Ventura, David. *De historia judía hispánica*. Barcelona: Universitat de Barcelona, 1991.

Roncero López, Victoriano. "Lazarillo, Guzmán, and Buffoon Literature." *Modern Language Notes* 116 (2001): 235–249.

——. "El tema del linaje en el Estebanillo González: La 'indignitas hominis.'" *Bulletin of Hispanic Studies* 70 (1993): 415–423.

Rose, Constance H. "The Marranos of the Seventeenth Century and the Case of the Merchant Writer Antonio Enríquez Gómez." In Alcalá Galve, *The Spanish Inquisition and the Inquisitorial Mind*, 53–71.

Roth, Cecil. Introduction to *The Philosophy of Love*, by Leone Ebreo, ix–xv.

——. "João Pinto Delgado: A Literary Disentanglement." *Modern Language Review* 30 (1935): 19–25.

——. "Les marranes à Rouen: Un chapitre ignoré de l'histoire des juifs en France." *Revue des Études Juives* 88 (1929): 113–155.

——. *The Spanish Inquisition*. New York: Norton, 1996.

Roth, Norman. *Conversos, Inquisition and the Expulsion of the Jews from Spain*. Madison: University of Wisconsin Press, 1995.

Round, Nicholas G. "La 'peculiaridad literaria' de los conversos: ¿Unicornio o 'snark'?" In Alcalá Galve, *Judíos, sefarditas, conversos*, 557–576.

Rozen, Minna. *A History of the Jewish Community of Istanbul: The Formative Years, 1453–1566*. Leiden/Boston: Brill, 2002.

Ruderman, David B. "The Community of Converso Physicians: Race, Medicine, and the Shaping of a Cultural Identity." In Ruderman, *Jewish Thought and Scientific Discovery in Early Modern Europe*, 273–309. New Haven, Conn.: Yale University Press, 1995.

——. "Italian Renaissance and Jewish Thought." In *Renaissance Humanism: Foundations, Forms, and Legacy*, edited by Albert Rabil, Jr., 1:382–433. Philadelphia: University of Pennsylvania Press, 1988.

——. *The World of a Renaissance Jew: The Life and Thought of Abraham ben Mordechai Farissol*. Cincinnati, Ohio: Hebrew Union College, 1983.

Ruffinatto, Aldo. *Las dos caras del Lazarillo: Texto y mensaje*. Madrid: Editorial Castalia, 2000.

Sachar, Howard M. *Farewell España: The World of the Sephardim Remembered*. New York: Vintage, 1994.

Sáenz-Badillos, Ángel, and Judit Targarona Borras. *Diccionario de autores judíos*. Córdoba: El Almendro, 1988.

Saffar, Ruth El. "The 'I' of the Beholder: Self and Other in Some Golden Age Texts." In Brownlee and Gumbrecht, *Cultural Authority in Golden Age Spain*, 178–205.

Salomon, Herman Prins. "The 'De Pinto' Manuscript: A Seventeenth-Century Marrano Family History." *Studia Rosenthaliana* 9, no. 1 (1975): 1–62.

Salvador Miguel, Nicasio. "La identidad de Fernando de Rojas." In *La Celestina*, edited by Gonzalo Santonja, 71–103. Madrid: Sociedad Estatal España Nuevo Milenio, 2001.

———. "El presunto judaismo de *La Celestina*." In *The Age of the Catholic Monarchs, 1474–1516*, edited by Alan Deyermond and Ian Macpherson, 162–177. Liverpool: Liverpool University Press, 1989.

Sánchez-Albornoz, Claudio. *España: Un enigma histórico*. 4th ed. Buenos Aires: Edhasa, 1973.

Saraiva, António José. *The Marrano Factory: The Portuguese Inquisition and Its New Christians, 1536–1765*. Leiden/Boston: Brill, 2001.

Sasson, Jack M. *Ruth: A New Translation with a Philological Commentary and a Formalist-Folklorist Interpretation*. 2nd ed. Sheffield, UK: Sheffield University Press, 1989.

Schärf, Christian. *Geschichte des Essays: Von Montaigne bis Adorno*. Göttingen: Vandenhoeck & Ruprecht, 1999.

Schlanger, Jacques. *La philosophie de Salomon Ibn Gabirol: Étude d'un néoplatonisme*. Leiden: Brill, 1968.

Schmauser, Caroline, and Monika Walter. *¡Bon compaño, jura Di! El encuentro de moros, judíos y cristianos en la obra cervantina*. Frankfurt a.M.: Iberoamericana, 1998.

Schreckenberg, Heinz. *Die christlichen Adversus-Judaeos-Texte und ihr literarisches und historisches Umfeld (1.–11. Jh.)*. 4th ed. Frankfurt a.M. / Vienna: Peter Lang, 1999.

Schreiber, Markus. *Marranen in Madrid 1600–1670*. Stuttgart: Steiner, 1994.

Schulte, Hans Gerd. *El desengaño: Wort und Thema in der spanischen Literatur des Goldenen Zeitalters*. Munich: Wilhelm Fink Verlag, 1969.

Schultz, Uwe. *Michel de Montaigne*. Reinbek: Rowohlt, 1989.

Schumacher-Wolfgarten, Renate. "Rose." In *Lexikon der christlichen Ikonographie*, edited by Engelbert Kirschbaum, vol. 3, cols. 563–568. Rome: Verlag Herder, 1971.

Schwerhoff, Gerd. *Die Inquisition: Ketzerverfolgung in Mittelalter und Neuzeit*. Munich: C. H. Beck, 2004.

Seidenspinner-Núñez, Dayle. "Inflecting the Converso Voice: A Commentary on Recent Theories." *La Corónica* 25 (1996): 6–18.

Seidenspinner-Núñez, Dayle, and Gregory Hutcheson. "Responses from the Authors: 'Navigating the Minefield.'" *La Corónica* 25 (1996): 195–205.

Serrano Mangas, Fernando. *El secreto de los Peñaranda: El universo judeoconverso de la Biblioteca de Barcarrota (siglos XVI y XVII)*. Huelva: Universidad de Huelva, 2004.

Serrano Poncela, Segundo. *El secreto de Melibea y otros ensayos*. Madrid: Taurus, 1959.

Serrano y Sanz, Manuel. "Noticias biográficas de Fernando de Rojas, autor de *La Celestina*, y del impresor Juan de Lucena." *Revista de Archivos, Bibliotecas y Museos* 6 (1902): 245–299.

Severin, Dorothy Sherman. *Witchcraft in "La Celestina."* London: Department of Hispanic Studies, Queen Mary & Westfield College, 1995.

Sextus Empiricus. *Outlines of Scepticism*. Translated by Julia Annas and Jonathan Barnes. Cambridge: Cambridge University Press, 1994.

Shell, Marc. "Marranos (Pigs), or from Coexistence to Toleration." *Critical Inquiry* 17 (1991): 306–335.

Shipley, George A. "The Critic as Witness for the Prosecution: Making the Case against Lázaro de Tormes." *Publications of the Modern Language Association* 97, no. 2 (1982): 179–194.

Shmuelevitz, Aryeh. *The Jews of the Ottoman Empire in the Late Fifteenth and the Sixteenth Centuries: Administrative, Economic, Legal and Social Relations as Reflected in the Responsa*. Leiden: Brill, 1984.

Sicroff, Albert A. *Los estatutos de limpieza de sangre: Controversias entre los siglos XV y XVII*. Madrid: Taurus, 1985.

Silverman, Joseph H. "Del otro teatro nacional de Lope de Vega: El caso insólito de 'El galán escarmentado.'" *Hispania* 67 (1984): 23–27.

——. "Personaje y tipo literario: El converso." In *El personaje dramático*, edited by Luciano García Lorenzo, 253–266. Madrid: Taurus, 1985.

Singer, Hans-Rudolf. "Der Maghreb und die Pyrenäenhalbinsel bis zum Ausgang des Mittelalters." In *Geschichte der arabischen Welt*, edited by Ulrich Haarmann, 264–322. Munich: C. H. Beck, 1987.

Singerman, Robert. *Jews in Spain and Portugal: A Bibliography*. New York: Oak Knoll Press, 1975.

——. *Spanish and Portuguese Jewry: A Classified Bibliography*. Westport, Conn.: Greenwood, 1993.

Sitler, Robert. "The Presence of Jesus Christ in *Lazarillo de Tormes*." *Dactylus* 12 (1993): 85–97.

Smith, Gilbert. "Christian Attitudes toward the Jews in Spanish Literature." *Judaism* (1970): 444–451.

Sola Pool, David de. "The Marranos." *Jewish Quarterly Review* 24 (1933): 247–250.

Solá-Solé, Josep María. *Sobre árabes, judíos y marranos y su impacto en la lengua y literatura españolas*. Barcelona: Puvill, 1983.

Sonne, Isaiah. *Intorno alla vita di Leone Ebreo*. Florence: Civiltà Moderna, 1934.

Sousa Viterbo, Francisco Marquez de. *Notícia acerca a vida e obras de João Pinto Delgado*. Lisbon: Typ. da Academia, 1910.

Stampfer, Joshua, ed. *The Sephardim: A Cultural Journey from Spain to the Pacific Coast*. Portland, Ore.: Institute for Judaic Studies, 1987.

Starobinski, Jean. *Montaigne: Denken und Existenz*. Frankfurt a.M.: Fischer Taschenbuch Verlag, 1989.

———. *Montaigne en mouvement*. Paris: Gallimard, 1982.

Starr-LeBeau, Gretchen D. *In the Shadow of the Virgin: Inquisitors, Friars, and* Conversos *in Guadalupe, Spain*. Princeton, N.J.: Princeton University Press, 2003.

Stenzel, Hartmut. *Einführung in die spanische Literaturwissenschaft*. Stuttgart/Weimar: Metzler, 2001.

Stern, Samuel M. "Spanish Literature and the Jews." *Judaisme Sephardi* 22 (1961): 974.

Stierle, Karlheinz. *Petrarca-Fragmente eines Selbstentwurfs: Essay*. Darmstadt: Carl Hanser, 1998.

Stillman, Yedida K., and Norman A. Stillman, eds. *From Iberia to Diaspora: Studies in Sephardic History and Culture*. Leiden/Boston: Brill, 1999.

Stoll, André. "Sepharads Widerstand: Zur poetischen Produktivität der jüdischen Kultur Spaniens nach dem Vertreibungsedikt." In *Sepharden, Morisken, Indianerinnen und ihresgleichen: Die andere Seite der hispanischen Kulturen*, edited by André Stoll, 15–46. Bielefeld: Aisthesis-Verlag, 1995.

Stolz, Christiane. *Die Ironie im Roman des Siglo de Oro: Untersuchungen zur Narrativik im Don Quijote, im Guzmán de Alfarache und im Buscón*. Frankfurt a.M.: Peter Lang, 1980.

Strosetzki, Christoph. "*Lex divina* und *lex positiva* im Drama und in der Traktatliteratur des Siglo de Oro." In Nitsch and Teuber, *Zwischen dem Heiligen und dem Profanen*, 41–56.

Strosetzki, Christoph, and Manfred Tietz, eds. *Einheit und Vielfalt der Iberoromania: Geschichte und Gegenwart*. Akten des Deutschen Hispanistentages Passau [Proceedings of the German Hispanists' meeting], February 26–March 1, 1987. Hamburg: Buske, 1989.

Stuczynski, Claude Bernard. "El antisemitismo de Francisco de Quevedo-obsesivo o residual? Apuntes crítico-bibliográficos en torno a la publicación de la *Execración contra los judíos*." *Sefarad* 57, no. 1 (1997): 195–204.

Suárez Bilbao, Fernando. *Judíos castellanos entre 1432 y 1492: Ensayo de una prosopografía*. Madrid: Antiqua et Mediaevalia, 1990.

Sviri, Sara. "Spiritual Trends in Pre-Kabbalistic Judeo-Spanish Literature: The Cases of Bahya Ibn Paquda and Judah Halevi." *Donaire* 6 (1996): 78–84.

Swetschinski, Daniel M. *Reluctant Cosmopolitans: The Portuguese Jews of Seventeenth-Century Amsterdam*. London / Portland, Ore.: Littman Library of Jewish Civilization, 2000.

Talmage, Frank. "The Francesc de Sant Jordi-Solomon Bonafed Letters." In *Studies in Medieval Jewish History and Literature*, edited by Isadore Twersky, 1:337–364. Cambridge, Mass.: Center for Jewish Studies, Harvard University, 1979.

Tavares, Maria José Ferro. "Expulsion or Integration? The Portuguese Jewish Problem." In *Crisis and Creativity in the Sephardic World, 1391–1648*, edited by Benjamin R. Gampel, 95–103. New York: Columbia University Press, 1997.

——. *Los judíos en Portugal*. Madrid: Mapfre Editorial, 1992.

Tietz, Manfred. "Mittelalter und Spätmittelalter." In *Spanische Literaturgeschichte*, edited by Hans-Jörg Neuschäfer, 1–68. Stuttgart/Weimar: Metzler, 1997.

——. "Profane Literatur und religiöse Kultur im Siglo de Oro." In Nitsch and Teuber, *Zwischen dem Heiligen und dem Profanen*, 23–40.

Tigay, Jeffrey Howard, Alan Cooper, and Bathja Bayer. "Lamentations, Book of." In Berenbaum and Skolnik, *Encyclopedia Judaica*, 12:446–451.

Tirosh-Rothschild, Hava. "Jewish Culture in Renaissance Italy: A Methodological Survey." *Italia* 9, nos. 1–2 (1990): 63–96.

——. "Jewish Philosophy on the Eve of Modernity." In *History of Jewish Philosophy*, edited by Daniel H. Frank and Oliver Leaman, 499–573. London / New York: Routledge, 1997.

Trebilco, Paul R. *Jewish Communities in Asia Minor*. Cambridge / New York: Cambridge University Press, 1991.

Valle Lersundi, Fernando del. "Testamento de Fernando de Rojas, autor de *La Celestina*." *Revista de Filología Española* 16 (1929): 366–388.

Veit, Philipp F. "Heine: The Marrano Pose." *Monatshefte für Deutschen Unterricht, Deutsche Sprache und Literatur* 66 (1974): 145–156.

Veltri, Giuseppe. "Leone Ebreo's Concept of Jewish Philosophy." In *Renaissance Philosophy in Jewish Garb: Foundations and Challenges in Judaism on the Eve of Modernity*, edited by Giuseppe Veltri, 60–72. Leiden/Boston: Brill, 2009.

Vendrell de Millas, Francisca. "Retrato irónico de un funcionario converso." *Sefarad* 28 (1968): 40–44.

Verd, Gabriel María. "Las biblias romanzadas: Criterios de traducción." *Sefarad* 36 (1971): 319–351.

Vermeylen, Alfonso. "*La Celestina*, objeto de una enconada sospecha de judaísmo." In *Studia Hispanica Medievalia*, edited by Rosa E. Penna and María A. Rosarossa, 3:215–222. Buenos Aires: Editorial Ergon, 1995.

Vieira, António, and Sébastien Lapaque. *Sur les procédés de la Sainte Inquisition: Propositions en faveur des gens de la nation juive*. Paris: Bayard, 2004.

Vila-Chã, João José Miranda. *Amor intellectualis? Leone Ebreo (Judah Abravanel) and the Intelligibility of Love*. Braga: Publicaçóes de Faculdade de Filosofia de Braga, 2006.

Vivarelli, Vivetta. "Montaigne und der 'Freie Geist': Nietzsche im Übergang." *Nietzsche-Studien* 23 (1994): 79–101.

Vones, Ludwig. *Geschichte der Iberischen Halbinsel im Mittelalter 711–1480*. Sigmaringen: Jan Thorbecke Verlag, 1993.

Walfish, Barry Dov. *Esther in Medieval Garb: Jewish Interpretation of the Book of Esther in the Middle Ages*. Albany, N.Y.: SUNY Press, 1993.

Wardropper, Bruce W. "The Strange Case of Lázaro Gonzales Pérez." *Modern Language Notes* 92, no. 2 (1997): 202–212.

Warshawsky, Matthew. "A Spanish Converso's Quest for Justice: The Life and Dream Fiction of Antonio Enriquez Gómez." *Shofar: An Interdisciplinary Journal of Jewish Studies* 23 (2005): 1–24.

Weimann, Robert. *Realismus in der Renaissance: Aneignung der Welt in der erzählenden Prosa*. Berlin/Weimar: Aufbau-Verlag, 1977.

Weinfeld, Moshe S., David Sperling, and Aaron Rothkoff. "Ruth, Book of." In Berenbaum and Skolnik, *Encyclopedia Judaica*, 17:592–596.

Wendehorst, Stephan, ed. *The Roman Inquisition, the Index and the Jews*. Leiden: Brill, 2004.

Wexler, Paul. "Marrano Ibero-Romance: Classification and Research Tasks." *Zeitschrift fur Romanische Philologie* 98 (1982): 59–108.

Whinnom, Keith. "Was Diego de San Pedro a Converso?" *Bulletin of Hispanic Studies* 34 (1957): 187–200.

Whitenack, Judith A. *Confession and Conversion in Guzmán de Alfarache*. Madison: University of Wisconsin Press, 1980.

Wilke, Carsten. "Conversion ou retour? La métamorphose du nouveau-chrétien en juif portugais dans l'imaginaire sépharade du XVIIe siècle." In *Mémoires juives d'Espagne et du Portugal*, edited by Esther Benbassa, 53–67. Paris: Publisud, 1996.

———. *Jüdisch-christliches Doppelleben im Barock: Zur Biographie des Kaufmanns und Dichters Antonio Enríquez Gómez*. Frankfurt a.M.: Peter Lang, 1994.

Williams, Patrick. "A Jewish Councillor of the Inquisition? Luis de Mercado, the Statutes of Limpieza de Sangre and the Politics of Vendetta (1598–1601)." *Bulletin of Hispanic Studies* 67 (1990): 253–264.

Wilson, Edward W. "The Poetry of João Pinto Delgado." *Journal of Jewish Studies* 1, no. 3 (1949): 131–142.

Wiltrout, Ann. "The *Lazarillo de Tormes* and Erasmus' *Opulentia sordida*." *Romanische Forschungen* 81 (1969): 550–564.

Wolf, Hubert. *Römische Inquisition und Indexkongregation: Grundlagenforschung 1814–1915*. Paderborn: Ferdinand Schöningh Verlag, 2005.

Yerushalmi, Yosef Hayim. "L'antisémitisme racial est-il apparu au XXe siècle? De la limpieza de sangre espagnole au nazisme: Continuité et ruptures." *Esprit* (1993): 5–35.

———. *Assimilation and Racial Anti-Semitism: The Iberian and the German Models*. New York: Leo Baeck Institute, 1982.

———. "Assimilierung und rassischer Antisemitismus: Die iberischen und die deutschen Modelle." In Yerushalmi, *Ein Feld in Anatot*, 53–80.

———. "Conversos Returning to Judaism in the Seventeenth Century: Their Jewish Knowledge and Psychological Readiness." In *Proceedings of the Fifth World Congress of Jewish Studies*, edited by Pinchas Peli. 4 vols. Jerusalem: World Union of Jewish Studies, 1972 (Hebr.).

———. *De la Cour d'Espagne au ghetto italien*. Paris: Fayard, 1987.

———. *Diener von Königen und nicht Diener von Dienern: Einige Aspekte der politischen Geschichte der Juden*. Munich: Carl Friedrich von Siemens Stiftung, 1995.

———. *Ein Feld in Anatot: Versuche über jüdische Geschichte*. Berlin: Wagenbach, 1993.

———. *From Spanish Court to Italian Ghetto: Isaac Cardoso–A Study in Seventeenth-Century Marranism and Jewish Apologetics*. 2nd ed. Seattle: University of Washington Press, 1981.

———. *Sefardica: Essais sur l'histoire des juifs, des marranes et des nouveaux-chrétiens d'origine hispano-portugaise*. Paris: Éditions Chandeigne, 1998.

Ynduráin, Domingo. "El renacimiento de Lázaro." *Hispania* 75 (1992): 474–483.

Yovel, Yirmiyahu. "Converso Dualities in the First Generation: The Cancioneros." *Jewish Social Studies* 4, no. 3 (1998): 1–28.

———. *The Other Within: Split Identity and Emerging Modernity*. Princeton, N.J.: Princeton University Press, 2009.

Zagorin, Perez. *Ways of Lying: Dissimulation, Persecution, and Conformity in Early Modern Europe*. Cambridge, Mass.: Harvard University Press, 1990.

Zelson, Louis G. "*The Celestina* and Its Jewish Authorship." *Jewish Forum* 8 (1930): 459–466.

Zepp, Susanne. "Ironie, Inquisition und Konversion: Parodien von Inklusionsdispositiven im *Lazarillo de Tormes*." *Romanistisches Jahrbuch* 56 (2005): 368–392.

Zimic, Stanislav. *Apuntes sobre la estructura paródica y satírica de "Lazarillo de Tormes."* Madrid / Frankfurt a.M.: Iberoamericana, 2000.

Zimmels, Bernhard. *Leo Hebraeus, ein jüdischer Philosoph der Renaissance: Sein Leben, seine Werke und seine Lehren*. Breslau, 1886.

———. *Leone Hebreo: Neue Studien*. Vienna, 1892.

Zimmels, Hirsch Jakob. *Die Marranen in der rabbinischen Literatur*. Berlin: Buchhandlung Rubin Mass, 1932.

Zweig, Stefan. *Montaigne*. Frankfurt a.M.: Fischer, 1995.

Index